THE ENGLISH COUNTRY INN

Also by Garry Hogg:

(frontispiece, overleaf)
Ye Olde Masons Arms, Branscombe, Devon

GARRY HOGG

THE ENGLISH COUNTRY INN

B. T. Batsford Ltd

London & Sydney

First published 1974

Copyright © Garry Hogg, 1974

Printed in Great Britain by Bristol Typesetting Co. Ltd,
Barton Manor, St Philips, for the publishers,
B. T. Batsford Ltd, 4 Fitzhardinge Street, London W.1.
and 23 Cross Street, Brookvale, N.S.W. 2100, Australia.

ISBN 0 7134 2855 4

CONTENTS

ILLUSTRATIONS

ACKNOWLEDGEMENTS

The author wishes to thank Messrs Swallow Hotels Ltd, of Sunderland, for permission to include the photographs of the *Blue Bell Hotel*, Belford, and the *Lord Crewe Arms*, Blanchland, on page 200. The remaining photographs were taken especially for this book by the author.

for
C.M.S.
and
the Staff
of
The Intensive Care Unit
Torbay General Hospital
but for whom
This Book
would never have been
completed

FOREWORD

Dr Samuel Johnson, a regular patron of *Ye Olde Cheshire Cheese* in Wine Office Court, Fleet Street, declared: 'There is nothing which has yet been contrived by man by which so much happiness is produced as by a good tavern or inn'. The great man's observations, on matters whether trivial or vital, were always forthright, so that though his prowess as a tea drinker was legendary during his own lifetime this statement should not be summarily dismissed. Perhaps, however, it was just one of those utterances to which he was prone when a chance remark made in his presence by some lesser mortal seemed to him to call for a challenging reply; perhaps it was some rabid teetotaller venturing an opinion, who needed to be slapped down.

There is a footnote to this utterance which has, so to speak, a 'dying fall'; it comes from the late G. K. Chesterton (does anyone, these days, read that minor masterpiece of his, *The Flying Inn*?). Though more given to paradox than the worthy Doctor, he could speak with equal emphasis (albeit often tongue-in-cheek). He declared: 'The decay of the taverns (the two noblest words in all poetry being Public and House) is part of the general decay of democracy'. Perhaps this declaration, too, should not be taken too seriously; certainly the portion in parenthesis can be dismissed.

Tavern, Inn and Public House are the three terms so far used. There are others, including Hotel and Hostelry. The latter is the most euphonious of them all, but the dictionaries state: 'an archaic word meaning inn'. It is not only euphonious; it conveys a sense of nostalgia, and romance. Also, I suppose it is the only term that can fairly claim to embrace the whole gamut: hotel, tavern, pub, guest-house, public house, inn. The total number of these must run, in England alone, into tens of thousands. At the one end, the *Hotel Ritz-Royal-Imperial-Splendide* in Megalopolis; at the other, the *Pig & Whisker*, Little Slobworth.

Whole shelves of books have been written about the first category. The traditions, the historical and literary associations, the archi-tectural features, the names of notabilities, royalty and rascals, who have stayed beneath their roofs, the menus made available to them, the resources of their cellars, the luxury of their ambience: all these have been catalogued, extolled, indeed written-up sometimes with a degree of uninhibited enthusiasm that might lead the cynical at any rate to suspect that the authors had in advance been dined and wined and accommodated with, in Kipling's phrase, 'more-than-oriental-splendour'.

There are innumerable examples of such hostelries up and down the country; I have visited most of them, dined and wined at more than a few of them, slept at some of them. They bear names well known not only to English travellers but to overseas visitors recom-mended to them. Among them, one thinks immediately of *The Old Ship* at Brighton and *The Dolphin* at Southampton; of the *Angel & Royal* at Grantham and *The George* at Stamford, both on the Great North Road; of *The Rose & Crown*, Tonbridge and *The Great White Horse* at Ipswich; of *The Royal Victoria & Bull* at Rochester and *The Feathers*, Ludlow; of *The Lygon Arms* at Broadway and *The Luttrell Arms* at Dunster; of *The George* at Norton St Philip and *The George & Pilgrims* at Glastonbury; of *The White Harte*, Salisbury and *The White Horse*, Dorking; of *The Bell* at Thetford and *The Lion* at Shrewsbury; of *The Royal Anchor*, Liphook and *The Mermaid*, Rye; of *The Bull*, at Long Melford and *The Royal George* at Knutsford; of—but the list is endless!

However, it is not of such hostelries as these that I am about to write; as I say, they have all had their virtues sung; the bibliography of books about them is already extensive. I have not consulted any of these, for my concern is, quite simply, The English Country Inn.

Country inns are as essential a feature of the rural scene as the parish church, the village green, the market cross. Down the years, the centuries, they have been focal points in the day-to-day lives of country folk. They vary in importance, it is true, according to where they are situated. If in the heart of some village, then they are places where the menfolk (and increasingly their womenfolk) meet to drink in an atmosphere of good-fellowship; if they are relatively isolated, on some highway, then they have been ports-of-call for travellers, whether on foot, in the saddle, riding in (or on) stage-coaches, leading packhorse-trains or driving heavy long-distance wagons. They have served as, not merely ports-of-call but, in emergency or in isolated areas, something more: places of refuge. One of the less important passages in *Macbeth*, but at the same time one of the most evocative, is that spoken by the First Murderer as he and his companions await the approach of the fated Banquo:

> The west yet glimmers with some streaks of day;
> Now spurs the 'lated traveller apace
> To gain the timely inn . . .

'The timely inn': there you have it in a nutshell.

It should not be supposed that just because an inn is to be found in the heart of some village, or isolated on a roadside between two widely-spaced towns, it does not merit inclusion in a book devoted to hostelries; it is rather the reverse. Unobtrusive, even secretive they very often are; but as I hope I shall have shown in the succeeding pages, of the two hundred described, scattered through some thirty counties, not one should be lightly dismissed. They may be of some interest architecturally; they may have historical or literary associations; there may be something unusual, memorable, about their siting, or about what is to be seen once you have crossed the threshold. In quite a number of cases all these qualifications will be seen to apply.

Furthermore, almost without exception, every one I have mentioned is photogenic. I took some hundreds of photographs during the time I spent travelling about in search of them or renewing acquaintance with those with which I was already familiar. Very few of these, in the event, served no more useful purpose than to illustrate notes made about their appearance at the time of my visit or to remind me of some detail I had missed, or forgotten when I came to write about them; they form a gallery of small, often intimate, pictures from which I can derive pleasure in retrospect. I make this point because few of us these days travel anywhere at home or abroad without our cameras; one's own pictorial record is worth so much more than memory alone.

The question may be posed: On what basis have you made your selection of two hundred out of a potential that runs into thousands? The answer is simple, but twofold. I wanted to make the distribution of these country inns as wide as was practicable; and I wanted to make their variety, so far as outward appearance is concerned, as pronounced as possible. In fact, of course, the two aims neatly interlocked. You do not find, for example, granite buildings in Suffolk or Kent; you do not look for half-timbering in Cornwall or on the Pennines; you do not expect to see tile-hung brick in the Lake District; you do not encounter oolitic limestone (perhaps the most perfect of building materials) in Northumberland or Devon. And so on.

As for variety of information relevant to the inns finally selected from the many, this of course has little or no particular regional basis. An inn could have been originally the Guest House of an abbey, whether in Berkshire or in Sussex; it could have been a haunt of highwaymen, whether in Wiltshire or in Essex; it could have been frequented by smugglers whether in Devon or in Kent; it could have been notorious for cock-fighting, whether in Hertfordshire or in Yorkshire; it could have served the needs of fleeing monarchs, or Pretenders to the Throne, whether in Hampshire or in Dorset.

In addition to the problem of making the ultimate selection as comprehensive as possible, there was the problem of arrangement, of order. I decided to distribute the inns of my choice from the south northwards, by regions and also by counties. Even the most perfunctory glance at a map of England in which the counties are marked by colour shows that they do not readily lend themselves to lateral distinction; the purist and the geographer will almost certainly take exception to some of my groupings. For this I must plead *force majeur*. I know perfectly well that Surrey, for example, is one of the Home Counties; nevertheless, because after disposing of The West Country I had decided to include in one group all the counties that lay to the south of the Thames, starting with those with an English Channel coastline, Surrey had to be included. (Gloucestershire, of course, complicated this issue since the Thames rises to the south-west of Cirencester and more than half the county lies to the north!) East Anglia offered no problem at all. North of the Thames I took the Home Counties and allowed them to merge gradually into the Midlands as a whole until they themselves gave place to the true North Country.

So much, then, for the book's pattern. As to its authenticity, I can say, hand on heart, that I have revisited every one of those included (as well as very many which for one reason or another had to be omitted) especially for this book. I have collected information about them in my own way, talking at each with the landlord or with some customer who proved to be interested in something more than the mere availability of his favourite beverage. I may well have been led more than once, and for no ascertainable reason, 'up the garden path', but I do not think very often. I have the pleasantest memories of my visits to practically every one of these inns.

Many of them, of course, had changed in various respects since I first knew them, some of them forty-odd years ago. Their owners have 'moved with the times' in order to cater for the requirements of a changing clientele while keeping their regulars' goodwill as best they can. As the landlord of the *Smith's Arms*, Godmanstone, Dorset, said to me, 'These days you've got to keep up with modern trends if you want to satisfy your customers'.

Rather too many of them, in my opinion at least, are tending these days to call themselves Hotels rather than Inns, to seek the *cachet* of the motoring organisations and diners' clubs. But those included in this book (and, happily, countless others) remain fundamentally inns rather than hotels; it is as such that I approached them, entered them, and remember them. I hope that readers of this book may feel stimulated by what I have had to say about them to go and visit them for themselves, and enjoy the experience as much as I myself have done—and shall continue to do.

Groombridge   G.H.

1 First and Last, Sennen

2 Ye Olde Punch Bowl & Ladle, near Feock

3 Jamaica Inn, Bolventor

4   The New Inn, Sampford Courtenay

5   Church House Inn, Harberton

CHAPTER ONE

The West Country

Cornwall

Men build, or at any rate did so in olden times, in the raw materials readiest to hand; in Cornwall this is granite and slate. Almost every building in the Duchy, whether cart-shed or Cothele House, demonstrates this. Along the stormy Atlantic coast the two materials are often married: the windward side will have its granite slate-hung for added protection. You can see this well at the *Boscaswell Inn* near St Just. It is a pity, therefore, that the *First & Last* inn in England, within a stone's throw of Land's End, should be untypical, unrepresentative.

Whatever its basic material, the whole of it is plastered and painted dazzling white save for the tall, narrow windows whose frames are glossy black. This strongly contrasted black and white paintwork is of course typical of buildings close to the sea, whether lighthouses or coastguard stations. But in such a setting, so close to the craggy bastion of granite that is the seaward-facing extremity of south-western England, this, ideally, should be of granite, naked and unadorned. The point is emphasised by the squat granite tower of the church, immediately behind the inn.

To find my first granite inn, I went three miles east by south to the microscopic hamlet of Treen. Its boldly painted sign, *Logan Rock*, caught my eye as I climbed the steep lane. But for the sign-board you would hardly recognise it as an inn. It is an L-shaped, cottage-like building that butts on to the road, with a short arm at right angles to it part-enclosing a diminutive courtyard. The two halves are linked by an archway, through which the garden can be seen; a small room sits on the archway, and a row of hitching-rings are set in the walls, used by the pack-ponies while their drivers regaled themselves inside. I asked the landlord about the odd name, and he told me the story of Treen's Logan—or 'Rocking'—stone; but only after exacting a promise from me that I would go and see it for myself. It was a promise I was later to regret!

Granite, of course, was the answer. A gigantic boulder, estimated to weigh some sixty tons, topped an outcrop of rock overlooking Porthcurno Bay. Owing to centuries of weathering, it is finely balanced on a boss of hard rock beneath; indeed, so finely balanced that it could be set in pendulum motion with little more than a well-calculated shove from one side. 'Surprising that some young vandal in the mood of today hasn't toppled it over once and for all,' I remarked.

He grinned. 'There were vandals a hundred and fifty years ago,' he answered, 'and that's just what they did, in 1824. Tipped it right off its perch, down on to the rocks at the foot.' I passed over my glass for refilling, for this looked like being quite a story. Licensing hours, I thought as he filled it, and another for himself, must be fairly freely interpreted hereabouts, since mid-afternoon was certainly not a normal time for being open.

It seems that a mischievous-minded young naval lieutenant named Goldsmith (incidentally, as I found out later, a nephew of Oliver Goldsmith), having obtained shore leave and, with some cronies from his ship, having drunk rather more than he should at this very inn then set off along what I was to discover to my cost was a difficult and very strenuous rock track beyond the cliff, on mischief bent. The young men succeeded in dislodging the Logan Stone so that it thundered down on to the rocks at the bottom. The noise awoke the sleeping citizens of Treen, all twenty of them. They tumbled from their beds and intercepted the trio of young officers and virtually held them to ransom: 'Put back our Rock where it belongs—or else!' was the burden of their challenge. Goldsmith and his friends were in a spot, and knew it, for they had already long outstayed their leave.

What their punishment had been, the landlord could not say;
but the Logan Stone had to be replaced. The crew of H.M.S. *Nimble*
brought tackle ashore: a massive set of sheer-legs, ropes, pulley-
blocks and, above all, man-power. It was some weeks before the
Rock had been laboriously hauled back into position. Crew members
were paid a bonus on their regulation wages, at the expense, I
suspect, of the three young officers. Able-bodied Treen men were
co-opted, and paid for their services. By the standards of the day,
they received good money. One brawny Cornishman earned 2/- a
day for forty-seven days; another earned 3/- a night for fifty-three
nights' work; a small army of fifty-eight men laboured over one
particularly awkward stage and ended the day with £5 16 0 in
their communal pocket. This detailed information came from a
crumpled piece of paper the landlord produced from a drawer by
the beer-pump. All in all, the cost to those young officers amounted
to £130-odd. 'A dear evening out, I reckon,' he commented, folding
up the paper, 'and a joke hard earned. Go and have a look at our
Rock for yourself, and you'll be welcome to a drink on your return!'

I started out enthusiastically enough, but gave up part way along
that saw-toothed track amid the granite blocks. Those three junior
officers had made that trip in the half light, and achieved their
objective; I admit to a sneaking respect for them! But it would never
do to say so in Treen. I never claimed that free glass of beer; I never
got near enough to the Rock even to touch it, let alone set it rocking.

On the opposite side of Mounts Bay, beyond Penzance and
screened from St Michael's Mount by Trewavas Head, is Porthleven,
its snug harbour dominated by *The Ship*, an inn which gives a strong
impression of literally growing out of the granite cliff behind. In
fact, its Cellar Bar is hewn from the solid rock. Rough granite steps
lead up to the entrance; you feel that you are entering a lighthouse.
It claims to be three hundred years old. Some years ago, when
redecoration of the upper bar was in progress, more than half a
dozen layers of wallpaper were stripped off. Behind these was some
unusual wallpaper that excited the interest of a chance customer.
He took a sample of it away with him and, after some inquiry,
established that it was almost certainly of French origin and at

least two hundred years old. In the now reconditioned bar a handful of customers were vying with one another to down in the shortest possible time the contents of a copper-and-brass 'yard-of-ale'. All about them were the marine objects typical of inns of this kind: lifebelts, binnacles, riding-lights, marline-spikes, old pulley-blocks and similar reminders of the old days of sail.

At Penryn, just north of Falmouth, the *Seven Stars* is, unusually, one of a row of granite-built terrace houses fronting on to a raised, slabstone footway lining the steep main street. I should have passed it without a second glance, for outwardly it is unprepossessing enough, but for a chance conversation the evening before with a young couple staying at the same farmhouse. Also, I have learned during a lifetime of touring both at home and abroad, and especially in France, never to be put off a place simply by its outward appearance. 'The landlord's got *everything* there!' the young man had said: 'You name it, he's got it. Go and see for yourself!' I did so. As I passed beneath the low lintel of the *Seven Stars* I entered a veritable Aladdin's cave.

The single bar is immediately inside the door, on two levels. It was crowded, but through the fug and tobacco smoke I saw that every inch of wall space and every inch of the low ceiling was covered with brass and copperware in every conceivable form, glinting warmly, richly, from a hundred angles; the very smoke shimmered with ruddy light. The landlord has been there for some thirty years, and his lifelong hobby has been collecting the unusual. True, any number of inns up and down the country have their horse-brasses, copper jugs, pewterware, and so forth; but few, surely, can rival this collection in number or, more important, in variety.

I asked him if he had any idea how many articles he had accumulated. 'Seven hundred-odd at the last count, sir,' he said, briskly wiping a fistful of pint-pots simultaneously. 'But that was a year or two back. I've no time, these days, to keep tabs on 'em, though the wife has a go now and then, when we're giving 'em a rub over.'

It must be a whole-time job! And a tricky one at that. For they are by no means all copper or brass. An unexpected item is what the landlord claims to be 'one of the smallest Bibles in the world'. If

22

there exists a smaller one, it would fit inside a matchbox. Another
and equally unexpected item, at the opposite end of the scale in
both size and character, is the tiller from a Chinese junk. But it is
really the sheer mass of glowing brass and copper that dominates
this small bar, every item, large and small alike, burnished to within
an inch of its life. Every item, too, eminently covetable. I spotted
the very twin of a copper-and-brass snuff-box that I have prized
ever since I picked it up in an Amsterdam junk shop. I remember
that I paid a guilder for it, feeling a sense of triumph at having
beaten down the Dutchman from the initial asking-price. Beautifully
inscribed, it must be worth something today.

Warmed by the glow of the copperware and the friendly atmosphere of the bar, I walked out into drizzling rain. Looking up at the
façade, I noticed that the granite wall bulged from about the level
of the ground-floor ceiling, the bulge emphasised by the curve of
the guttering at the eaves and the slight twist of the windows. The
fact that the wall bulged still did not convince me that the *Seven
Stars* was, as I had been assured, more than five centuries old. It
lacked the 'feel' of an inn of that age. Probably the landlord had
meant that there had been a licensed house on this site since 1454.
Though even this is unlikely, it is possible; there are plenty of such
records up and down the country, from Cornwall and Kent to
Northumberland.

You could hardly find a greater contrast than at the *Norway Inn*,
Perranarworthal, only five miles away. Its signboard was swinging
in the breeze as I pulled up there, giving the curious impression that
the Viking longship painted on it was in motion. Why the name,
here in a remote corner of England? And why the Norwegian flag on
the tall mast? Norway is writ large all over it; another longship,
in wrought-ironwork, graces the main entrance and is repeated elsewhere in miniature on the walls.

The answer is a pleasing one. In the days when the River Fal was
navigable much farther than it is today, Norwegian ships unloaded
their cargoes of timber at a quay near by, exchanging pit-props for
tin from the mines then being worked in Cornwall. This inn became
a centre for traders in divers commodities; not all of them were

English-speaking. The landlord had the wit to build up a serving staff that could cope with other languages and, since Norwegian is such a difficult language, that one in particular. The tradition has persisted. Enter this brightly painted inn and you will find that several languages are spoken and understood by one or more of the staff. Norwegian, of course; but also German, Spanish, Italian and French. The full benefit of this forward-looking policy will be increasingly felt in the years ahead as the European Common Market, for better or worse, becomes increasingly a reality.

This part of Cornwall is among the most picturesque and least exploited in the Duchy. Estuaries abound: that of the Fal; Carrick Roads; King Harry's Reach; the Truro and Tressilian Rivers; Percuil Creek, between the mainland and the peninsula of St Anthony in Roseland. Tiny 'lost' villages and their approach-roads offer unsuspected and usually memorable rewards. Feock, for example.

A mile or so short of it is *Ye Olde Punch Bowl & Ladle*. True, it smacks of Devonshire rather than of Cornwall, but this is not granite country hereabouts. It is elaborately thatched, instead of being slate-roofed. The thatch undulates along the roof between the two chimneys and over its two porches set a-symmetrically among its 'staggered' windows. These carry what might be called shaggy eyebrows, curving deeply also over dark doorways standing out against white-painted walls. The landlord claims that his inn not only has a name unique in the country but dates back to the eleventh century. It is difficult to accept, however, for few buildings other than churches and castles can substantiate such a claim.

Inside, however, the impression of age is very strong. In addition to the usual old oak beams there is a huge fireplace with an unusual chimney; it bears the curious name, the 'Bosun's Pipe'. To my inquiry I received an answer as convincing as it was prompt. Here the Revenue Men held their regular meetings, and in this hearth all combustible contraband seized from the legion of smugglers who used these tortuous inlets to land their goods by night was duly burned. Duly burned? Tradition stoutly maintains that the Revenue Men were not all as honest as they were expected to be and that many a consignment of tobacco and similar commodities was transferred into their possession rather than going up the Bosun's Pipe in smoke! There is an echo of this at Falmouth: the thirty-foot detached chimney on Customs Quay known as the 'King's Pipe'. It was built for the express purpose of burning contraband tobacco smuggled into the port. Here again, one suspects. . . .

From Feock you take the King Harry ferry to the cottage-style *Roseland Inn* at Philleigh, with flower-filled garden, to the *Plume of Feathers* at Portscatho and thence to the landlocked harbour of Portloe in Veryan Bay. Here *The Lugger* must surely be everyone's notion of the perfect smuggler's sea-edge inn, a smuggler's paradise comparable with, say, the *Cod & Lobster* at Staithes in Yorkshire. It stands, squat and uncompromising, on the hard itself, on to which the lobstermen's boats are drawn up while they sit repairing their pots and other gear. To reach it you descend a steep, ever-narrowing lane that dips on to the hard so that you must brake in good time to avoid being inadvertently launched into deep water.

The small inn's balcony offers all that the lazy visitor could ask for, in miniature: tar barrels, coils of rope, cork floats and 'witch-balls', nets, lobster-pots, grapnels, rusty old-style anchors, fragments of torn sail-cloth, tins of paint, lobster claws, the odd discarded sou'-wester; all this greatly enhanced by the composite smell of stale fish, diesel oil, paint, tar, seaweed—the lot; *multum in parvo*, in fact! The older members of this tiny community may just remember the days when smugglers used the craggy shelter offered by this natural harbour, strangely reminiscent of Ghar Lapsi, in Malta, and the resources of the inn. It has now been somewhat 'tarted up' to meet the demands of the holiday-maker; but not too much. Nor does Portloe lend itself to expansion: the few cottages cling to the rocks wherever a perch offers room; ideal in many respects, *The Lugger* is not, perhaps, for the claustrophobe.

Climb the steep lane over the headland and you come soon to St Ewe. Here is the *Crown Inn*, a sixteenth-century farmhouse that obtained a licence to sell spirituous liquor so long ago that the land-lord, whose forbears have owned it for generations back, cannot put a date to it. The inn is not striking in appearance, but inside you tread on a stone-flagged floor that is certainly original; four centuries of use have given it a patina associated more with antique mahogany than stone. In the ancient fireplace is a roasting-spit operated by a complex system of pulleys and weights and maintained in full working order. Every Christmas it is brought into use when an outsize turkey is skewered on to it and the landlord entertains his many friends to dinner. There is no small-boy 'turnspit' on hand today, but friends and family are always ready to manipulate the elaborate system of weight adjustment that is necessary every quarter-hour or so.

Heading next cross-country for St Agnes, I came to Tressilian Bridge, the last of the old-style toll-bridges left. Just behind it is the *Wheel Inn*. The feature that immediately strikes you is the huge straw wagon-wheel incorporated in the heavy thatch. Did this give the inn its name, or is some obscure origin pictorialised in it? No one seems to know. But history was enacted here, for the *Wheel Inn* was used as his headquarters by General Fairfax when he was campaigning in the region and it was the setting for the surrender of the Royalists in Cornwall to the Roundheads.

The thatch wheel apart, the inn is less picturesque than many hereabouts. One evocative feature is the stable-like 'split' main doorway. Tradition holds that, like Cromwell elsewhere, the general housed his horse here as well as himself. And here, until only a few years ago, a tradition was maintained that has now, regrettably, elapsed. Annually on New Year's Eve one hundred 'regulars' would sit down to eat their way through that most traditional of local dishes, the Cornish pasty. And what a pasty! Six feet in length from one 'twist' to the other, oozing good solid meat, belly-filling potato, onions and other ingredients, it was served not merely on the huge refectory table but 'on the house'.

Just short of St Agnes is the homely little *Miners' Arms* at Mithian (there is another so named close to the *Castle of Comfort*, on the Mendips). This is tin-mining country; all the way eastwards from Cape Cornwall may be seen relics of this once-flourishing industry, notably the fine, rugged, engine-house and chimney opposite the *Boscaswell Inn* near Morvah. But the *Miners' Arms*, Mithian, was originally a retreat for monks; the date 1577 is still to be read on a ceiling beam. It is one of those odd buildings that appear larger inside than out. Behind one fireplace a secret chamber was recently found, and also the entrance to a tunnel which, according to local tradition, linked the inn with a neighbouring manor house. There are so many stories of this kind relating English inns to monasteries and manor houses (and nunneries) that most of them must be taken with the proverbial pinch of salt. But this inn has obviously been put to other uses during its four centuries of life. What is now a bed-room was once a tiny chapel; Mithian was sufficiently off the beaten track to have served as a place of refuge in post-Reformation times.

On the far side of Perran Bay but within sight of St Agnes Head is Holywell Bay. Here you will come upon the *Treguth Inn,* a strong contrast in immediate appeal to the *Miners' Arms* ten miles away. Its impact is immediate; it is the sort of inn that silently forces you to pull up and look at it. Until some twenty years ago it was a farm-house—and had been so for many centuries, if not the seven that the landlord claims. White walls, one carrying an attractive wrought-iron sign; a square-cut porch with stone seats, almost concealing the low-lintelled door. A small-paned window on the other side, almost completely obscured by a creeper that has already climbed up the wall, over the low eaves and more than half way up the thatched roof. Though thatch is not rare in Cornwall, it is not often seen quite as elaborately finished as here. Ornamental work runs along the ridge line, neatly edging the squat chimney and patterned with an ornate trellis-work of spars. The thatch, too, reaches down-wards right over the porch and across the outbuildings, so that it forms an integral whole, reminiscent of the great spreading roofs of the Emmental region of the Bernese Oberland.

The main bar is thatched, too. If the ornamental brass and copper-ware is not comparable with that at Penryn's *Seven Stars,* it is never-theless a goodly collection. But it is surpassed in interest by the unique display of no fewer than two hundred army cap badges on the ceiling beams. These were adroitly 'won' from the caps of servicemen from a large number of regiments stationed at one time or another in a camp near by who naturally came to regard this inn as their 'local'. There is a parallel to this feature many hundreds of miles to the north in the bar of the *Collingwood Arms* at Cornhill-on-Tweed, Northumberland, though in that case it is the crests and actual caps of the five Guards regiments which are on display.

In the village of Crantock, five miles to the north beyond the Gannel estuary, is the *Old Albion*, an inn that certainly dates back four hundred years. Its whitewashed walls are stone and cob, roofed with thatch. Holding pride of place on its end wall is a sign depicting a full-rigged 90-gun frigate, H.M.S. *Albion*; in fact the inn was named after a schooner built here before neighbouring Newquay was ever heard of, though Crantock was a thriving seaport and shipyard. It was also, of course, a hideout for smugglers and there is evidence of this. Beside one of the fireplaces there is a blue-tinted stone which seals-off what was the entrance to the smugglers' cellar retreat, carved out of the solid slate. Beneath the floor, too, is the head of the well from which, until a few years ago, the landlord drew up his own water by bucket and rope, as he did at the *Fox & Hounds*, Beauworth, Hampshire, and at the *Red Lion*, Avebury, in Wiltshire, and elsewhere up and down the country.

Beneath the sea, according to tradition, lies the 'lost city' of Langurroc. It is said to have been so populous that it had seven churches. But the inhabitants fell into evil ways and, as a result, one night a storm terrible even by Atlantic coastline standards, blew up and the wind swept so much sand across the area that Langurroc vanished from sight. This type of legend persists round the Cornish coast, as it does round that of 'Cornwall-across-the-water', Corn-ouaille, Brittany, too. But here, oddly, there is no tradition of bells from those churches to be heard on windless nights; Debussy would not have derived inspiration for *La Cathédrale Engloutie* at Crantock, Cornwall, though he might have done at Dunwich, Suffolk.

None the less, at the *Old Albion* you are standing on, or very near to, hallowed ground. Immediately beyond the inn, a fine cedar shadows a lych-gate leading into the churchyard; the church is believed to stand on the very site of a small oratory in which St Carantocus, a companion of St Patrick, established himself in the fifth century. Today's Crantock is, without question, a variant of the saint's name.

It was a morning of great heat and utter stillness when I revisited the village to refresh my memory after a lapse of many years. It seemed to me virtually unchanged from the days when, as a small boy during World War One, I used to walk there from Newquay with a favourite maiden aunt who knew my appetite for saffron buns and 'splits' with strawberry jam and clotted cream. I located without difficulty the cottage, almost opposite the *Old Albion*, in the garden of which we had eaten those delectable teas. True, there were now striped sunshades over garden tables, and people drinking iced drinks from a refrigerator visible inside the kitchen doorway where in my childhood days such things were undreamt of. Had it been nearing teatime, I might have lingered and ordered 'splits' and jam and cream; but I shrewdly suspected that these would no longer taste the same. *Sic transit gloria. . . .*

Such inns as you will find along the coast northwards to Padstow and beyond are steadily adjusting to the requirements of the tourist-by-car; a few miles inland, however, they are slower to change their image. There is the *Ring o' Bells* at St Issey, for example; or the *Earl St Vincent* at Egloshayle, whose modest appearance completely belies the distinction of its name. The *Ring o' Bells* obviously started life as a row of two or three linked cottages, one of which became a tap-room for the locals. It is L-shaped, facing two roads, one of which dips to a tributary of the River Camel. The upper floor of its seaward-facing side and the flattened angle that links it with the other, are neatly slate-hung, for they stand high, exposed to westerly winds. A delightful wrought-iron and painted 'ring' of bells stands out well against the strong white paintwork whose staring whiteness is broken noticeably by the louvred shutters on each side of the windows.

Due north, across the estuary, lies Port Isaac, now matching, in its somewhat self-conscious perfection, *the* Cornish fishing village of Polperro, on the opposite coast. Here you will come upon the *Golden Lion*, dating from 1715, which lifts its gaunt flanks sheer from the harbour immediately below. It was for long, unquestionably, a smugglers' haunt. The grisly-named Bloody Bones Bar is located at the inner end of a tunnel, long since bricked-up by the

Customs & Excise Authorities, that in the heyday of smuggling served both as secret entrance and vital escape-route for the gangs of smugglers (rivals rather than colleagues) who had found this tight cove exactly suited to their nefarious purposes and a succession of landlords whom they could 'keep sweet' either by rake-off from their contraband or by threat of pistol.

Loath to leave this coast, though I knew how much more awaited me on the other, I pressed on northwards to Boscastle to have a look at an inn that can have few rivals in the ugliness league. Nor is this surprising, for it was built as a warehouse, with a rock-hewn cellar for the storage of wine; it fulfilled these two functions for two hundred years or so, not obtaining a licence to sell liquor until twenty-odd years ago. It possesses, however, one virtually unique feature, for which it is famous, or notorious, according to your feelings: for many, many years, when it was not in use, it was taken over by—spiders. Spiders' webs are not only intricately spun but remarkably durable; you can check this for yourself here at Boscastle's *Cobweb Inn*. You can, incidentally, do so likewise, though on a much smaller scale, at the *Victoria & Albert*, Netherhampton, near Salisbury.

I stayed no longer than was necessary to establish that the name of this hideous inn was justified. I have an idiotic but in-built dread of spiders. Years ago, in an attempt to eradicate this fear, I wrote a story about a giant spider; it was published in an illustrated magazine; the illustration was so lifelike that I could not put my hand to the page; far from exorcising my fear, the effort had deepened it; my pathological fear remains, and every autumn in this cottage in the country where I live it is once more grimly put to the test. There are few spiders today among the festooned webs in the bar of this inn; with an eye to his trade, no doubt, the landlord recognises that this phobia is fairly widespread, and allows for it among his customers. One of them, at any rate, will certainly not pay a return visit.

There is no direct road south-eastwards over Bodmin Moor to Bolventor, where one of the loneliest and most windswept inns in all England (and I am not forgetting *Tan Hill* on Arkengarthdale

Moor) is to be found. It overlooks the main road between London
and Land's End. To reach it I took a virtually unmarked road that
led eventually to Altarnun. A five-mile climb brought me to the
Jamaica Inn, my objective.

It is as sinister looking an inn as you could expect to find anywhere: dark grey granite, the upper half of its long façade slate-
hung beneath a heavy slate roof and slate-hung chimneys; a slate-
roofed porch more forbidding than inviting; a massive granite wall
topped by a signboard so forbidding that it alone is sufficient to
daunt the potential caller in search of bed and board or even a quick
glass of ale. The only comparable signboard that I know is that of
the *Rattlebone Inn* at Sherston, in Wiltshire. But in that, even the
brandished, bloodstained sword is somehow less fearsome than the
scowl on the face of the villainous Joss Merlin who glares at you
through his one eye beneath the great tricorn, the embodiment
of evil.

The inn achieved fame in the present century because Daphne du
Maurier used it for inspiration in her best-selling novel of that name,
but it was notorious long, long before that. East- and west-bound
stage-coaches and wagons drew into the huge courtyard, trundling
over the self-same cobbles that are there today, to change horses
between London and Falmouth or Truro. They might or might not
have escaped the highwaymen who frequented these windswept,
desolate heights; they might yet meet them. The inn was almost
certainly a rendezvous for smugglers plying their trade between
coast and coast, along tracks which only they would risk taking in
the dark and which can be treacherous today even in broad day-
light. Curiously, some research has been done into the practicability
of these moorland tracks, and experiments have been carried out
with sure-footed pack-ponies, timing the distances that would have
to be covered both from the north and from the south coast.

The *Jamaica Inn* is not old, by prevailing standards; the year
1780 is generally accepted. Enter it, however, and you will find it
hard to believe that it is so relatively young. It smells of antiquity;
you breathe antiquity. The ceiling of the huge main room is supported by oak pillars like rough-hewn tree-trunks; the joists between

them are hardly less massive. You are surrounded by relics of the age when smugglers and highwaymen flourished: horse-pistols, brandy-kegs, dark-lanterns, powder-flasks, daggers, even short, now rusting swords. A vast granite-block fireplace dominates the room, the huge log fire kept permanently burning. And well it might be, for at no time the whole year round is the temperature here on the near-summit of Bodmin Moor equable, let alone truly warm. Strangely, even if on rare occasions it is warm outside, with the sun shining and the wind temporarily in abeyance, the air strikes chill immediately you cross the threshold of this inn.

I slept there once, many years ago. I forget in which room it was—the narrow doorways to the bedrooms are all inscribed with names from characters in the novel, carved in suitably Gothic lettering. I had seen, and touched, the iron hook from which, in the story, Mary Yellan was persuaded that she could discern a dangling corpse. I did not sleep well, and was not sorry to be on my way next morning as soon as possible, having eaten a rough-and-ready breakfast of home-cured bacon, fried potato and tea strong enough, as they say, 'to trot a mouse on'.

A greater contrast to Bolventor than Lanreath, to the south of Bodmin Moor and in the lush country just short of Polperro, would be hard to find in a distance of less than fifteen miles. To have slept on two consecutive nights in the *Jamaica Inn* and at Lanreath's *Punch Bowl Inn* would have been to sample the two extremes. Perhaps with a subconscious desire to remind myself of this difference, I did stay here overnight; it offers everything that is lacking at the *Jamaica Inn*—save, of course, that sense of brooding menace.

The façade is white-painted with contrasting black window-frames, no two of the same size or at the same level. From an out-thrust oak beam there hangs a wrought-iron sign depicting Mr Punch bearing a bowl and ladle invitingly towards the entrance. Who could resist such a sign? The entrance to this four-centuries-old inn has satin-smooth flagstones leading straight through to a wholly enclosed small courtyard in which you may drink at a table composed of a millstone mounted on a squat granite pillar. An outside staircase climbs the wall to the upper floor. Let into the wall is a window constructed from a wagon wheel, the interstices between its spokes neatly glazed—a most unusual feature. In the centre of the small courtyard is the oddly named St Monarch's Well, the waters of which are believed, locally at any rate, to possess curative properties. Try it for yourself, and decide whether this justifies the somewhat odd taste!

Loving care has been devoted to converting the interior as discreetly as possible from the original function of the house, when it served as the Court House for the region, with a room for thirsty individuals as an ancillary feature. The old bars are still known respectively as the Men's Kitchen and the Farmers' Kitchen, as they were three centuries ago; I know of no other inn with these names. It is also one of the very few inns where mead is still served; it is somehow typical that this traditional drink should survive in a county that has maintained so many traditions that the 'furriners' east of the Tamar have long abandoned.

Upstairs, too, a tradition is maintained. Two or three of the bedrooms contain not only four-poster beds but that rarity, the Cornish half-tester. You might stop overnight in some hundreds of inns before you found one of these; I have done so myself, but the only one I can call to mind is the one I slept in at Lanreath. Here the inn has been brought sufficiently up to date to meet the requirements of the more exacting visitor, as I found when I had my evening meal; it could well have had its status changed to 'Hotel', but happily the owner has retained the homelier term.

Probably the easternmost inn in this westernmost county is to be found in one of its smallest 'lost' hamlets, St John. The winding lane that leads to it skirts Whitesand Bay, passes through the hamlet of Crafthole, where you will find the fantastically named *Finnygook Inn*. What an address to have on one's notepaper: Finnygook, Crafthole, Cornwall! The name derives from the story that a smuggler, Finny by name, was run to earth here and, in the course of a struggle with the Preventive Men, killed. With his last dying breath he swore that he would haunt the place. One of Cornwall's many names for ghost, or poltergeist, is 'gook'. Tradition has it that Finny's gook was as good as his word, and the fact that the house has passed through the hands of so many short-term owners suggests that there is something in it.

A mile or two beyond is the even smaller hamlet of St John, over-looking Whitesand Bay to the south and the estuary to the east that separates Devonport from Plymouth, Cornwall from Devon. Here on the crest of a hill stands the *St John's Inn*. Like the *Roseland* at Philleigh, it could be just a cottage; but its remarkable sign indicates otherwise. It is probably unique: a Maltese Cross painted bright red with, in the centre of it, the head of St John. Beneath the saint's head lies an ornate fish.

I went inside and bought the last Cornish pasty I was to eat before I crossed the Tamar into Devon. The little inn was busier than I would have expected, the bar crowded with naval types from Devonport. The landlord dismissed my inquiry about the fish with a laconic 'St John was a fisherman, wasn't he?' I do not know whether in fact he followed the same calling as Simon and Peter, and ought to have taken the trouble to find out. A naval type at my elbow offered an alternative explanation, with a grin. 'It's a bass, that fish. And this is a Bass-Charrington pub, you see.'

I ate my pasty and swallowed my lager. As I left, I spotted by the door a notice headed RULES OF THIS TAVERN. Briefly it informed potential customers that they must pay '4d a night for Bed; 6d with Pot Luck; 2d for Horsekeeping. No more than 5 to sleep in a Bed; no Boots to be worn in Bed; no Razor-Grinders or Tinkers taken in; Organ-Grinders to sleep in the Wash-House.' I took the hint, and departed. After all, I was—at least by Cornishmen's standards—a 'furriner', and so must watch my step. I could hardly imagine a warning notice of this kind at the *Punch Bowl Inn*, Lanreath; it was conceivable, however, at the *Jamaica Inn*, Bolventor; and these were the last two Cornish inns that I had revisited.

Devonshire

One of the most interesting groups of inns in all England is to be found in the southernmost corner of Devon, north of Kingsbridge and inland from Torquay and Brixham. 'Group', not because they are all owned by the same brewery but because they have in common the fact that they are 'church house inns', built expressly to house the masons—sometimes monk-masons—employed in building medieval churches. They almost always immediately adjoin the church; as good an example as any is the *Church House Inn*, Harberton, a couple of miles south-west of Totnes.

It stands so close to the magnificent tower of St Andrew's that in the early part of the day the shadow of the tower lies across its slated roof and for an hour or two darkens its white-painted façade. It contains some stone, but more obviously the characteristic Devonshire building material of cob, strengthened with reed brought here from Slapton Sands. Nine or ten windows, no two of the same size and few at the same level, break the long line of the façade, the lower part of which is screened by a sloping half-roof that runs its full length. Over each window is a rough-hewn oak beam, dark against the paintwork, uneven, varying in length, occasionally tilted; these are a foretaste of the magnificent oak timbers to be seen when you pass through the doorway inset in the thick, solid wall at the end nearest the church.

The abbot who ordered the building stipulated that once it had served the masons, and they had departed, it should serve as a Chantry House; this it did for several centuries. The community of monks was relatively large for so remote a corner of the country, and the Great Chamber (as it is still called) extends almost the full length of the inn, with what was originally their chapel at the far end. There was even a small workshop for the craftsmen-monks to use; it is now the inn's dart room.

Evidence of the care that went to the building of the *Church House Inn* is to be seen on every hand. The great beams constituting joists and wall-ties are, many of them, beautifully moulded instead of being just roughly adze-hewn. Some years ago, when some plasterwork had to be renewed, a magnificent oak screen was discovered; it had been hidden for centuries and is now a reminder of the purpose for which the inn was built long, long before it became a licensed house. More interesting still is the small double lattice window in the thickness of the inner wall of the main bar, part of the Great Chamber: it contains glass which experts declare to be thirteenth-century in origin, rarely found except in some well-preserved church.

Not all church house inns were designed on quite such a lavish scale. Torbryan's *Church House Inn*, a few miles to the north, is an example of the lowlier type, though it possesses a charm essentially its own. It lies in the heart of one of Devon's least spoiled villages, opposite the church built in the fifteenth century when the earlier one had been destroyed by fire. One of its ceiling beams carries the date 1485, which suggests that the inn was built to house the masons who built the second church.

At this particular inn what are known as 'Church Ales' took place in far-off days. In remote corners of the country like this, worshippers had often to travel considerable distances and it was sometimes the practice to offer them sustenance at the Church Houses, perhaps on arrival and always before they set off again, usually on foot, to their homes. The ale they drank, either free or for a token payment, was normally brewed on the premises, and the dispensing of this 'parish ale' was a useful source of income to the ecclesiastical authorities in the diocese through the fifteenth and sixteenth centuries and even later than that.

This particular inn is more picturesque than that at Harberton: one of a row of three linked cottages, white-painted with small windows picked out in black and dominated by a chimney that, curiously, rises from ground level, standing proud from the façade and cutting through the overhanging eaves of the lichen-covered slate roof. Each window has an irregularly shaped oak beam, sometimes oddly 'dished', and heavy enough, you might think, to cause the glass panes beneath to crack. There is no room here comparable with the Great Chamber at Harberton, but this was not designed for use as a Chantry House. Its link with the church beyond the hedge at the end of the garden, however, is clear enough. It possesses an oak-panelling screen that could have been salvaged from the original church, destroyed by fire six centuries ago. It possesses, too, an inventory drawn up by the owners, the church, in the year 1617

6   Rose & Crown, Lyng

7   Ye Olde Kings Arms, Litton

8 George & Crown, Speldhurst

9 The Crown Point, Seal Chart

which includes mention of two 'chittles'—an old word for kettle—
that had doubtless been used in the entertainment of the deserving
parishioners. The purely secular use to which the inn was eventually
put is emphasised by a row of skittles hanging from one of the
beams; the landlord assured me that they were three hundred years
old and more, though now there is no skittle-alley as there once
had been.

Another of these Church Houses may be found a few miles west
of Kingsbridge, on the road to Aveton Gifford. This *Church House
Inn*, or at least some portions of it, may date back to the mid-
thirteenth century. Its ancient fireplace is remarkable. It was originally designed as a Rest House for the monks from the neighbouring
Benedictine Abbey, though it was also used by the masons who
built a number of churches in the district; the very name of the
village, Churchstow, indicates a 'place of churches' and this inn is
but one of those in the district built by the men who ate, drank and
slept here while they were engaged on church building. There is yet
another at Marldon, almost within the boundaries of sophisticated
Paignton; this one is more substantial than the others, and was
occupied by a succession of vicars.

This county is not unique in possessing these Church Houses. A
mile or two on the other side of the Tamar at Pillaton, in Cornwall,
there is *The Weary Friar*, an L-shaped, low-slung building hard up
against the grassy mound on which the church was built. It claims
to date from the twelfth century, but this date is suspect; however,
it *was* built to house the masons, though obviously it has since been
enlarged and much altered. Unlike the Devon Church Houses, it is
differently named; on the corner of its white-painted exterior, at
first-floor level, it carries a charming near-life-size black silhouette
of a friar in tattered gown, staff in hand, making his laborious way
towards the bracket lamp that invites him to rest his weary bones.

Very few of the inns in this book are to be found located in
towns, or even in townships. An exception, however, must be made
for the *Kingsbridge*, on the outskirts of Totnes. It is truly more rural
than urban: white-and-black-painted, at an angle to the road and
overlooking the rooftops below. It is owned by enthusiasts who are

lovingly working on it during such time as they can spare from the business of the bar. The man who runs it with his wife is a former member of the D'Oyly Carte Opera Company, and at the slightest hint will break out into one of Sullivan's airs.

The inn was used by shepherds who found themselves benighted on the wrong side of the old town walls; by Elizabethan times it was well established, and it may well be on account of that tradition that the 'management' have thrown themselves in whole-heartedly with Totnes's traditional 'Elizabethan Nights'. These take place every Tuesday from June to September. As many as will, attired in Elizabethan costumes, meet in the Great Barn behind the inn, to indulge in madrigals and folk-singing and the playing of contemporary as well as more modern instruments.

The interior of the inn is rich in the unexpected. Just inside the entrance is an old stone trough, backed by a cast-iron water-pump from which, until the mains were laid on, the earlier generations of landlords laboriously drew their water. Today the trough is kept full, and bright goldfish bring a touch of colour to the sombre stone. In the small bar there is a fireplace whose stonework is believed to be of Saxon origin, though this cannot be proved. Above it is a locally-made 'faggot' of willow wands and ash stems, bound by knotted rings of hazel. Such bundles, when dry, are known to 'explode' when thrown on to an open fire. When this happens, drinks are 'on the house'. Canny innkeepers where the tradition is maintained take care to use green hazel for the 'knots', for these do not explode but burn slowly.

North of Totnes, at the end of a narrow and twisting lane is the hamlet of Littlehempston: two or three cottages, a church, and the *Tally Ho*. None of your Devonshire cob walls here, but good solid granite blocks throughout, for you are on the eastern fringe of Dartmoor. The stone has happily been left in its natural state, unpainted, only the porch being picked out in white; but almost the whole building is Virginia creeper-clad, a glory of russet, dark red, near-purple in the autumn.

Though its name hardly suggests this, the inn was originally a Church House; as long ago as the fourteenth century it was granted a licence to dispense ale, and among the many who appreciated this later on were the magistrates and their minions who used an upper room as their official Court House until they removed to Totnes Guildhall. The room is there still, entered by way of granite steps that climb to it from ground level. Examples of the use of such inns for this purpose abound throughout the country: one thinks of the *Red Lion* at Kingham, Kent, of the *Church House Inn* at Torver, close to Coniston Water in the Lake District, and the *Hundred House* near Great Witley in Worcestershire, among many others.

Centuries after this small inn was built for the church masons it was purchased by a local squire and re-named the *Bolton Arms*. Much more recently it became the meeting-place of the local otter hunt and the then landlord was induced to change the name to its present one. Happily the present landlord is, as we should all be, strongly against otter hunting and has had the courage to request the Master to meet elsewhere. He talked about the cruelty of this so-called sport as he busily polished his fine collection of brass and copperware which runs almost the full length of the bar beneath the former Court Room. The burnishing of his three hundred individual pieces is his Wednesday morning chore. I was tactless enough to mention the famous collection at the *Seven Stars*, Penryn, and what I told him was not too well received.

South-west of this covey of Church House Inns and others there are individual inns of charm and interest such as the *Crabshell* at Kingsbridge, where cider has been brewed since the seventeenth century, though I found it over-sophisticated for my taste today; in another of the many creeks and minor estuaries between Prawle Point and Stoke Point there is the *Hope Anchor* at Hope Cove where also you may watch people in Kenneth Grahame's classic phrase 'messing about in boats'; from the windows of both *The Swan* and the *Old Ship* at Noss Mayo you may employ yourself in the same way, as I did on one unhappily wet day. More interesting, however, to me at any rate, is the little inn at Ringmore, between Kingsbridge and Noss Mayo, so secluded that you must study your map carefully to locate it. It fully justifies the effort.

This is *Journey's End*. Not necessarily yours, and certainly not mine, for I had yet many hundreds of miles of travel ahead of me, with my own journey's end somewhere in the North Country. The inn stands almost at the end of a track that leads tortuously down to a tight little cove from a mere lane on the outskirts of a hamlet, a cove that has been used by smugglers for centuries. It is white-painted, with black-framed windows and flower-baskets suspended beside the little porch. It was originally the *New Inn*, built, it is said, at the command of the first Elizabeth, as were so many of the same name. If so, it certainly does not look its age. The name it bears today is more obviously appropriate, for it is virtually 'at the end of the road'. In fact, it is so named because here R. C. Sherriff wrote that play, *Journey's End*, a slice-of-life from World War One that became one of the most popular plays of the century; so, it is hardly surprising that the then landlord cashed-in on the name and took it for his inn.

The great mass of Dartmoor naturally offers few inns; but there is a scatter of them up the western fringe, as up the eastern fringe. At Clearbrook, for instance, eight miles north of Plymouth and uphill all the way, there is the unpretentious *Skylark*. It stands on a stretch of rough, bracken-covered ground from which, improbable as it may seem in such a region, the lark's sweet cry is often to be heard—hence the name. While looking at the old bread-ovens that are a feature of this one-time farmhouse, and in the bar now called the Lark's Nest, I listened in vain for it 'in the clear air ascending'.

A couple of miles to the north, and more difficult to locate, is the *Royal Oak* at Meavy. It is a truly modest little place: a long, low, whitewashed building immediately overlooking the village green, whose chief feature is an oak tree (hence the inn's name) of indeterminate age whose lower boughs, big as tree-trunks themselves, have had to be supported by iron posts which are braced against the lych-gate of the church beside the inn. The *Royal Oak* is as unpretentious within as without; but it must be older than the tree, for it is actually mentioned in Domesday. As a property, it belongs to the parish of Meavy, and a proportion of its takings go to the upkeep of the church; the fact is symbolised by the physical link between the iron braces of the oak tree and the lych-gate leading into the churchyard.

Northwards from here, beyond Tavistock, you will come to Peter Tavy and Mary Tavy, on opposite sides of the stream from which they, and the market town below, take their name. At the first is the *Peter Tavy Inn*, a small, compact building of whitewashed granite reminiscent in shape, though on a smaller scale, of the *Treguth Inn* at Holywell Bay. In the sixteenth century, and for long afterwards, it was a farmhouse where cider was brewed for local consumption only; being so far off the beaten track, it is unlikely that its clientele is other than local even today. Its bar is so minuscule that if more than three people want to drink there the later customers have to take their glasses out into the small courtyard.

Beyond Mary Tavy, again up a narrow lane that climbs steeply for a couple of miles and then fades out on the lower slopes of Nat Tor, you come upon an inn with what surely is one of the most improbable names in the country, if not unique: *Elephant's Nest*. Why that extraordinary name? According to the landlord it is the outcome of ribaldry among the tin-miners who operated hereabouts until the industry came to an end. The building was originally a pair of miners' cottages; at some time the party-wall was removed and a licence was granted to sell ale and cider at this *New Inn*. But some time in the last century the landlord happened to be a man of enormous size, weighing almost twenty stone. The bar was so small that he virtually 'overflowed' it with his sheer bulk. Some tin-miner, over a quart of home-brewed, had the wit to dub him 'an elephant in the nest', and the nickname stuck. Far from taking offence, the landlord recognised the publicity-value of the joke and promptly renamed his inn.

Northwards again and you will come to the *Castle Inn* at Lydford, another of these long, low-pitched, hospitable looking inns, white-painted and creeper-clad; it looks all the more welcoming by contrast with the remains of the sombre stonework of Lydford Castle close by. Hard up against the inn is the old stannary prison into which, as far back as the twelfth century, offenders against the tin-mining statutes would be thrown to await trial at the nearest Stannary

Court. Small as it seems today, Lydford was important right back to Saxon times; in the *Castle Inn*, among other local relics, you may see two 'Lydford Pennys', struck in the local mint in the far-distant days of King Ethelred the Unready.

On the northern fringe of Dartmoor there are a number of small inns, most of which I already knew though I intended to revisit them to refresh not only myself but my memory. However, there was a handful of inns along the coastline of Devon and overlapping into the northernmost tip of Cornwall that I had yet to revisit, and I decided to go and look at these before returning to the eastern part of Devonshire. I made therefore in the direction of Welcombe, on the border of the two counties, as obviously attractive an objective as any on the map. Taking a very minor road, so as to avoid holiday traffic, I found myself bound in the first instance for Sheepwash.

Here, overlooking a neat square, is the *Half Moon*, as picturesque and charming a rural inn as I can call to mind, at least in the category of cottages-turned-inns. If it does have a signboard, I do not remember it; nor does it appear in any of the photographs I took of it. Its cream-washed, rough-cast façade has four small windows above and two below, with a little gabled porch between them; the whole is creeper-clad and embowered with roses beneath a lichen-encrusted slate roof. As its name implies, Sheepwash is in a sheep-farming district; it was the local market and both the sloping square and the yard behind the inn served the needs of buyers and vendors. Today, however, motor transport makes it possible for sheep to be conveyed to larger and busier markets; Sheepwash sleeps in the sun and the *Half Moon*, with its five-mile stretch of the River Torridge, renowned for its trout, caters for the angler. I learned this when, having looked in to get the feel of the interior where, against the large open fireplace with its inviting ingle-nook, I saw an assembly of fly-fishers' rods in one corner and, in the window, a heavily moustachioed individual engrossed in the all-absorbing task of creating a trout-fly to his own delicate design.

To reach the Cornwall-Devon border at the coast I travelled due west as far as Stratton, still in the first-named county. There, the *Tree Inn* was temporarily closed for renovation. I remember it well from a night I spent beneath its roof some years ago. The beams spanning the main room were four centuries old; the twisting stair that led up to my bedroom brought me on to a corridor that, as I walked along it, felt like a trampoline, and, what is more, a trampoline that creaked with every step. Remembering this, I speculated as I stood outside the great double doors that seal off the courtyard that perhaps those vast beams had finally proved unequal to their span. The Cornish giant Anthony Payne was born here and spent much of his life, when he was not soldiering, beneath this roof. At thirty-eight stone (almost *double* the weight of that landlord of the *Elephant's Nest* near Horndon), he must have imposed a near-intolerable strain on those oak timbers.

So, I drove on some five or six miles to the most northerly inn in Cornwall, the *Bush Inn*, Morwenstow. Just short of the church of Rev. Robert Stephen Hawker fame, on your left, is a somewhat crude looking, cottage-like stone building with a thatched roof, crouching from the Atlantic gales at the far side of an open common. Is it truly, as they claim, of thirteenth-century origin? If so, how often has that roof had to be replaced, even if the stonework is original? It began life as a monastic cell, or small oratory; it was probably occupied by Cistercians, for they yielded to none in their asceticism, choosing whenever possible the bleakest, most exposed of sites. Evidence of its original monastic nature is to be found in the fact that in an inner wall, now that of the Kitchen Bar, there is a piscina, emphatically of Celtic origin, carved out of the serpentine for which Cornwall is noted.

It did not remain a monastic establishment; for three centuries past it has held a liquor licence. It cannot have had a large clientele, for this is a deserted area to this day. But if you care to explore the cliffs near by you will find a track that leads upwards from the cliff base to the top; it is known as the Smugglers' Track—a self-explanatory name! Who knows how many of these contrabandists have over the years trodden the stone-slab floor of the *Bush Inn*, sheltered within its solid walls, and drunk to the success of their latest escapade? The very name indicates the function of this squat building near the cliff edge. One of the oldest signs on a licensed house—

earlier by far than the now familiar fixed or swinging signboard—was an actual bush. Three centuries ago a couplet appeared in the *Perambulations of Poor Robin*:

> Some ale-houses upon the road I saw,
> And some whose *bushes* showed that wine they draw . . .

The simple lines echo the old proverb: 'Good wine needs no bush'.

Immediately to the north and only a few yards over the border into Devonshire again is the *Old Smithy Inn*. This, too, stands at the end of a narrow road, just short of the cliff edge and, with a cottage or two, constitutes the whole of the hamlet of Welcombe. The village must surely have been larger than it is today, or it would hardly have needed its own smithy. The inn which bears its name does not look old, but its link with the original building is to be seen in the anvil on which the older inhabitants will tell you that the sledge-hammers of Caleb Wakely and his son once rang from dawn to dusk. Old man Caleb had a sideline that must seem to us macabre. Among the tools that he, like all smiths, had fashioned for himself was a small pair of pincers. With these, for the price of a quart of ale, he would extract a rotten tooth, sitting astride his anvil and gripping his client's head between his knees, the poor man's face buried deep in the leather apron so that his cries were muffled.

Back on to the A39 you come to the *Hoops Inn* at Horns Cross, one of the most immediately attractive inns for many miles around, at least on a main road. Long enough to have three porches, each thatched like the roof that spans it from end to end, this many-windowed inn was a staging-post on this North Devonshire main road throughout the heyday of long-distance horse-drawn travelling. It stands some five hundred feet above sea level, near enough to the sea to have been also the haunt of contrabandists in their day. It was long famed for the ale brewed on the premises—stronger as well as cheaper than what you buy today. You drink beneath a low ceiling spanned by heavy beams and contained within walls some of which are four feet thick; indeed, one is so thick that a pair of bake-ovens by the fireplace were hollowed out of it.

Strangely, there is more headroom in one at any rate of the upstairs chambers, one in which there is an enormous four-poster no less than eight feet high, almost comparable with Shakespeare's Great Bed of Ware that was alleged to sleep twelve in comfort. From its window you look out across the road at a stage-coach appropriately named *Lorna Doone*, the heavy wheels of which long knew the steep hills and treacherous bends of this coastal road on which it used to ply, taking in Minehead and Lynton, Combe Martin and Ilfracombe. It was in regular use until the end of last century, and a craftsman at work on a rear spring the day I was there told me that no fewer than six trace-horses were required in addition to the shaft-horses to negotiate the Lynmouth, Porlock and Countisbury hills.

This area is rich in small inns; you can perambulate for days on end, finding something new at every other turn. A few miles inland from Horns Cross, at Buckland Brewer, is the *Coach & Horses*, a smaller version of the *Hoops Inn*. During the seventeenth century one of its rooms served as Court House, as at Littlehempston's *Tally Ho* on the diametrically opposite side of the county. An unusual exhibit here is a beadle's staff, or truncheon, found in that very room during the course of renovation. Another exhibit is a cannonball said to date back to the Civil War, found embedded in an outer wall.

Due north of Barnstaple, if you leave the main road, a narrow lane between high banks will take you steeply downhill into the hamlet of Berrynarbour and its seventeenth-century *Olde Globe Inn*. Do not be put off by its rather commonplace exterior, for it is well worth a look inside. It has an unusual lime-ash floor, from which upright beams support cross-beams and the floor above your head. At one end of the bar is a curious semi-circular length of wall which curves half way round a vast open fireplace to form a most inviting inglenook. It is virtually cut out of the immensely thick stone wall of the building, which was originally a row of small cottages.

There is an echo here, incidentally, of the unusual feature of the *Kingsbridge* at Totnes, though at Berrynarbour it is a custom preserved that goes back to pre-Christian times, one which is to be found in various forms in many parts of the world. Here it is known as the ceremony of the Ashen Faggot.

Annually on Christmas Eve a bundle of ash wands, bound with nine—it must always be nine—withies, is brought to the fireplace in which the fire has been deliberately allowed to die. Into the faintly glowing embers the Ashen Faggot is thrown; it ignites and the fire is then said to be re-born. Any churchman will tell you that this symbolises the Resurrection—and so of course it does. But you will find in Frazer's *Golden Bough* and elsewhere irrefutable evidence that this was a world-wide ceremony in pagan times: the Old Year was dying; the New Year, with its hope and promise, was born, arising phoenix-like from the ashes.

From Berrynarbour it is a stone's throw across the bay to Combe Martin, and here you cannot miss that monstrosity, the *Pack of Cards* inn. It is the antithesis of all that the Devonshire inn so far has offered; nevertheless it should not be missed, for it tells an odd, three-dimensional story.

Squire Ley had a passion for gambling and won a fortune at the card table. He celebrated his fortune by building a memorial to himself and his run of luck, and this inn is the result, as its name suggests. Four storeys (for the four suits) and thirteen windows to each storey. You can count them for yourself, though some were boarded up after his death in 1716, when his memorial became an inn. As you might expect, inside this glaring white-and-black edifice there is quite a display of odd relics. The most unusual, and the largest—one which I have never yet found duplicated elsewhere—is a huge refectory-type table supported on four massive legs. Ten feet in length and some five feet wide, it is also eighteen inches deep. Why the unexpected depth rather than the usual solid slab of oak, maybe two inches thick? I was given the answer. This is a Press-Gang Table. Its 'lid' can be raised, to reveal a long, wide, shallow 'coffin'. At the warning of the approach of a Press Gang, potential victims clambered inside, the lid was closed, and other customers, too old for possible press-ganging, sat round the table, beer mugs in hand, drinking as men do drink, and almost invariably allaying suspicion—an effective ruse.

It was time, now, to turn inland again, south-eastwards, to pick up my earlier tracks, for I wished to finish with Devon before looking round Somerset. Since most of Exmoor is in the latter county, I skirted it to the west once more and made for Umberleigh, where the *Rising Sun* looks due east across the River Taw, a somewhat complacent smile on its face, as though hiding a secret that no one would suspect. It was, in fact, originally a monastery Rest House. It knew periods of harassment, too, and behind the fireplace behind one of its bars there is the entrance to what was once a priest's hide. The beams are old, very old. They are believed to have been taken from the monastery when it was abandoned; certainly they have that 'feel' about them. The landlord pointed to a date carved in one of them. It read: 1010. Only an expert could prove whether that was the date when the beam was hewn; for my own part, sceptic that I have become after a long succession of these claims and counter-claims, I suspect that the date was inscribed on that beam long, long after it was cut from the living tree, seasoned and set in place, whether in the monastery or in the inn.

Southwards from Umberleigh is the tiny village of Winkleigh (-leigh is a particularly common suffix hereabouts, with Warkleigh, Chulmleigh, Chawleigh, Kennerleigh and Bondleigh among other close neighbours). Here is the charming *Ring o' Bells*, as obvious an example of a church house inn as any in the Harberton group far to the south, though it does not specifically call itself one. It stands right against the church gate, truly a church house, though built, as its records show, to accommodate the masons who rebuilt the thirteenth-century church a century or so later. It is thatched, and one window-ear is cocked, as it were, for the chimes of the mellifluous bells near by from which it has taken its name.

Five miles to the south is Sampford Courtenay; on the angle of the road by which I approached it and the B3216 stands the *New Inn*. Not 'new' at all, of course; sixteenth-century in fact. But it is memorable not so much for its age, which is not obvious, as for the quite extraordinary assemblage of agricultural and other implements and relics displayed not merely within but across the face of its impressive exterior. Against a white-painted façade reaching up to a high gable and well thatched roof there stand out, imaginatively arranged and mounted, scythes and besoms, wicked-looking hay-knives, two-handed cross-cut tree-felling saws, saddlery and harness-work, ox-yokes and milkmaids' yokes, pitchforks, hay-rakes, ox-horns, antlers, man-traps, wagon-wheels, ploughs and ploughshares, delicately fashioned pony-trap wheels, curved shafts, carriage-lamps, thatch-rakes and goodness-knows-what-else.

The collecting of these has been a labour of love on the part of the landlord over many years; everything on view comes from the immediate neighbourhood, with the exception of a lifebelt, which here strikes a false note. On the roof ridge there is a well-preserved specimen of a 'penny-farthing'; solidly on the ground close to the inn wall is a set of blacksmith's pear-shaped bellows and an old-world man-operated fire-engine which was in use locally until the turn of the century. Its services had been much in demand as the thatched roofs of the cottages caught fire.

Southwards again and a narrow road dips into the hamlet of South Zeal. There is the *Oxenham Arms*, and your mind leaps back to your childhood reading of Kingsley's *Westward Ho!*, to Amyas Leigh and Salvation Yeo, 'flower and pattern of all bold mariners'. But this inn dates back many centuries before the action of that fine novel. Eight centuries ago it was what is known as a 'lay monastery'; it has held a licence to sell liquor for the past five hundred years. Immediately you cross the threshold you are almost overwhelmed by the pervading sense of antiquity. Atmosphere apart, it has a most striking feature: two granite monoliths rise from the stone floor, each supporting the enormous beam that spans the hearth; one of them is not part of the wall but stands proud from the fireplace; you can walk round it. It resembles any one of the innumerable 'standing stones' on neighbouring Dartmoor; more than one archaeologist has suggested that it was already *in situ* when the house was built around it, for it is embedded far more deeply below the floor than would normally be the case. These monoliths are rugged, naked, challenging; to see them on the open moor is one thing; to encounter them beneath a roof is another thing altogether!

The huge slabstones constituting the floor give the impression of having been there, like the monoliths, since the beginning of time. The massive black oak beams immediately over your head support ceiling, stairs and gallery; the entire framework of this lay-monastery-turned-inn was conceived on the heroic scale. One of the open fireplaces consists of a single eight-foot granite lintel two feet thick supported on two shorter but equally massive granite columns, suggestive of a dolmen that was once the grave of some chieftain in megalithic times. So thick is the outer wall that a spiral staircase has been carved out of it, a feature reminiscent, if on a smaller scale, of the *brochs* in Shetland such as Mousa.

Beyond Chagford and Moretonhampstead, still on the fringe of Dartmoor, is the picturesque hamlet of North Bovey, with yet another *Ring o' Bells*. But for its sign you might well take it for a cottage or small farmhouse. I came to it at dusk, enchanted by its setting: a small church, a village green, some gnarled trees, a cottage or two and a delightful little post office. One cottager told me, as I inquired for the unobtrusive inn, that North Bovey had recently won the prize for the best-kept village in the county. At that moment my eye was caught by a string of garish electric bulbs, multicoloured, that had just lit up along the frontage of a building tucked away on the opposite side of the green. 'There's the *Ring o' Bells*, if you want it,' she said, and from the tone of her voice I could guess that she disapproved of this form of self-advertisement. I did, too. Were those electric lights installed before, or after, this village won its coveted award? I would like to think that someone with moral courage might drop a hint about this to the landlord. But, in these competitive days, self-advertisement has become a *sine qua non*.

The landscape between Ashburton and Exeter is currently being altered out of all recognition, in the interest of the motorist-in-a-hurry; village after village is being swallowed up; those that survive tend to take some finding. One of these is Doddiscombsleigh. It is worth the search, if only to locate the *Nobody Inn*, which looks less like an inn than even the *Roseland* at Philleigh. It is one of a row of small cottages, the one adjoining the inn being the post office, probably the smallest in the country. Flowers and shrubs overflow along the white-painted frontages of all the cottages, beneath their lichened roofs. Rustic fences are intermingled with walls of uneven granite blocks. Immediately opposite, a field slopes steeply upwards. It would seem that visitors are a rarity, for the mild-eyed cows grazing in it were so interested in the man-with-the-camera trying to find a vantage-point behind the hedge that I was continuously nuzzled out of balance.

The cows were the only evidence of any life in sleepy Doddis-combsleigh—the very name suggests drowsiness! It was only as I turned the corner to follow the lane away from the village that I spotted the picture-sign that amplifies the name of the inn. It was a mysterious looking cloaked figure on horseback, obviously be-nighted. He was leaning out of his saddle and knocking urgently on the door of the *Nobody Inn*. ' "Is there anybody there?" said the Traveller, Knocking on the moonlit door,' wrote Walter de la Mare in *The Listeners*. Here, apart may be from the ghosts, there was Nobody In. . . .

On the other side of the estuary of the River Exe there is a handful of inns that call for mention, though because this is a more sophisti-cated area they mostly lack the charm and atmosphere of those to the west. At Tipton St John's, just inland from Sidmouth, is the *Bowd Inn*. It appears to have started life as a pair of cottages linked back-to-back instead of in tandem, for there is a 'valley' in the thatch running lengthwise between them. Its exterior is white and glossy black paintwork on the typical cob walls, but it is the interior that is the more memorable. The huge fireplace has two bread-ovens attached to it and its solid appearance gives the probably erroneous impression that the place was built around it. No one there could explain the name, which reminded me of the so-called 'Bowder Stone' in the Lake District, which itself is a North Country version of Treen's Logan Rock. But there are no boulders in this south-east corner of the county from which it could take its name.

Nearer to Exeter, at Broad Clyst, is the *Red Lion*, an inn much older than it looks, parts of it at any rate seventeenth century. It is not a church house inn, but shares with the church close by a cobbled courtyard overlooked by a lych-gate that gives the impression of being shared between them. The roof is no longer thatched, as it used to be. A century or so ago the thatch caught fire and, because of the strong wind at the time, more than half of the thatched roofs in the village were destroyed by the sparks. The memory of this disaster survives to this day. So great was the conflagration that sparks were carried to the neighbouring hamlets, as far as the Woodburys, and farmers had to get busy throwing water over their ricks and barns. The *Red Lion*'s fabric escaped, for the wind that carried the sparks so far afield kept them clear of the structure itself, an irony that was not overlooked.

This small corner of Devonshire is thick with Clysts-this-and-that and Woodburys-this-and-that. One of these is Woodbury Salterton, where the *Digger's Rest* catches the eye. Four, possibly five, centuries ago this was a farmhouse. The farmer used to brew his own cider, for which he became well-known far and wide. In due course he obtained a licence and the house became the *Salterton Inn*. Why the change of name? No one could answer my question. Certainly an obvious labourer is shown 'at rest' on the signboard, but he does not look the typical Australian 'digger'. Behind him is the lightly curving façade of creamy-pink-washed cob wall, its upper windows almost obliterated by the thick thatch that overhangs them. Baskets of flowers hang on it. Inside, there is a fine fireplace constructed of stone taken from a mason's yard when the church nearly opposite was being restored. More interesting: comparatively recently a magnificent oak screen was revealed when plaster and no fewer than twenty layers of old wallpaper were stripped away.

I was anxious to obtain my own photographs of the *Digger's Rest*, but came to it when the sky was overcast and rain imminent. I had foolishly left my pocket compass behind and had no means of knowing in which direction the inn faced so that I could gauge the best time for a return visit in better conditions. Astonishingly, no one could answer my question. I put it more simply: 'Where does the sun rise?' Blank looks by way of response. Perhaps no one in Woodbury Salterton gets out of bed before the middle of the day? Eventually I solved the problem quite simply. I took my bearings from the church, knowing that it would be aligned west-east. I found that the inn faces roughly north-east. This meant that I must be there pretty early in order to get the benefit of sunlight on its curving façade. There was no accommodation available, so this involved an early-morning dash to the village from where I put up for the night. The early morning dawned fine. I raced to Woodbury Salterton and got my photographs. And so early a start to the day suggested as good an excuse as any for saying goodbye to Devonshire and heading north into Somerset, the third in my trio of West Country counties.

Somerset

A Devonian will always maintain that you do not enter the true West Country until you have crossed the River Axe, just west of Lyme Regis. Maybe. But I have always held that you have entered the West Country when you have crossed the Mendips, with the Quantocks and the Brendon Hills immediately ahead. You can attempt to placate him by reminding him that there is another River Axe, which flows off the Mendips to enter the Bristol Channel at Weston-super-Mare, but he will remain unpersuaded. In any case, I was now on my way out of, not entering, the West Country. I was in a bit of a hurry, too. The weather that had complicated matters for me at Woodbury Salterton was still threatening; a south-westerly wind was banking up cloud, and I wanted to keep ahead of this. So, I took the main road almost due northwards from Exeter. I crossed the border just north of Bampton and made straight for Winsford, nestling between the western slopes of the Brendon Hills and the eastern slopes of Exmoor.

Here, in as pretty a village as you will find in all Somerset (though Bicknoller, with its *Bicknoller Inn*, runs it pretty close), is what must surely be one of England's most picturesque inns, the *Royal Oak*. For the record, it was selected as the 'typical English inn' to represent this country in the British Exhibition staged in New York some twelve years ago, where a replica was appropriately named *Britannia Inn*!

Deep, curving thatch fits so closely over the small upper windows

10   Hay Waggon Inn, Hartfield

11   The Tiger Inn, East Dean

12   Blacksmiths Arms, Adversane

13   The Fox, Charlton

that they might be said to be eyes half-hidden by shaggy eyebrows. Last time I was there, and had stayed the night, the thatch was in process of being renewed. I had sat on the green and watched the thatcher at work throughout much of the day, fascinated by his craftsmanship. That was ten years or so ago. Then, the new thatch was straw-gold; now it had darkened to the true thatch colour of a well-baked, crusty loaf, almost tobacco-brown.

Inside, you will find a twist in almost every one of its walls, in which true right angles are rare. Beneath your feet the floors seem to undulate, though they have not the trampoline-like effect of those at the *Tree Inn*, Stratton; there is no vast room beneath them. Massive beams project at odd angles, appearing and disappearing through the inner walls; from these, you can guess at the main lines of the roof rafters, though these are hidden by the spread of white plaster. From any one of the small, secretive windows you look out at the green: an open-air skittle-alley shadowed by a stand of trees; just beyond this, a medieval pack-horse bridge alongside a shallow ford; both lead to the centuries-old church that dominates the village.

I was tempted to continue northwards, if only to re-visit the *Ship Inn* at Porlock where, forty years ago, I had been foolish enough to drink a glass of rough cider before beginning to push my bicycle from sea level to the summit of Porlock Hill, 1,400-odd feet above; I had appreciated my folly within the first hundred yards. A glance at the sky, however, induced me to change my mind and, instead, to turn east, away from the wind-borne clouds. I glanced perfunctorily at the *Foresters' Arms* at Williton and the *Bicknoller Inn*, both on the west side of the Quantocks, and made instead for Combe Florey and the *Farmers' Arms*.

Not only its massively buttressed, white-painted walls and small windows beneath wide-spreading, deep thatch but its open hearths and massive beams make it easy enough to accept the claim that the place is more than four hundred years old. The feature that immediately catches the eye is the notable collection of horse-brasses. The landlord regards these with a peculiar satisfaction; it is not so much that they are all genuine as that every one of them has been presented to him by one or other of his appreciative customers. The first gift dates back forty years, and still they come along: proof of the good relationship that has persisted between men on each side of the bar during four decades. Did I use the word bar? I should not have done. This inn is one of the very few in the country that do not have a bar, as such, but serve direct from dark, cool cellars. Among the traditional ornaments on walls and beams are firkins and other small specimens of the cooper's art (now sadly dying, with the advent of the metal keg), such as those that harvesters used to take their cider out to the fields. Another feature is a 'wag-o'-the-wall' clock that quietly ticks away the long, leisurely hours beneath this roof.

Ten miles to the south-east, at Henlade, is the *Blackbrook Inn*, an almost blindingly white-painted building whose tall white chimneys are silhouetted against a dark tiled roof. Its chief feature is a great bow-window that rises through both storeys, to be capped by a conical gable that merges well with the lines of the roof. The designer must have been a man of some originality. Between the high bow-window block and the small, gabled porch there is a smaller, single-storeyed bow-window, trapped as it were between the two but stoutly holding its own. An odd feature of the staring façade is an array of deer antlers large and small, irregularly placed among the various windows. Within, you step on to a slabstone floor with the patina of age; here, in days gone by, the Court Leet, or Manorial Court, used to be held and justice (or injustice) dispensed in cases deemed not serious enough to be taken to the Assizes at the County Town, Taunton.

Once again, with the weather in mind, I had to choose between alternatives: either to continue on to look again at the *Volunteer Inn* at Seavington St Michael, with its gay and arresting signboard, and thence to the *Devonshire Arms* at Long Sutton and the *Half Moon* at Somerton; or to go northwards by way of Lyng, Emborough, Litton and Stanton Wick (alias, most charmingly, Compton Dando). I plumped for this alternative as it would enable me to run up and over the Mendip Hills.

The *Rose & Crown* at Lyng was originally a pair of cottages; the pair were knocked into one, to become a farmhouse on foundations that date back some four hundred years. Overlooking a road that carried a good deal of wagon traffic as well as pack-horse trains to and from Taunton, it became a favourite stopping-place, and in due course an ale licence was granted and farming became a sideline. Like the inn, at Henlade, this is painted white, but the impact is relieved by trelliswork on which roses climb luxuriously.

The contrast within is even more striking. One noteworthy feature is a fine oak screen, almost certainly originating in some manor house though no one seems able to confirm this positively. On one wall is a fine specimen of what is known as a 'Parliamentary Clock', a large and relatively rare cousin of the more common 'wag-o'-the-wall' version. Its black and gilt dial is almost a yard in diameter, with hands and figures to match; its characteristic squat 'tail', containing the weights, bears its maker's signature; Ant'y March, London. Such clocks are a slow-ticking reminder of the days when there was a tax on timepieces and only the affluent could afford them. Poorer folk had to rely on clocks in public places—including public houses. After two hundred-odd years of constant use, it still keeps remarkably good time.

Before you leave the *Rose & Crown*, glance up at the beams immediately overhead. It is perfectly true that most buildings of this age have oak beams supporting the floorboards above. But here the pattern is most unusual, possibly even unique. Instead of the customary long main beams and occasional cross-tie, here you have a chequer-board of bold six-foot squares composed of wedge-shaped beams beautifully interlocked. And again, before you leave, step down from the bar into a small room at a lower level. Inset in the fireplace is a stone mask which was brought to light during structural alterations and is believed to represent King Alfred.

The hamlet of Emborough, what there is of it, stands close to two important roads that cross the Mendips. At their junction is an imposing building known today as *Old Down Inn*. With its classic portico and well-spaced windows it looks more like a gentleman's country seat than an inn. Nevertheless it was a posting-house in the eighteenth century, when it was already a hundred and fifty years old. Its chief claim to distinction—for there were posting-houses on every road of importance at that time—is that for decades it served as the official franking office handling long-distance mail and packages entering the country from ports such as Falmouth. In fact, it was so important as to be given the name *Post Town*. When the first issue of the famous Bradshaw Railway Guide appeared in 1840 the *Post Town* was the only inn to appear in its voluminous pages, though in fact it was featured as a landmark and given the name it bears today, *Old Down*, a puzzling point I have not elucidated yet.

Just to the north, where the slope of the Mendips begins to flatten out, in a hollow that makes it easy enough to miss, lies *Ye Olde King's Arms*, Litton. The inn presents a curious contrast in styles. The pantiled roof spans a long, white-painted façade whose windows are topped by gently curved oak beams. Two cottages linked, at a guess; but some time later, its owner built on to the front of them a porch out of all keeping with the modest appearance of the main structure. It is castellated, as though designed for defence. 'Defence against what?' I asked. The landlord shrugged. 'They do say Charles II took refuge here,' he told me. 'My daughter can probably give you the date, if you don't mind waiting till she comes in from school.' I had heard the tale so often, and so rarely had it substantiated. That monarch must have stayed in just about as many country inns as had provided overnight accommodation for Elizabeth I, if all these claims were in fact true. Which, of course, they are not.

The inn certainly looks older inside than out. The slabstone floor is original. It must be at least three hundred years since the last peg was driven into the framework of the enormous settle over there by the wall. Looking at it, I speculated as to how it had been installed there. Either it had been made in sections and assembled *in situ* or (and I think this more likely) it had been constructed actually within the walls. Whether or no, the joiner who made it was a craftsman of undoubted skill and not a little imagination besides.

There is another piece of outstanding craftsmanship here: a massive oak table whose top bears a patina at once silky and glasslike. The landlord is much more proud of this than he is of the dubious claim about Charles II. He pointed out the elaborate pattern

of lines on the table top. 'They used to play a game called "Tippet",'
he explained. 'Something like Shove-ha'penny, it was, only more
complicated as you might say. And it involved gambling, of course,
too. I doubt there's anyone left in the country that would even
remember the game today. We call this room the Tippet Room, but
there's not many that bother to ask me why, as you did.' Chalk and
beer were the traditional ingredients for keeping the right running-
surface on a Shove-ha'penny board down the years, together with
the copper coins that were so deftly slid by practised hands along
it. Some subtler polishing agent, I think, had produced the remarkable patina on this particular table. Glancing over my shoulder as
I left the inn I looked again at its unusual sign: a three-dimensional
'book' outspread on the wall, larger than some of the windows, with
the name and the alleged date printed boldly across it in glossy black
medieval script.

Less than ten miles north of Litton I came to the last of the Somerset inns on my chosen itinerary. Curiously enough, it appears to have
two addresses: the *Carpenter's Arms* is variously ascribed to Stanton
Wick and to Compton Dando. The hamlets are so small that you
are through either of them almost before you realise the fact, though
several miles of open country separate them. Signposts hereabouts
seemed particularly thin on the ground and I got myself lost. I asked
a lad leaning over the parapet of a bridge if he could direct me, and
became so interested in what he said, or rather, in the sort of lad
he was, that when I went on my way I lost myself all over again.
Eventually I must have done what a friend of mine in such circumstances refers to as 'eleven sides of a duodecagon' before I reached
my objective.

The lad was a fitter in some engineering works in Bath. 'I come
out here on my bike,' he told me earnestly, 'every day after leaving
work and before going home to my tea. It's quiet, here. Now and
then a fish pops its head out of the water, but that's the only sound,
once I've switched off the engine. I like quiet. I like to think. I
can't at work. And at home there's always my kid brother wanting
me to do something for him, or my older sister nattering away with
my mum.' He elaborated the simple theme, proving himself to be

something of a philosopher though he was barely out of his teens. A nice lad. And a nice spot he had found for contemplation, too : a medieval arched bridge over a silent, weed-filled stream, with a church tower lifting above the trees just beyond.

It would have been easy enough to miss the *Carpenter's Arms* even when I did eventually, and more by good luck than by good management, come upon it. Obviously, once again, a pair of linked cottages, stone-built and slate-roofed, converted at some period during its near-four hundred years of life and bearing its tally of years modestly enough. Within, you stand on a stone-flagged floor, smoothed by the feet of more than a dozen generations of boots, a low ceiling close over your head. Open fireplaces, with the bread-ovens that were essential to the cottagers and the innkeepers who succeeded them when the ale licences were granted. Above one of the hearths there is an array of pewter mugs that many a connoisseur would be glad enough to own, but not one of them is for sale. You may or may not like the fresco that has been painted on a length of solid interior wall, but that is—to my mind—the only false note struck here; and I have to confess (what may already have become obvious) that in these matters as in so many others I am, un-ashamedly, a traditionalist.

Within a very short time of leaving the *Carpenter's Arms* at Stanton Wick (or was it Compton Dando?) I had visited the last inn that I was to visit, for the time being at least, in the West Country.

CHAPTER TWO

The Southern Counties

Kent

You cannot drive far along any of Kent's major or minor roads without coming across an inn that catches the eye. This proliferation may partly result from the fact that it is our chief hop-growing county, and hops are essential to the brewing of beer. They may be like the sixteenth-century *Crown Inn* overlooking Groombridge green, tile-hung—a characteristic of Kentish building; they may be mellow brick with mullioned windows, like the *Black Horse* at Pluckley; they may be creeper-clad brick with dormer windows, like the *Crown Point* at Seal Chart; they may be white-painted weather-boarded, like *The Chequers*, Smarden, or the *Walnut Tree* at Lewson Street; they may be splendid examples of ancient half-timbering, such as the *George & Dragon* at Speldhurst or *The Abbot's Fireside* at Elham. Their variety in style is as wide-ranging as the stories they have to tell are, so often, memorable.

Midway between Canterbury and Margate, for example, you will find *The Crown*, at Sarre. Most unusually, it is known by three names. Because of its location it is aptly named the *Halfway House*, for it stands practically on the site of the ford by which travellers had to cross the Stour which separated the 'Isle of Thanet' from the rest of Kent. But its third name is its best-known: *Cherry Brandy House*. One of the conditions of its licence is that this particular brandy must be permanently 'on tap'. It is made from a unique recipe, concocted by a Huguenot refugee who sought sanctuary here three hundred years ago. You will probably relish it; but whether or no, it is not to be tasted in any other of England's many thousands of country inns.

The exterior of the inn does not rank high for picturesqueness; it is neither of mellow brickwork, weather-boarding, nor half-timbered; its brickwork is white-painted and topped by a good tiled roof, the neat dormer and main windows picked out boldly in black. The interior is more rewarding. In addition to the beams and low ceiling that bespeak its age, it possesses—surprisingly—an Adam fireplace, installed, of course, long after the inn was built. Notable in the hearth is a magnificent specimen of a cast-iron fire-back, the work of some Sussex Wealden ironsmith, bearing the Royal Crown and the Rose of England insignia and the date 1650. The inn is some forty miles from the *Leather Bottle*, at Cobham, with its *Pickwick Papers* associations; many miles further still from the *King's Head* at Chigwell, Essex, with its *Barnaby Rudge* associations; but here, too, Dickens left his mark. In a room overlooking the garden the novelist, who had such a love of Kent, wrote much of his *Bleak House*; appropriately, the room in question has been named after him.

A minor road leads southwards to Wingham, five miles distant. Right on the corner of a short, steep, main street is the *Red Lion*. Together with the *Dog Inn*, just along the road, and a curiously shaped group of buildings that fill the space between them, it survives as part of what was an 'Ecclesiastical College for One Rector and Six Canons' founded by Archbishop Peckham some time prior to the fourteenth century. The interior is most impressive. The great oak beams not only support the ceilings and inner walls but in some cases were left standing detached from the party-walls when the building was reorganised to become a residential inn; this enables one to appreciate what may be termed the skeleton. Whoever was responsible for this brought imagination as well as skill to the task.

From the reign of Queen Anne until well into the nineteenth century a large upper chamber set in the corner of the building was utilised as a Magistrates' Court. In the wall of what is now a bedroom there is a cupboard which in those days was the doorway to a smaller chamber that served as the Magistrates' Retiring-Room. On one wall of the bar there are some framed original pages from the

'Minutes of Her Majesty's Justices of the Peace'. These include warrants in respect of apprentices who misbehaved during the period of their indentures; offences committed by local ale-house keepers; a list of penalties imposed for varying degrees of obscene language; others imposed on women who had given birth to bastards; the permissible treatment of unruly servants; edicts relating to the upkeep of highways; misbehaviour on feast days; a warning against treasonable acts; and much else. There is a specific reference to one Ann Hammond, 'an idle person and a liar, with a bastard child, that must be sent to a House of Correction for a second spell in that, having once been so corrected, she had been released, permitted to go into service, and had again misbehaved and must therefore be adjudged an Incorrigible Rogue'. Her misdemeanours appear to have been noted and dealt with over a period of no less than nine years, ending—we are not told how—in 1712. Interesting side-glances for the social historian. But perhaps the most noteworthy feature of the *Red Lion* is its lovingly cared-for staircase. It was installed during the reign of Queen Anne as the original one, already some three hundred years old, was 'deemed unfit for the use of Her Majesty's Justices of the Peace'.

Ten miles farther on, near a gap in the North Downs by which you make for Hythe, is the village of Elham. Here are two inns, and rarely will you see two inns facing one another so completely different in style. On one side, the *Rose & Crown*: a white-painted façade rising from a black plinth, the motif sustained in the glossy black window-sills beneath the inset windows; white chimneys soaring above a dark tiled roof; hanging flower-baskets introducing touches of colour on either side of the swinging signboard. From the exterior, you would say mid-eighteenth-century at latest. Look inside, however, and the old beams—which you would never suspect from the façade—tell you that the main fabric must be some centuries earlier. Beneath this roof for many years, as at Wingham's *Red Lion*, the Justices of the Peace met to hold their Court.

From the large-paned windows you look straight across at an inn which is in every respect its complete antithesis. *The Abbot's Fireside* is a magnificent example of late-fifteenth-century half-timbering.

Here enormous exposed timbers are supported by even larger oak beams that run its full length below and above the diamond-shaped, lead-paned windows. These are half concealed beneath jutting rafters supported by no fewer than fourteen carved angels alternating with carved grotesques, each more fantastic than the last, and all reminiscent of Gothic-inspired gargoyles.

You enter by way of a short flight of well-worn stone steps leading to solid oak doors which give access to the oak-beamed interior. As you climb the steps you are aware that the whole façade seems to be leaning outwards overhead; in fact, it is doing so. It has probably done so for the better part of five hundred years, for the date of the building has been established as 1485. Clearly it was granted a liquor licence early on in its career, for as far back as Stuart times it was known as the *Smithies Arms* and it retained that name until well into the eighteenth century. Then, somewhat unusually, the licence was withdrawn and the building converted into three linked dwellings. Modest as these were, they were known for a period as Keeler's Mansions. But not long afterwards it was reconverted into its original state and a new liquor licence granted to its owner.

Among its most treasured features is its huge fireplace. It is believed to have originally been that of the Abbot's House in a small monastery at Lyminge, probably carved by a monk-mason. Happily, it was salvaged at the time of the Dissolution, and installed here; this will account for the change of name, the *Smithies Arms* becoming *The Abbot's Fireside*. Another interesting relic is a chain-mail coat alleged to have been worn by the Black Prince at the Battle of Crécy in 1346. But surely, if this really is the case, so precious a relic would now be housed in some major museum. Another interesting feature is an eighteenth-century 'Parliamentary Clock', reminiscent of the one at the *Rose & Crown* at Lyng, Somerset.

Before crossing the North Downs, which divide East Kent from West Kent and the border with neighbouring Sussex, a handful of inns on the other side of Canterbury call for mention. The *Grove Ferry* at Upstreet, for instance, known as *Ferry House* in 1831 when a boat was the only means of crossing the Stour at this point and the bridge had yet to be built. It is a distinguished looking building with a pillared portico, more country gentleman's house, you would say, than a public house. Local tradition has it that it was a place-of-call for contrabandists and that the landlord, who also operated the ferry-boat, could be 'kept sweet' and have 'mislaid' the key of the padlock when the Preventive Men arrived on their heels. Sitting on its lawn and considering its somewhat staid appearance, I found it difficult to imagine it involved in such goings-on!

The Stour is navigable still, beyond Upstreet to Fordwich. Here, where stone from Caen was off-loaded for the building of Canterbury Cathedral, sailers of small boats occupy themselves as such men (and women) do, and slake their thirst at the *George & Dragon* in between whiles. Here, too, Izaak Walton, he of *The Compleat Angler*, fished, for he mentions the excellence of the 'Fordidge Trout'. But unless the inn is a good deal older than it looks, with its yellow-painted rough-cast and doors with bottle-glass panes, he will not have enjoyed a glass of ale beneath this roof. Close by the inn and the little hump-backed bridge adjoining is one of the few surviving 'ducking-stools' in which over-garrulous women, and women suspected of nameless crimes, used to be dipped into the Stour, held there until they were on the point of drowning, then levered out again and dipped again, a specified number of times according to their alleged sins.

Farther to the north, a mile or two inshore from Herne Bay, is the *Smugglers Inn*. It is to be found at a spot shown on large-scale maps as Smugglers Corner, which lends authenticity to the tradition. The bar is liberally adorned with relics of those days, and with maritime exhibits ranging from a small lifeboat suspended from a ceiling beam to binnacles and riding-lights. Beneath the bar is the cellar, in the wall of which not long ago a store of bottles were uncovered. These were almost certainly contraband, secreted there when the alarm was given of the approach of the Excise Men, and either forgotten (which is improbable!) or abandoned because the smugglers were apprehended, or even killed. The chance discovery led to a more careful search, and this revealed a crypt-like recess in the cellar in which a number of casks, containing rum of extreme potency, were literally unearthed.

A few miles to the west, in the middle of nowhere, is the *Red Lion*, Hernhill. Small-paned windows light the façade beneath a steeply sloping roof that seems disproportionately large for the building. Its most attractive feature is the sort of alcove that fills the space between the two jutting wings and contains two a-symmetrically placed windows. The 'knee-joint' oak beams take the weight of the overhanging part of the roof that spans it, as in the case of *The Bell* at Waltham St Lawrence in Berkshire or that strange building in Bignor, Sussex, known as 'The Old Shop', which dates from 1485.

Farther to the west by seven or eight miles is *The Plough*, at Lewson Street, so tucked away that you must deliberately look for it, for it makes no attempt to draw attention to itself. Modest as it is, it is a little gem of an inn, whether considered from the outside or from the inside. It is screened by a huge walnut tree, a withdrawn character altogether. Most weather-boarded buildings are brick-built to their first floor; *The Plough* breaks this rule. Part only of its façade is weather-boarded, and that is at ground level, with lath-and-plasterwork on the upper storey; the left-hand side of the front, however, reverses the process: brickwork below, and weather-boarding above. A reminder that Kent is hop-growing country *par excellence* is to be found in the fact that a hop-garden (hop-*field* in Herefordshire) comes right up to its left-hand corner.

It claims to date from the fourteenth century, though this is improbable. It has served as a vicarage, though it was a licensed house in the seventeenth century. The landlord was not prepared to say whether the vicar was in residence at the time: 'He'd be more use to his parishioners behind the bar than up there in his pulpit!' was his gratuitous comment. Today you can see in the bar a huge brick fireplace, with a priest's 'hide' adjoining it. Such a thing was not even suspected by the generations of drinkers who have patronised the bar of *The Plough* for so long, and indeed the discovery was not made until as recently as 1971. Since then, experts have looked into it and come to the conclusion that the fireplace is almost certainly original and has been sealed over for at least two hundred years. It is large enough to accommodate logs of quite remarkable size, a great stack of which leans up against an end wall.

The fire, I was told, is kept burning for eight months out of the twelve, and once every week spit-roasting is done at *The Plough*, as it was of yore.

A stronger contrast could hardly be found than the seventeenth-century *Leather Bottle*, Cobham, near Rochester. No white-painted weather-boarding and red brick here, but half-timbering and small, diamond-paned windows. From here the unhappy Tracy Tupman wrote his despairing *cri-de-coeur* to Mr Samuel Pickwick. 'Any letter addressed to me at the *Leather Bottle*, Cobham, will be forwarded—supposing I still exist. Life, my dear Pickwick, has become insupportable to me. You may tell Rachel—ah, that name!'

The signboard portrays Pickwick, precariously balanced on a chair, one hand behind his coat-tails, holding forth; above the signboard is a replica of the ancient 'leather bottle', the original of which, crammed with gold sovereigns, was found by chance in the building many years ago and may be seen—minus the bullion—in the dining-room. Within these heavily timbered walls you 'breathe' Dickens; sketches and prints of characters and episodes from his novels meet you at every turn, though so dark is the interior that often you must peer closely to identify them. He knew the inn well, and indeed stayed beneath its roof. His well-loved home, Gadshill Place, is only two or three miles distant along the road by which he used to bring his intimates to enjoy a glass of punch with him at the *Leather Bottle*.

Westwards again from Cobham, indeed within ten miles from the heart of London, though still just in Kent, is one of the most charming of all weather-boarded inns, the *Ramblers Rest* at Chislehurst. It is very small indeed, formerly a single cottage, built on a steepish slope so that the depth of the weather-boarding on its left-hand side is considerably greater than that of the right-hand side. It is white-painted, little porch and all, with black-painted window-frames beneath a pantiled roof. Step inside, and you find the customary oak beams and low ceiling and must take a step or two downwards into the second room. Even in the small main bar you are partly below ground level, and there is artificial lighting on all but the brightest days. This enables you to spot the unusual feature: an extensive array of variegated, decorative silk ties, every one of them auto-graphed by the donor before being presented to the inn.

So far, all these inns have been to the north of the North Downs, that slope south-eastwards from Rochester to Folkestone. It is time now to cross them at their southern end, beyond the *Rose & Crown* and *The Abbot's Fireside* at Elham. Just over their gentle rise, on lower ground inland from Hythe, is the *Walnut Tree* at Aldington. In its air of secrecy it is reminiscent of *The Plough*, Lewson Street; its small, lead-paned windows emphasise this quality of withdrawn-ness. In the early nineteenth century it was the headquarters of one of the rival gangs of smugglers that operated along this stretch of the Channel coastline, the notorious Ransley Gang. From a small window still visible today a look-out was constantly maintained across the wide expanse; from it, signals could be given by night if there was rumour of the Excise Men being on their trail in the neighbourhood, for from Aldington the whole way to the coast the low-lying Romney Marshes fill the triangle to Dungeness and Rye.

The exterior is unprepossessing, apart from the natural beauty of the aged walnut tree from which it takes its name. The interior, as so often in these rural inns, offers an emphatic contrast. Its most notable feature is the huge fireplace, with a massive overmantel that is 'stepped-back' upwards to the low ceiling. On the left of this, above head height, is a small room, hardly more than a cupboard, to which access could be obtained by a ladder that could then be drawn away so that there was nothing to indicate its existence once the trapdoor was closed. The prime function of that hiding-place is obvious; no doubt the ghosts of the long-dead, but still remembered, sinister Ransley Gang haunt its narrow confines to this day.

Beyond Ashford there is a little group of strangely named ham-lets: Boughton Monchelsea, Boughton Malherbe, Boughton Aluph and Boughton Lees. Here, overlooking a spacious green, is the *Flying Horse*, a dignified building of mellow brick not unlike the *Crown Point* at Seal Chart. Its five stone-mullioned windows, one of them a small one set between the gable of the porch and the shadowing eaves of the fine roof, contrast effectively with the varying-hued brickwork. Somewhat improbably, the name of the inn is said to derive from the horses that were a feature of the fair held annually on the green opposite, where now only cricket-matches are played. Alternatively, since the old Pilgrims' Way passed close by the inn, it may have taken its name from the horses ridden by the Wife of Bath and the more affluent of the countless pilgrims making for the shrine of St Thomas à Becket in Canterbury, ten miles to the north-east.

To me, this seems the less likely explanation. A feature of Chaucer's *Canterbury Tales* is surely that his pilgrims travelled leisurely, beguiling the lazy hours by story-telling; there can have been no 'flying horses' among them. In any case the name is common enough, though more often to be found on major highways along which fast coaches and riders sped on horseback, on errands legitimate or nefarious, between town and town. I did not like to challenge the landlord's claim when I asked him—landlords can be very touchy when doubts are thrown on their assertions! I accepted readily enough his statement that the humbler pilgrims often dossed down in the part-Saxon Church of All Saints nearby, for free, and slaked their thirst beneath his roof. But these were certainly not Chaucer's pilgrims, he agreed, for the *Flying Horse's* oldest foundations date back only four hundred years—two centuries after Chaucer's day.

A few miles west of the quartet of Boughtons is the hamlet of Pluckley; overlooking a small square is the *Black Horse*, notable for its steeply pitched roof in which three gabled dormer windows are neatly set between its well matched chimneys, and for the impressive main windows of two, three, and four lights apiece, heavily mullioned and each topped by an appropriate number of semi-circular arches all set within the curved span of ornamental brickwork. The effect is odd, but becomes more acceptable when you note that every house and cottage in this small community possesses the same style of window, so that homogeneity is achieved. In fact, this style is to be observed in farmhouses and cottages alike, scattered round the village, for all of it belongs to the Dering estate. Were it not for the black horse displayed in full canter on the sign you might well take this tall building for a private house; indeed, until a generation or so ago it was the residence of a senior member of the Dering estate staff.

Behind the brick façade and the end walls as far as the exterior chimney which rises through three storeys to beyond the roof ridge, half-timbering with cob and plaster infilling replaces the brickwork, constituting an emphatic contrast; but even this rear section of the inn has its Norman-arched window, a pair-light this time, like the one over the porch and looking wholly out of place in a form of construction that is always associated in the mind with rectangular (if lop-sided) windows filled with rectangular or diamond-shaped lead-paned glass. It is through this part of the building that the customer enters the *Black Horse*, whether to stand at the bar, to take his ease in a comfortable chair in front of the fireplace, or to help himself from a generous display of cold dishes set on wide, free-standing shelves and then eat at any one of the elm-topped tables in the bar-cum-dining-room. In a little more than a generation, the true atmosphere of an inn has replaced that of a family residence: private house, in brief, turned public house. A Maltese friend was my guest there a year or so ago; it was his introduction to the resources of an English rural inn.

Standing at the dog's-leg turn that takes you westwards out of the village of Smarden, three or four miles from Pluckley, is *The Chequers*, as neat an example of a Kentish inn as any you will find if you are looking not for a tile-hung specimen but for a mixture of brick and weather-boarding. Here there is brickwork to the ground-floor section at the right-hand end and the protruding porch; the remainder of the ground floor and the whole of the upper storey, including the porch, the gable of which lifts so high that it breaks the line of the tiled roof and is in fact commodious enough to contain a room whose window is neatly set in it, is white weather-boarding. And the unusual feature of this is that it is carried round the corner, not butt-ended in the usual fashion but in a curve as strong and withal pleasing to the eye as that of a clinker-built vessel. How many visitors to this inn, I wonder, have noticed this quite distinctive feature? It is the only example I can recall to mind in any part of the country where weather-boarding is widely used, though there

14 The Tudor Rose, Upper Burgate

15 The Bat & Ball, Broadhalfpenny Down

16   Wise Man Inn, West Stafford

17   Brace of Pheasants, Plush

may well be some isolated inns in Essex, Hertfordshire and Cambridgeshire that I have not seen or do not remember as possessing this feature. The landlord himself did not seem to have been aware of its unusualness when I drew his attention to it.

He does, however, claim that *The Chequers* is all of four hundred years old—though it certainly does not look it. He also claims the existence of a tunnel that links his cellars with the church, a 'get-away tunnel' much used by smugglers in the past. The tradition is stoutly maintained locally, in spite of lack of evidence, for neither entrance nor exit has as yet been located. And why, anyway, would the tunnel lead to the church? Did the law of 'Sanctuary' obtain in smugglers' days? Also, the soil here has rock close to the surface— we are not far from the famous Bethersden Marble quarries; would it have been worth anyone's while to carve a tunnel out of rock? I found it easier to accept another tradition: that one of the bedrooms here is haunted by the ghost of a prisoner-of-war who died in the locality during the Napoleonic Wars, though here again the evidence was as insubstantial as his alleged ghost. Such traditions are best left to more highly romantic books than this professes to be.

With every mile covered westwards from Smarden you come closer to the true heart of the hop-growing region of west Kent. As you approach Beltring, on the upper reaches of the Medway, hop-gardens extend seemingly to the horizon in all directions. Here is the enormous complex of square (as opposed to the more usual round) oast-houses that are the headquarters of one of our major brewery groups. Facing them is the *Blue Bell*, Beltring, almost hidden by a row of ancient, heavily pollarded elms. It appears to be white-painted weather-boarding, but in fact it is bastard Kentish tile-hung; I use the term because I firmly hold that tiles should be left *au naturel*, as should wrought-ironwork.

The inn does not (for once!) claim to be old. It is early-eighteenth-century, and first held an ale licence in 1757. At that time there was a toll-house nearby, though no sign of this survives today. It is believed that the owner of the inn obtained a licence in order to be able to make money out of wayfarers and vehicle drivers temporarily delayed while dues were being exacted from them. The *Blue*

Bell is surrounded by hop-gardens. Elderly hop-pickers sourly watch the development of mechanical hop-picking equipment which has now almost entirely replaced the traditional East-Enders who used to inundate the area, combining holiday-making with piecework money-making. One of them told me that he could recall the days when the spigots of the *Blue Bell*'s beer casks were left permanently turned on, permitting their contents to flow into a large trough; and so ready with their containers were the thirsty pickers that the trough was never known to overflow! Reflecting on this, I ignored the notice, DUCK OR GROWSE, to be found in so many of these low-ceilinged inns, and cracked my head as I stepped up over the threshold and out into the clear air; one of my less happy memories of an inn visited, though it was nobody's fault but my own.

More elegant by far is the *Crown Point*, at Seal Chart, on the A25 two or three miles short of Sevenoaks. Like Pluckley's *Black Horse* and the *Flying Horse* at Boughton Lees, this elegant building of Kentish brick and tiled roof looks more like a private than a public house. In fact, this is what it originally was: a residence closely linked with a once-famous name which, confusingly, appears also on the sign-board: Sir Jeffrey Amherst.

Sir Jeffrey was a local landowner who rose to be Commander-in-Chief of forces campaigning in Canada, among whom was James Wolfe, who was born in neighbouring Westerham, captured Quebec, and died on the Heights of Abraham. Sir Jeffrey was responsible for the capture from the French of Montreal. A lesser triumph of his, during that campaign, was the taking of a French fort situated on Lake Champlain and known as Crown Point. Amherst retired, full of honours, returned to his house and named it after the fort; he died there at the age of eighty, in 1797. So, the house bears his name as well as that which he gave it. A beautifully proportioned building of warm brick, lit by bold windows, the upper ones reaching to the eaves. In the roof are two trim dormers, exactly proportioned to its pitch, the upper part of each one lightly curved. The louvred shutters to the main windows above and on either side of the gabled porch lend an air of privacy and self-sufficiency to the façade; here Sir Jeffrey, full of years, must have died well content.

There is one odd feature, exterior but not immediately noticeable. Indeed, I had not spotted it until the young landlord drew my attention to it. On the right-hand side, close to the foot of a steeply roofed outbuilding, there is a solid ground-level timber roof. Today it is opened for the delivery of barrels and kegs of beer; in the years immediately following the old Commander-in-Chief's death it served as a lock-up for vagrants apprehended by the authorities and awaiting trial at the local Assizes.

On your way westwards from Seal Chart you actually pass the house where General Wolfe was born, on the outskirts of Westerham; at the top of the hill, in Westerham, is the early-seventeenth-century *George & Dragon*. It is obviously a former posting-house, with a high archway at the right-hand end, over which, close beneath a low section of the otherwise high roof, is a windowed room. The brilliant white paintwork of the frontage is strikingly set off by the glossy black plinth from which it rises and further emphasised by the glossy black woodwork of the many windows, three of which are spaced out as dormers midway up the slope of the roof. Between two of the windows at first-floor level is an ornate plaque inscribed in bold lettering: 'General James Wolfe, on His Last Visit to Westerham, stayed at this inn, December 1758.' He died at Quebec a year later, and fifty years younger than his Commander-in-Chief, Sir Jeffrey Amherst, but already a general though barely into his thirties.

Beyond Westerham, the B2026 meanders southwards, interweaving with the Kent-Sussex border. Branch off it to the left and you will come upon a number of cosy, unobtrusive, attractive little inns. At Smarts Hill, near Penshurst, for instance, there is the *Bottle House*. In its hundreds of years of existence it has changed both ownership and function several times. It was once a small shop, bakehouse and cottage all in one, bought for £600—a tolerable sum at the time. In the eighties of last century it had 'outbuildings consisting of a coal lodge, a paraffin lodge and a zinc lodge, (whatever that might be!), and a licence to sell ale. A later owner, to attract more trade, invested in a monkey, which he kept chained in the bar, and for many years the inn was generally known as the

Monkey House. Its owner bore the very odd name of Mole Mules.

Once inside, you will no longer find a monkey chained to the fireplace, but you will probably notice that one side of the stonework is curiously smoothed; there are also a number of narrow, vertical incisions, like scars. Puzzled about these, I asked for an explanation. The smooth stonework, apparently, is the result of much unofficial honing of clasp-knives and even possibly sickles by customers who found the smooth-grained stone a handy whetstone as they swilled their ale. As for the incisions: these had apparently been cut when blades were being sharpened to a point. In fact, here at the fireside of a homely inn was an echo of the *polissoirs* that are such a remarkable feature in the churchyards at Stokesay in Shropshire and Alkborough, Lincolnshire, and Chedzoy in Somerset. These vertical clefts are reminiscent, on a miniature scale, of the grooves in the so-called Devil's Arrows near Boroughbridge, Yorkshire.

More unexpected than the customary brass and copperware and corn-dollies, which are in evidence, is a remarkable array of small, faded prints of 'Ladies' Fashions from the Seventeenth Century' and some reproductions of Rowlandson cartoons. These meet the eye at every turn, a pleasant change from the more usual hunting scenes. Behind the bar there is a most interesting set of hand-bells which originated in a Tibetan temple: half a dozen or so, graduated from bottom to top, from soup-plate size to that of a coffee-cup. On the opposite wall is a whole turtle-shell, lovingly polished to a marvellous patina. In fact, the interior is more sophisticated than you might have anticipated from outside, where a truly homely note is struck by the verse on the tall inn-sign below the terraced flower-garden:

> From this Bottle I am Sure
> You'll Get a Glass both Good and Pure;
> Each Goodman, and eke His Spouse,
> Drink to Each Other and This House.

I was on my own at the time, though so near home; but, the day being hot, took the hint.

It is surprising that so small a community as this can support two inns. Only a few hundred yards down the hill is the smaller, older, *Spotted Dog*, hidden behind the fruit trees and rioting shrubs of an old-world type garden which stand out against its white weather-boarding. Within, low ceiling, heavy beams, small windows letting in the minimum of light. But a rear doorway admits you to a narrow terrace on which you can sit, glass in hand, feasting your eyes the while on one of the finest views of the Kentish Weald I know. I sat there once with three visiting American friends who had just completed a fortnight's high-speed tour of England. As we got up to leave, one of them said quietly: 'For me, this will always remain the most perfect view of what I think of as the *real* England.' She could hardly have made a better choice.

And so to the *George & Dragon*, Speldhurst, within three miles of the *Spotted Dog*, within a couple of miles of the Sussex border; it could not offer a stronger contrast. Massively half-timbered, it is impressive enough from the outside; within, its low ceilings and heavy beams are what you have long recognised as typical of the truly ancient English inn. But here, as at *The Ship*, at Mere in Wiltshire, it is the upstairs timberwork that is its chief glory. In what is now the dining-room are some of the noblest black oak timbers to be found in any building, sacred or secular, in the whole country. Enormous cross-beams, interlocking with one another, unencumbered by plasterwork, span the large room at less than head height, supporting great king-posts thrusting upwards into the great roof. It is of craftsmanship such as this that James Kenward wrote so memorably in his book, *The Roof Tree*, which I treasure on my shelves along with Sturt's *The Wheelwright's Shop* and Walter Rose's *The Village Carpenter*, and other books of their ilk. I sat beneath that roof not so long ago, with the daughter, son-in-law and granddaughter of the American who had spoken so appreciatively of the view from the terrace of the *Spotted Dog* some years before. And there we tape-recorded part of our conversation, in the ambience of that candle-lit room, filled with diners, for them to play-back to the older folk on their return to California.

Having been so close to such timbers, it is not difficult to accept the statement on the signboard that the *George & Dragon*'s date is 'circa 1212 A.D.'. Checking this with the landlord, I was told: 'That date's a lie. In fact it should be 1189.' He spoke with such emphasis that it seemed as though he had been present at its building. He went on to talk about the place of which he was so justifiably proud. 'That fireback,' he said, jerking over his shoulder with his thumb while he filled a glass for a customer, '1669. Wealden iron, of course. My inn was already almost five centuries old when that was made.' I did not challenge him, whatever my thoughts.

He went on: 'We were more than two hundred years old' (he was identifying with his inn) 'at the time of Agincourt. That was 1415, as you probably know. The Kentish bowmen celebrated the victory right here, at the *George & Dragon*.' I had the impression that he had poured their beer for them, joined in their celebrations. 'And of course their bows—well, some of them at any rate—had been made from the yews across the way.' I looked across at the mighty yews in the churchyard of St Mary the Virgin, built ten feet above the road level facing the inn. They are said to be 1,000 years old; but then, I reflected, every churchyard yew tree is claimed to be that age, and I thought of the enormous ones in the churchyard at Gilbert White's Selborne, Hampshire.

I remembered also the strong denials I had read about the making of bows from such yews, in books by experts who ought to know. But certainly this was no moment to question so positive a statement. Anyway, I was interrupting the flow of beer, which to the crowd around the two bars was far more important than his flow of information directed solely at an inquisitive customer. So, I ordered a modest half-pint for myself, drank it meditatively, and set off for home down the hill past the sixteenth-century *Crown Inn* opposite moated Groombridge Place, and there crossed the border once more, out of Kent and into Sussex.

Sussex

Within a hundred yards of the *Crown Inn*, Groombridge, you can literally stand with one foot in each county. Not waiting to do so, I went on south-westwards to Hartfield and the *Hay Waggon*, four or five miles away. It is near enough to the border to feel the Kentish influence, being largely tile-hung; but its Sussex birth is emphasised by the true and, to the *cognoscenti* unmistakable, Sussex wagon, painted in the traditional colours, hitched to the signpost immediately in front of the inn. The wagon is echoed, in miniature, in a glass-fronted niche, floodlit, in the wall beside the bar : a perfect scale-model, perhaps half-inch to the foot, complete with team of Shires.

There is a good reason for this emphasis on farm wagonry, for the inn was a farm, more than four hundred years ago; though the exterior belies the fact, the interior confirms it. The framework is of massive oak timbers, the majority of them adze-hewn though one of them is most beautifully fluted along its length, reminiscent of those in, among others, the *Royal Oak* at Cerne Abbas, Dorset and *The Star*, Alfriston, Sussex, and other hostelries which were either associated with abbeys and monasteries or built of materials salvaged from them after the Dissolution. There is no question that this fine central beam was carved by some highly skilled Tudor craftsman.

The oak skeleton of this farm-turned-hostelry is in-filled with the traditional wattle-and-daub of buildings of this age, though this has long been covered over. But the framework of oak beams, cross-ties and king-posts has happily been left uncovered in the main room beyond the bar, reminiscent of the upper floor of the *George Inn* at Speldhurst though on a somewhat less ambitious scale. A further reminder of the original domestic nature of the building is to be found in the carefully preserved bread-oven alongside the open hearth.

Beyond Hartfield is the great expanse of Ashdown Forest and on its edge is Fletching and its three-centuries-old *Griffin*. Again, as at Hartfield, its exterior belies its age; indeed, with its three neat gables it has a faintly Victorian look about it. But I saw a document there which reads : 'Ye Sum of Four Pence was paid for a Piece of Land at Ye Griffin Ale-House, Fletching, formerly a Nine-pin Alley.' It is a good while since parcels of land of any size, even if only skittle-alleys, changed hands for one groat! Another document states that the then landlord proposed installing bread-ovens 'Large enough to Bake for the Whole County of Sussex'. This puzzles me still. Surely in his day every housewife baked her own bread? And how, if he was to fulfil his promise, did he propose to distribute his loaves throughout a county not far short of a million acres in extent, eighty miles in length from east to west? I put the question to the present landlord. He was non-committal, but drew my attention to a remarkable pair of fire-dogs in his copper-canopied hearth: appropriately enough they bear a griffin's head apiece.

I turned south-eastwards, next, for a look at the *Queen's Head*, Icklesham, a couple of miles from Winchelsea. I have often seen, and been irritated by, the blatant 'sky-sign': huge white letters sprawled across the whole roof. The advertising is perhaps justifiable, since the inn cannot be seen from the road and takes more than a little finding at the end of a narrow lane. A mixture of styles, here: one white-painted and one, larger, tile-hung gable overlook the diminutive gravelled courtyard, with a low-lintelled black doorway between them; a wheel from a long disused binder, and a scythe or two, leaning against the white brickwork stress the rural nature of the place, and you step through the narrow doorway straight on to a floor of well polished red brick. The bar was formerly a butcher's shop; behind it, a couple of steps lead down into a tiny 'snug', originally, the barmaid (an elderly woman) told me, 'a snog', or cobbler's shop. It was just about large enough to contain his small workbench, last and stool.

The dominant feature of the inn, however, is a most remarkable collection of 'bygones'. Mostly small, they dangle from the low rafters, make patterns along the beams, cover the walls, drape the bar itself: harness equipment, wheels of various types, butchers' cleavers obviously hand wrought, rat-traps, a man-trap, eel-spears, mole-traps, yokes, corn-dollies, pewter, brass and copperware, oddments unidentifiable by me at least, and the landlord who had assembled them over the years was not present to enlighten me, absent 'on business' the woman told me; perhaps tracking down some new item for his ever-growing collection. It had taken him twenty years, and he was still not satisfied, she said, obviously considering it all a thorough waste of time. There may exist an even larger collection of, essentially, 'bygones'—as opposed, for instance, to the heterogeneous collection at the *Seven Stars*, Penryn; but if there is, I have yet to encounter it.

Ten miles to the west is *The Lamb*, Hooe. As at Winchelsea and Rye, the sea here receded long ago and the inn stands isolated on low-lying ground that somewhat resembles the salt-marshes of Romney. Like most inns built near the sea, it is of white-painted brick on a black plinth. It is a great deal older than it looks. Polishing his glasses in readiness for midday custom, the landlord told me something of its story. In the early sixteenth century it was (as indeed it still looks) a pair of cottages. In 1520 the Prior of nearby Battle Abbey granted the then owner an ale-licence on a dual proviso: first, the left-hand door must be kept permanently unlocked day and night during the lambing season; second, a substantial fire must be kept burning in one or other of the hearths. At that time huge flocks were continuously grazed on what were true salt-marshes, the sea having not long departed from them. The interior of the inn is virtually one long room today, with the original and enormous black-painted fireplace at the far end; it was not difficult to visualise the shepherds warming their half-frozen hands and feet, and the newly-born lambs, during the long hours of late-winter and early-spring darkness.

Smugglers, too, undoubtedly made use of *The Lamb*, as they did of the *Walnut Tree* in Aldington and so many of the smaller, out-of-the-way hostelries to be found not too far inland from this much-frequented coastline from Kent to Cornwall. There may have been a tunnel exit, for use in emergency; if so, there is no sign of it today. Did they share the warmth and comfort of that open hearth by night? If so, it would be with less ease of mind than that of the shepherds availing themselves of refuge provided on the specific authority of the Prior of Battle Abbey only six miles away. But at least they had three separate exits from the building. They are interspersed, as at the *George & Dragon* at Houghton, in the same county, by enormous sloping brick buttresses.

A mile or so inland from Beachy Head is the hamlet of East Dean, tilting downhill to Birling Gap. It is a village complete with green and flagpole, or possibly permanent maypole, with a shop and cottage or two on its upper side and a row of cottages on the lower, the last two or three of which have been combined to form the *Tiger Inn*. It would indeed be difficult to challenge a claim that this is at once the most attractive and the most attractively sited rural inn in the whole county and even farther afield. White-painted brickwork beneath a red-tiled roof; a well-windowed façade ornamented with genuine wrought-iron mangers filled with flowers in season; flowers, too, climbing from long, narrow flower-beds forming the plinth of the building and spreading among the windows and up an iron staircase that slopes from left to right up one end of the wall; a wagon-wheel, painted in the traditional colours of a Sussex wagon, as at Hartfield, leaning against the wall beside the door.

The interior is as attractive as the exterior, the one complementary to the other. Notice especially the beautiful fireback, product of a Sussex Wealden iron foundry in full blast three and a half centuries ago; it bears the date 1622 and is believed to have come from nearby Friston Place. An unusual feature here, too, is a document recording that a levy of one penny was made on the landlord of *The Tiger* for every day that he had a fire burning in that fireplace. Such a levy would have fallen hard on the landlord of *The Lamb*, at Hooe, but it could hardly have been imposed since the fire was kept burning on the express orders of the Abbey's Prior.

Five miles to the west, in a fold of the Downs, is the village of Alfriston; in the heart of it is perhaps the most perfect example of a half-timbered inn in Sussex: *The Star*. Built some five centuries ago, it was designed to serve as Guest House for pilgrims making their way to the shrine of St Richard at Winchester, and also as a rest-house for monks from the Abbey at Battle. No ordinary workmen built it; those whose signatures lie upon its design and fabric were craftsmen of high order—some of them doubtless monks themselves. This is explicit in the workmanship both without and within. The upper storey, with its vertical timbers devoid of cross-braces, projects outwards over the half-timbered lower storey, carried by one enormous lateral beam not rough-hewn in the customary style but, as befits a building so closely associated with an abbey, moulded by expert craftsmen, a beam of oak so hard that to this day it shows hardly a sign of the effect of five hundred years of wind and weather. In spite of the weight of the Horsham slabstone roof that surmounts the upper storey, it does not seem to have given an inch.

Protruding from that upper storey are three oriel windows. In their oak sills there is intricate carving: a mitred bishop; two inter-twined snakes; St Michael fighting a basilisk; a lion, a monkey, a terrier. And at the corner, at ground level, facing outwards beneath the junction of half-timbered façade and gabled end wall consisting of mixed flint and brick, tile-hung above, is—The Beast.

It is my own term for the creature: you are unlikely to find it in any guidebook. Mundanely, this grotesque figure, carved in oak and reminiscent of the classic Gog or Magog in London's Guildhall, is said to have been taken from the stem of some sailing-ship wrecked off the Sussex coast three centuries ago. But it is as unlike the traditional ship's figure-head as could be imagined. I encountered it for the first time some twenty-five years ago, when, at the end of a solo long-distance walk that had started at Streatley, followed the Berkshire Ridge Way to its midway point at Old Sarum, on Salisbury Plain, and ended at Birling Gap after a glorious sixty miles along the crest of the South Downs from Butser Hill, I slept at *The Star*. I wrote of that walk, among others of comparable scale, in a book published soon afterwards and long since out of print. In it I wrote of this grotesque carved figure with its 'repellent mien, globular, basilisk eye, immense, implacable jaw and sensual lips'.

But there was, that night, staying beneath the same roof as I, a girl of such serene, dark beauty that I had difficulty in keeping my eyes off her. She was, it seemed to me, the perfect foil to that oaken grotesque. I toyed with an idea, the inevitable idea. Though her mother frowned, she was co-operative. I took a number of photo-graphs of 'Beauty and the Beast'. One of them was duly published, and aroused favourable comment. I look at it still, from time to time, and remember. It is beside me now, as I write these words; The Beast was there a few weeks ago when I went back to have a look at it—and perhaps dream a little sentimentally, romantically. The girl with the serene look, firmly modelled chin, high cheek-bones and upswept, smooth, dark hair, a half-smile playing about her mobile lips, is now, I suppose, a matron in her mid-forties, married almost certainly, and perhaps with a grown-up daughter as old as she herself was in 1946. She is less likely than I, I suspect, to recall the brief but, for me, very memorable encounter.

Sometimes the interior of a building as outstanding as this proves to be something of an anticlimax; it is not so at *The Star*. The craftsmanship that went into its structure went also into its interior fittings. It possesses perhaps the finest oak staircase to be found in any hostelry in the country, a match for many in our smaller Stately Homes where timber was preferred to stone. The staircase rises from a floor, much of which is of brick. Wherever you look, timbers of striking proportions and superb workmanship are to be seen, an integral, functional part of the inner fabric but objects of beauty in their own right. There is a magnificent specimen of a Tudor fireplace, and the roasting-jack, though no longer in use, is still in position. Such restoration as has been necessary over the centuries has been carried out with the greatest possible skill and imagination; something of the spirit in which this Abbey Guest House was designed and built remains encapsuled within it; it is worth noting that its original name was *Star of Bethlehem*, but common usage inevitably brought about the abbreviation.

As strong a contrast as you could well imagine is to be found at Rowhook, to the north-west of Horsham. *The Chequers* overlooks the A29, which here runs so straight that you will not be surprised to find it marked on road maps as the Romans' Stane Street. It still looks what it originally was: a cottage or small farmhouse somewhat enlarged, but nothing has been done to it to make it catch the eye. Apart from the smoke-blackened lintel of the fireplace with its cupboard-like loft above in which, the landlord told me, successive owners used to cure hams from their own pigs, its dominant feature—and it *is* a dominant one—is the bar itself; I have never seen another like it.

It consists of an enormous 'Welsh Dresser' (such dressers, however, do not always emanate from Wales). The upper half of this has been detached and fitted onto the wall. On its long oak shelves is the customary display of bottles and liquor-dispensers. The lower half, with its long, deep drawers, forms the actual counter, though it has wisely been covered with something that will preserve its antique top from beer-mug rings and cigarette-stub scars. Both halves of the dresser are ornately carved. As a single unit it must have been a magnificent specimen; the landlord has long lost count of the number of antique dealers who have tried to persuade him to part with it. It has been there for fifteen years and more: an unusual if not absolutely unique fitment to be found in a wholly unpretentious country inn.

A mile away, on the outskirts of Bucks Green, is the *Fox Inn*. This too has one unique feature, though it is not apparent to the eye. The line of its frontage, white-painted with diamond-paned windows outlined in black close beneath the overhanging eaves, is otherwise broken only by a doorway set in a modest porch; herein lies the unique feature. So far as is known, this is the only inn in England through which runs a right-of-way. It passes through that front door and out through another at the back. In the interests of peace and quiet, the right-of-way is rarely exercised, though now and then someone rides his bicycle through and out, not stopping for a drink. A case is recalled, however, with sardonic amusement, of the wag who elected to ride a horse in through that doorway. Nemesis overtook him: in his high spirits he omitted to note the low lintel and was knocked backwards off his horse, to fall on the floor. There he was ridiculed by the customers, not one of whom offered to stand him a drink for his exploit. He was not, they told me, a local man, anyway.

Five miles down Stane Street, between Billingshurst and Wisborough Green, the *Limeburners' Arms* stands just off the A272. Like so many others, it was originally a row of three cottages, occupied by men whose thirst-inducing task was the operating of the local lime-kilns. Many years ago chalk from the Downs was brought up the Arun in flat-bottomed boats and off-loaded here. There are vast chalk quarries not far away to this day, as many Downland lovers deplore; but once this was virtually a 'cottage industry'. The inn is a reminder of this. Long and low, white-painted and tile-hung, with small windows snug beneath the eaves, it has three yellow-painted doors and a number of flower-filled hanging baskets. At one end is an enormous chimney, forming practically the whole of the end wall from the ground upwards. An odd feature is that the roof is tiled normally from one end to the other for its lower and upper thirds; between them is a middle third composed of ornate tiles certainly much newer than the rest; the effect is not wholly appealing and adds to the impression that the inn is not really, as is claimed for it, three hundred years old. Nevertheless, not so long ago, when the floor was relaid to provide better headroom beneath the joists by lowering it a foot or so, a coin dated 1672 was picked out of the rubble.

Overlooking Stane Street a couple of miles to the south is the *Blacksmith's Arms*. Adjoining it is that rare survival these days, a smithy devoted to farriery alone; it has always been closely associated with the inn, where you may drink either in the Forge Bar or the Anvil Bar, both within earshot of the ringing note of hammer on anvil. As I selected a vantage-point for a photograph, I found the rump of a huge Shire horse in the immediate foreground, its owner grooming it while it waited for a shoe to be fitted; it seemed appropriate to include it in the picture. In the Anvil Bar there is an outstanding display of horse-brasses, with not a 'Brummagem-un' among them, all collected by the blacksmith and his father and grandfather before him over the years and lodged there for safe keeping.

Another occupation is commemorated at Fulking, a Downs village some miles to the south-east below the Devil's Dyke. The *Shepherd & Dog* is to be found at the foot of a lane so steep that the inn perches rather than stands beside it, the upper storey of its lower end roughly level with the lower storey of its upper end. The windows are inset, half into the cream-painted façade, half into the roof, which is stepped in a sequence of wedge-shaped, slanting, individual sections. One bay-window looks out over the narrow, tree-shaded lane, while a solid wall protects a homely terrace from passing traffic, such as it is.

The main 'traffic' here, down the years, has been that of huge flocks of sheep wending their way from the Downland pastures to market towns such as Lewes. They slaked their thirst at a trough just below the inn supplied by a spring that has never been known to fail even during the worst droughts. Meanwhile the shepherds and drovers slaked their own thirsts inside the inn, which has been a port-of-call for generations if not centuries. You are left in no doubt as to who its customers have chiefly been: no fewer than three distinct and different signs draw attention to it. In all three, of course, the shepherd is featured, with his dog. In one he is striding along a Downland track, crook in hand (probably made at neighbouring Pyecombe), sheepdog at heel; in another he is simply surveying the Downland scene; in the third he is sitting at the inn door with a mug of ale on his smocked knee and, of course, his dog lying patiently at his feet. The workmanship of these signs is exquisite.

At Old Shoreham, on the seaward side of the Downs, is *Ye Olde Red Lion*. With its trim roof, clean-cut gables and over-all white-painted exterior it looks much less old than it is. It stands on foundations dating back five centuries, but it is not until you cross the threshold that you sense its age. You spot the warning notice: BOB AND DUCK, a variant of the more usual punning DUCK OR GROWSE. Rarely has it been more necessary than here, for there can be few inns with lower ceilings than this one, and nobody seems to have thought it worth while doing what has been done at the *Limeburners' Arms*, lowering the floor. If you stand six feet or more, you must move about the saloon bar with head and shoulders bent, or meticulously follow the plastered spaces between the beams, thus gaining the necessary extra inches.

The inn occupies a corner site at the junction of the coastal road and one that climbs up and over the Downs to Horsham and beyond. One window pelmet carries a pictorial representation of a scene from the heyday of the stage-coaches that made regular use of the inn. It was here that coaches taking the north-bound route hitched on a trace-horse for the ascent to Upper Beeding. Immediately behind the inn there used to stand a gibbet. On this, a man was hanged a century or so ago. He was a local man, and his mother would visit the scene nightly, weeping at the foot of the gibbet as her son's body rotted away. Eventually it was cut down; she begged permission to bury him in the churchyard nearby, but because he had been hanged as a felon he had to be placed in unconsecrated ground. The grimly pathetic story is still remembered at the inn. It was told to me by a man drinking in a chair of carved oak, one of several bearing the initials W.P. and two hundred years old, once belonging to a family that produced generations of local squires. The macabre story did not seem to affect his enjoyment of the beer, though it did mine.

Just off the fast A27 road between Brighton and Arundel is the *Woodman*, Hammerpot. Rough brick and local flint beneath old thatch, it blends with its background, the last survivor of a row of cottages built three hundred years ago and occupied for most of its time by foresters working in the vast beechwoods, part of the estate of the Duke of Norfolk, England's Earl Marshal. Towards the end of the eighteenth century, when it was known as Harmer's Farm, an ale-licence was granted to it, and from that time onwards it prospered exceedingly. Not all connoisseurs of country inns will approve its sign: the name WOODMAN spelled out in huge white letters curving somewhat blatantly across the foliage of a tall tree that shades its exterior; in its way I found it more offensive than the name of the *Queen's Head* on the roof of the inn at Icklesham, where at least there was some justification for its boldness.

I sat on a long pole in a field opposite, worn smooth by the nuzzles of generations of horses that had been tethered to it, contemplating the best angle for a picture. Having decided on this, I got ready my camera. I had hardly focused it before a huge brewer's lorry slowed to a standstill immediately in front, virtually blotting-out the inn; this is an occupational hazard that I have not yet learned, in thirty years, to accept with a good grace. The driver proved co-operative, however, and moved his lorry out of range just long enough for me to complete my task before backing into position again. Less friendly, however, was the landlord, who stormed out demanding

18   Waggon & Horses, Beckhampton

19   The Bell Inn, Wylye

20 The Barley Mow, Long Wittenham

21 Ye Olde Bell, Hurley

to know what I meant by interfering. I was taken aback, but consoled by the friendly wink of the driver and his mate sitting in their cab, aloof from the fray. It prevented me from expressing out loud my hope that the landlord's rabbits might die and his beer turn sour on him. Such reactions as his are unusual.

Less than five miles away, in the minuscule hamlet of Burpham, approached by way of ominously named Warningcamp, is the *George & Dragon*. You come unexpectedly upon it at the end of a long, twisting, ever-narrowing lane, opposite the very ancient church; it looks a cottage and nothing more: a pair of small bay-windows, a small gabled porch, no sign at first visible, though you will find it almost completely obscured by a tall lilac tree growing luxuriantly on the corner and within inches of the roof. Everything suggests that, like *The Plough* at Lewson Street, Kent, it just does not want to be noticed.

It has held a licence for three hundred years. Six or seven miles inland from the coast at Littlehampton, it has been a hide-out for smugglers dodging the risk of capture on the vast Arundel Castle estate, through which the Arun meanders down to the sea. That they foregathered beneath this homely, unobtrusive roof is commemorated in the fact that the inn possesses a rare item, a Spinning Jenny. This is not one of Hargreaves's famous machines which, with the inventions of Richard Arkwright, transmuted a long-established cottage industry into that of a factory and so led to riots in the late eighteenth century. It is an ingenious device operated by smugglers for the purpose of dividing up the proceeds from their contraband in as equitable a manner as possible. There are very few of these to be found today, outside the museums; one of them may be seen if you look up at the ceiling of this 'lost' rural inn.

To find another of the same name, the *George & Dragon* at Houghton, you have to retrace your steps, for Burpham, as the road-sign indicates, is in truth a dead-end; Houghton lies not three miles away, if you are prepared to walk across fields and wade through the Arun. There are no bay-windows here, no climbing lilac tree on the corner; instead, a squat, fortress-like building of thick flint and brick walls reinforced by massive oak beams and braced by a trio of solid brickwork buttresses slanting against the wall that faces the road. The skill with which the tapering edges of these buttresses have been feathered into the brickwork is worth more than a perfunctory glance, if you are interested in different types of skill and practice.

But, as at Burpham and Lewson Street, there is a secret air to this inn. The small, low-slung windows peer out half-blindly among the beams; the steeply pitched roof of tiles is broken only by one squat chimney. The landlord could not tell me its age, but pointed to a plaque above the door stating that 'Charles II, on his ride to the coast after the Battle of Worcester, stopped to take ale at this inn, October 14th, 1651.' Obviously, then, the place held an ale-licence more than three hundred years ago, so that the defeated monarch was luckier here than he was at Godmanstone, Dorset, where he asked in vain for refreshment and eventually brought prosperity to the owner of what became the *Smith's Arms*.

Westwards along the north slope of the Downs you will come to Duncton and the *Cricketers' Arms*. Unlike the *Bat & Ball* at Broadhalfpenny Down just across the Hampshire border, where the game was allegedly 'born', it does not face a well-kept cricket-pitch. But to the dedicated player it is nevertheless something of a Mecca, for it was owned, a century ago, by one John Wisden, whose name the cricketer's bible bears to this day. Here, too 'Jemmy' Dean was born, and lived for much of his life, playing for Sussex for thirty years, and for England too. Jemmy was largely responsible for the popularisation of 'round-arm' bowling, which superseded the old-style under-arm. The inn is part-screened by a big tree, but the signboard stands proud by the roadside: a stalwart cricketer, bat in hand, facing just such a ball.

From Duncton the road lifts over the Downs and drops, by way of a narrow lane, to the hamlet of Charlton; on its outskirts is an admirable specimen of a Sussex flint-built inn, *The Fox*. Triple courses of mellow brick, with vertical brickwork interspersed along its L-shaped façade, break up the flintwork into irregular but nicely proportioned panels. The man who built the inn, perhaps three hundred years ago, no doubt worked solely by rule of thumb, but instinct guided him, and the result is no less satisfying to the eye than if some architect had made use of the rule-book.

The brick-and-flint wall encloses a grass and gravel courtyard, with the remains of the windlass of an old well in evidence. It is an immediately inviting inn, and the interior was just what I anticipated: a small bar, a low beamed ceiling, a cosy fireplace, an overriding impression that the clientele would be a local one rather than customers seeking 'chicken-in-basket' and scampi. There was little ornamentation: a fox-mask or two on the wall, a few corn-dollies that were obviously long-term residents since they had lost their initial straw-gold sheen and become tinged like weathered thatch.

Two men, one tall with a military-style moustache, the other just the reverse, were drinking at the bar. The first glanced up at me, my camera dangling at my chest. 'Ah,' he remarked, 'I see we are about to be photographed!' I told him I had got my photographs already. 'But not of *us*!' he retorted. I tossed off the light-hearted reply that I took interiors only if those at the bar were wearing top-hats. 'No problem!' was the unexpected reply. He glanced at the landlord, vanished behind the bar and reappeared thirty seconds later, complete with—grey topper! I had overlooked the fact that only a mile or so to the south of the inn, and actually visible from its windows, is Goodwood Racecourse.

Beyond Chichester, to the south-west, at the head of one of the fingers of water that constitute the harbour, is Dell Quay. Here is a miniature Lymington, a paradise for small-boat sailers, the focal point of which is the *Crown & Anchor*, standing at the upper end of the hard alongside which scores of small yachts are tied-up and on which men are at work in the boat-yards, painting, varnishing, building craft that will in due course be launched down one or other of the small slipways.

It has been the scene of maritime activity not just for a generation or two, or even a century or two, but for almost two thousand years. From here, I learned, the Roman Emperor Vespasian despatched his ships, legionaries crammed aboard them, for the conquest of Vectis—the Isle of Wight—twenty-odd miles distant. True, the *Crown & Anchor* did not stand here in his day, but there is little doubt that there was some sort of a building there, probably of timber, for this was an important base. Certainly there was an inn here four hundred years ago, dominating the inlet; this afforded a safe anchorage, a safer refuge for small vessels plying their trade along this coast than the wider, open reaches of Chichester Harbour as a whole.

There is good evidence for this to be seen at the inn. Here you may inspect Customs receipts dated 1597—only nine years after the defeat of the Spanish Armada in the English Channel beyond. They cover goods brought ashore here, the value of which amounted to no less than £1,234 14s. 6¼d.—a staggeringly large sum for a minor port's trade in those far-off days, and meticulously accounted. Smuggling was inevitably carried on here in a big way, for this complex pattern of waterways was to the advantage of the contrabandists rather than of the Excise Men, just as it would be in maritime guerrilla warfare. The smugglers had their own entrances and exits (particularly the latter!) here, for the *Crown & Anchor* stands so close to the water that part of its frontage practically overhangs it, and the cellars could be entered from the water as easily as those of the *Golden Lion* in Port Isaac, Cornwall.

It is unlikely that the Excise Men caught more than a fraction of their potential prey. On more than one occasion, as records show, they were badly the losers in the endless feuds. Tradition has it that one ruthless gang was powerful enough to turn the tables on them completely, hanged a round half-dozen of them and buried their bodies in the very cellars in which they themselves had so often hidden and where they stored their contraband until it was deemed safe to distribute it among their expectant customers in West Sussex and, often enough, farther afield than that.

A reminder of those stormy days lies in the fact that to this very day a light is kept burning in a seaward-facing window of the inn for the benefit of those seamen who may be in difficulties after darkness falls, or in a sea mist pervading the harbour generally. In another room you may still see the very old game of 'Ringing the Bull' being played—a game whose origins are lost in the mists of time. A facsimile bull's head on the wall has a hook on its muzzle;

an iron ring is suspended from the ceiling overhead. The object of the exercise is to swing this ring in such a way that it settles over the hook. This, as you will quickly realise if you attempt the feat, is very much more difficult than it looks, even though—as with darts, shove-ha'penny and other games still played in inns throughout the country—old hands make it look simple enough.

Hampshire

Unlike Sussex to the east and Dorset to the west, Hampshire (including the Isle of Wight) has its main axis running north-south. There are some pleasant enough rural inns to be found in the northern half, bounded by Surrey and Berkshire, and even in that area so completely dominated by the military, centred in Aldershot, you will find the odd one. The *Crown & Cushion* at Minley, for instance, whose close-set topiary-work immediately catches the eye, though it tends more and more to obscure the building itself, originally a couple of cottages probably built in the early seventeenth century. It was granted an ale-licence, and the name it assumed derives from the fact that it was intended by the Irish adventurer, Colonel Thomas Blood, as his hide-out when he had stolen the Crown Jewels from the Tower of London. He failed, as every schoolboy knows, was accused, convicted but, surprisingly, reprieved. That was in 1671. The inn-keeper, when the storm had blown over, cashed-in on the glory of what-might-have-been.

A few miles to the south is the *Plume of Feathers* at Crondall, a much more striking inn, old enough to have been mentioned in Domesday and looking its age. Many of the great oak beams are original, and a good deal of the brickwork too. One great gable is carried on twelve massive timber-ends, almost certainly once a ship's timbers.

To the west of both Minley and Crondall, at the junction of two roads that have been thoroughfares for centuries, one of them the A30 to Salisbury and Exeter, the other the A32 running from the coast between Portsmouth and Southampton, there is the *White*

Hart, at Hook. Here too the massive timbers suggest that they were selected in the first instance by shipwrights, who knew how to pick the best from the huge New Forest oaks, now dwindled to a shadow of its former self. The expert can have a field-day here, establishing where the oldest part of the fabric survives and where and how the replacement timbers merged with the original ones. No exact date seems available, but the landlord insists that he holds the fifth oldest licence in the country. When I tentatively challenged this, mentioning among others Nottingham's *Trip to Jerusalem* and the *Fighting Cocks* at St Albans, he became a little vague.

An even more obvious posting-house is the *White Hart* at Sherfield-upon-Loddon. Of cream-painted brickwork, it stands well back off the main south-bound road between Reading and Basingstoke, its courtyard ample enough to hold a good many coaches. Its outstanding feature is a polygonal window-block rising through both storeys and with a shapely tiled gable that merges with the main roof. The windows on the ground floor were designed so that the coachmen, while slaking their thirst, could keep one eye on their vehicles while the ostlers changed the horses. It was an inn in the seventeenth century, though it does not look its age. The large open fireplace will have been a feature welcomed by the chilled outside passengers seeking to accumulate sufficient warmth for their onward journey when the guard hailed them. A more unusual feature, hinting clearly at the importance of the place in the heyday of long-distance coach travel, is the 'mail-rack', divided into a number of pigeon-holes like a poste-restante today. It was designed to hold letters, instructions, bills-of-lading and similar documents and communications for the convenience of regular travellers calling at the inn when on business.

Midway down the county we come to the *Fox & Hounds*, Beauworth, a cottage-style inn that gives no hint as to what it uniquely contains. There was a small castle on this site as long ago as the twelfth century, though nothing of it is to be seen today. But like every castle, it had to be self-sufficient, and this meant first and foremost that it must have its own water-supply. The *Fox & Hounds* has been on mains water for many years, but it still has the original castle well, reputed to be two hundred feet deep, which was dug for the use of the garrison eight hundred years ago. It contains water to this day, so that the inn could be self-sufficient if its customers were content to quaff 'Adam's Ale'.

Entering the inn, you are immediately confronted by a 12-foot-diameter, eight-spoked wooden tread-wheel wide enough for a donkey, or two men side-by-side, to 'walk' inside it. Wound round the massive wooden axle is the cable which, until mains water arrived, hoisted and lowered the 18-gallon barrel. At roughly ten pounds to the gallon, this means that a load of something like a hundredweight-and-a-half had to be hoisted every time. During the many years when ale was brewed on the premises a donkey was used to turn the wheel and there was a resident donkey-boy. More recently the task was performed by the former landlord and anyone he could persuade to help out. 'I reckon that with each lowering and hoisting of that barrel,' the present landlord said to me, 'they had to walk the better part of half a mile—and walk hard, what's more! Thank God we've got the mains, now,' He shut down the heavy lid in the floor, which covers the top of the well; it forms part of the floor behind the bar, so there is no risk that a surplus of customers will break through it.

Even more than the *Cricketers' Arms* at Duncton, across the border in Sussex, the *Bat & Ball* at Broadhalfpenny Down, near Hambledon, is the cricket-lovers' Mecca. This white-painted, tile-hung inn stands on the corner of two minor roads, architecturally undistinguished, it is true, save for an enormous exterior chimney that rises from ground level to well above the roof against the end wall of the older portion, reminiscent of that of the *Limeburners' Arms* near Billingshurst. But more important by far, it stands facing a cricket-pitch and a massive square-hewn granite obelisk that bears on one smoothed face the representation of a pair (not a trio) of cricket-stumps topped by a single bail, with a cricket-ball beneath it and a shinty-stick-like cricket-bat leaning up against each. Below is the classic inscription:

This Marks the Site of the Ground of
The Hambledon Cricket Club
circa 1750-1787

Here, in 1770, the Hambledon Cricket Club, secretary Richard Nyren—landlord of the inn, then known simply as *The Hut*—gloriously defeated an all-England team by an innings and 168 runs. Tradition has it that the men of Hambledon celebrated their victory by drinking from a bowl of locally-brewed punch strong enough, as the landlord declared proudly, 'to make a a cat speak', and gallons of ale strong enough 'to put the souls of three butchers into one weaver'.

Why these odd, poetic metaphors? There is no obvious answer; but it will be remembered that in *Twelfth Night* Shakespeare makes Sir Toby Belch say to Maria and his crony Sir Andrew: 'Shall we rouse the night-owl in a catch that will draw three souls out of one weaver?' It would seem that spiritual transplants were the order of the day in the late eighteenth century as well as in Elizabethan times, as heart and kidney transplants are becoming today. It is on record, too, that in that same latter century 'eleven maids of Hambledon did beat eleven maids of Bramley by 127 notches to 119, and they bowled, ran, batted and catched as well as most men—if not those of Hambledon themselves—can do in this game'. There is a charming postscript to this, though whether it is true or not is not easy to confirm. In 1807 one Christina Willes, 'to avoid entanglement with her voluminous skirt, bowled around-arm to a batsman of Hambledon, and thus started such bowling in due course for all who played the game'.

To the north and west of Hambledon is the small, white-painted *Brushmaker's Arms*, so tucked away in the tiny hamlet of Upham that it takes more than a little finding. Its modest façade is gay with flower-filled window-boxes and there are bottle-glass panes in its yellow-painted door, with a coach lamp on either side. You will find there a room smaller than most, indeed hardly larger than a good-sized cupboard. If tradition is to be credited, however, it was large enough for Cromwell to have used it as a secret retreat in which he could work out the plans for his campaign prior to his attack on Winchester, not ten miles distant, My impression, after at long last running the village to earth, was that nothing there could have changed much since that day, three centuries ago, when he used the inn as a hide-out and, it is said, stabled his close companions' horses in the church opposite so that their whinnying would not give any hint that there was something afoot.

The name is unusual, but easily explained if you know the district. Here for generations a colony of besom makers found the raw materials of their trade, notably the hedge hazel, and produced this old-fashioned type of broom, used only for sweeping up leaves today; the besoms sold throughout this part of south Hampshire and maybe farther afield. Doubtless, being the type they were, they drank much of the proceeds of their labours beneath the roof of the inn to which they had given their name and, intermittently, made use of the skittle-alley which is still popular today.

West of Southampton lies the corner of the county squeezed in between Southampton Water, the southern edge of Wiltshire and the border with Dorset. For many people this is the most attractive part of a much under-estimated county: the New Forest, with Lyndhurst at its heart, Buckler's Hard, Lymington, Christchurch and Bournemouth as its lungs. Not surprisingly, in this area are to be found some of its most memorable inns. A few of them are on the water's edge; some lie in the Avon Valley, which very nearly forms the border with Dorset; others again are tucked away in such areas of true forest land as still remain after centuries of denudation by shipwrights seeking the finest oak timber for the vessels they were building.

At Cadnam, on the fringe of the New Forest, is the long, low, thatched *Sir John Barleycorn*, with its few windows and three well-spaced, thatched porches. There was a building on this site eight hundred years ago, and there is little doubt that many if not all the massive beams are the originals, of heart-of-oak from the great forest which at the time of building completely surrounded it. It must possess one of the longest thatched roofs in the whole country: straight from one end to the other without a break for gable or chimney, though two squat chimneys, do just protrude from behind the roof ridge. Today the thatch is in sad need of renewal, but I remember it as a glory of the thatcher's art last time it was renewed, perhaps thirty years ago.

A couple of miles to the west, much nearer to the true forest, is the *Green Dragon*, at Brook. Its exterior looks newish, and is far less attractive than that of *Sir John Barleycorn* (and what a good name for an inn that is!), but inside the dominant impression is immediately of great age. The enormous black oak beam that spans the great brick fireplace could well have come from some ship built at Buckler's Hard, or direct from the forest itself; certainly some of the other timbers, many of them oddly shaped, came from some vessel that was abandoned in a ship-breaker's yard as no longer sea-worthy: the 'knuckles' and other curiously shaped beams, sometimes called 'knees', are immediately recognisable to the tutored eye and it is known that the *Green Dragon* was enlarged some three centuries ago, the adjoining smithy being later incorporated in the main structure. Today it is a bar, and on one of its beams there is a horse-shoe confidently said to be the last to be hammered out on the anvil by the farrier who, like his father and grandfather before him, had worked there all his life. Unlike the *Blacksmith's Arms*, Adversane, no farrier works there today.

Not far to the south, set among great trees, is the *Sir Walter Tyrrell*. It stands within a hundred yards or so of the bronze 'Rufus Stone' that replaces the original stone marking the spot where William II, William 'the Red', or Rufus, was accidentally shot by one of his knights while stag-hunting in the forest. The inn sign depicts Sir Walter with his bow at full stretch, the arrow-head glinting in the sun. The inn itself, alas, is more 'stockbroker-Tudor' than fittingly ancient, but it does have an interesting porch consisting of eight octagonal pillars constructed of brick instead of stone.

The story of the tragedy is told in an elaborate mural in the bar: the fateful shot; the flight of the unwitting slayer across a stream at a point still known as Tyrrell's Ford; the discovery of the dying monarch by one Purkis, or Purkes, variously described as a charcoal burner and as a carrier; the conveying of the royal corpse in a wagon supplied by Purkis from the site of the tragedy to its burial in Winchester Cathedral, twenty miles to the north-east. It is odd that the room in which the mural is displayed is named after Purkis rather than after King William, while the inn itself is named after the man who shot his monarch.

Smaller by far than the two inns just mentioned is *The Trusty Servant* at Minstead, a short mile away among the trees. It is unfortunate that, unlike the charming little inn at Emery Down close by, where for your 'ploughman's lunch' you eat miniature cottage loaves so piping hot from the landlady's oven that the butter instantly melts into them and the cheese sizzles as you lay it on, this inn is 'homely' in the American sense rather than the English. It is of red brick, unmellowed by time, smooth-faced, indeed shiny, rather than rough-textured; it is, not to beat about the bush, unredeemably plain. Why then recommend a visit? For one reason only: its most unusual sign and the curious doggerel verse beneath it.

The painted signboard depicts a monstrous figure: the head of a boar on a blue-and-gold smocked dwarf-like figure with red, knobbly knees, white calves and cloven hooves. What sort of a creature is this? Why does the classic statement, MANNERS MAKYTH MAN, appear beneath those cloven hooves? It was lightly drizzling as I came to a halt in front of it, so I decided to sit in the car and copy the verses through the windscreen. I had written perhaps two lines when I suffered a repetition of what had befallen me outside the *Woodman* at Hammerpot, Sussex. This time, however, it was not a beer lorry that came between me and the object of my attention but the vanguard of passengers from a forty-eight-seater coach doing a 'mystery tour' in the district. They approached in ones and twos and threes, in no hurry, pausing in front of the sign (and me), lingering long enough to read the verses and make their comments and then dawdle on to climb the steps and enter the bar. It seemed an interminable procession, and I was frustrated to the point of quite unreasonable irritability. But the last of the lingerers eventually passed on, shaking their heads in mystification, and I was able to complete my task while they regaled themselves inside. The verses were set down in fancy, Gothic lettering:

A TRUSTY SERVANT'S Portrait would you see?
This Emblematic Figure well Survey!
  The Porker's Snout, not Nice in Diet shows;
  The Padlock Shut—no Secret he'll disclose.
Patient, the Ass his Master's Wrath will bear,
Swiftness in Errand, the Stagg's feet declare;
  Loaded, his Left Hand apt to Labour saith;
  The Vest his Neatness, Open Hand his Faith.
Girt with his Sword, his Shield upon his arm,
Himself & Master, he'll Protect from Harm . . .

The accoutrements amount, in fact, to a large fork, an odd looking brush, and some unidentifiable bits-and-bobs flourished in his grotesque left paw. Perhaps, I thought, the landlord could shed some light on all this? But there were forty-eight men and women in his homely bar and he was quite obviously far too busy with serving them to be willing, or even able, to answer my question. I ought, I suppose, to have waited till the coach party had left, but for once I preferred idle speculation to satisfying my curiosity; in any case, it was raining, and I had yet to find a bed for the night. So I went meditatively on my way, with Buckler's Hard as my goal.

There, the *Master Builder's House* stands on the very edge of Beaulieu River, a mile or two beyond Beaulieu Abbey. But for its very modestly lettered signboard you would never suspect this to be an inn at all. With its fine sash windows and dignified portico it resembles rather a very respectable private house. And that indeed is exactly what it was when it was built in the eighteenth century for Henry Adams, master shipwright, who designed and built some of the most famous naval vessels of his day: the 64-gun *Agamemnon* and the 74-gun *Swiftsure* among them. In this very house he drew their plans; the windows of the room in which he worked looked out, as they still do, over his shipyard and the estuary down which his ships sailed into the Solent. Some of these played their part in the Battle of Trafalgar in 1805, the year in which he died at the magnificent age of one hundred years.

The brickwork of this lovely building, now an inn, is mellow red and russet, changing in hue as the sun rises across the water, passes across the sky and sets behind it. The tiled roof, with its three equally spaced dormer windows, is mellow too. Roses climb the walls, half-embracing the lower parts of the upper windows. The interior is as gracious as the exterior; the 'feel' of it is that of a house that has been lived in and cherished, as indeed it has, for more than two centuries and a half. Henry Adams's son and nephew carried on the tradition of fine shipbuilding in that yard and the family were recognised and highly appreciated suppliers of naval vessels to My Lords of the Admiralty for many decades. To wander about its rooms, to look out through the windows over the running water, to contemplate the carefully graded hard down which giant oak boles had been led to the shipyard from the New Forest immediately inland, is to step back in time and sense something of a more spacious, less pressurised, age than that in which we are obliged to live today.

Three or four miles inland, on what is known today as Beaulieu Heath, though it was once thick forest land, I came next morning, in bright sunshine after the rain that had been falling as I contemplated the inn at Minstead the night before, to the *Fleur de Lys*, at Pilley, a village, or rather hamlet, as charming as its name. The inn is of white-painted brickwork roofed with thatch, the brilliance of the paint relieved by mangers filled, as at the *Tiger Inn*, East Dean, with gay flowers. At intervals, sturdy brick buttresses slope inwards to reinforce the wall, as they do at Houghton's *George & Dragon* and so many other places where the weight of the roof has threatened to cause the walls to spread dangerously outwards.

The inn claims to be the oldest in the New Forest. Maybe; such claims are difficult to substantiate, and I could name a dozen that look older, though the explanation may lie partly if not wholly in the fact that they have been less well looked after. The *Sir John Barleycorn* at Cadnam is an obvious candidate for seniority. But here, as so often, the interior is more suggestive of great age than the exterior. The noble fireplace, for instance, set about with the traditional copper and brassware, has a relatively unusual feature: a hollow designed to contain an hour-glass and with space for that essential and once expensive commodity, salt, to be kept dry. Perhaps if this village were more like lovely Emery Down in the true heart of the New Forest, instead of being, as it so obviously is, a place to which naval men have retired to settle down, buying up and refurbishing the old cottages, the *Fleur de Lys* would have been allowed to grow old gracefully, without too much face-lifting and (to mix the metaphor) spit-and-polish. Some attempt has, however, been made to emphasise its age: it displays a list of successive, named incumbents, much as many old churches do; the list dates back to the end of the fifteenth century—no mean record!

The A338 runs almost due south from Salisbury to Christchurch, following closely the shallow Avon valley, some twenty miles from the Wiltshire border to the coast. On or close to it are to be found the last four inns to be glanced at before crossing into Dorset a mile or two beyond Bournemouth. Coming as I did from the southern edge of the New Forest, I approached the road by way of the B3055, and came almost immediately to the *Cat & Fiddle* at the second of the Hintons, Hinton Admiral. It has a namesake high on Axe Edge, on the moors to the west of Buxton; I can think of no two inns sharing the same name yet more dissimilar in appearance in the whole country.

The *Cat & Fiddle* catches the eye immediately as being everything that a roadside inn should be—like the *Sir John Barleycorn*, or the *Hoops Inn* at Horns Cross, Devon. It is a long, low-slung, white-painted building with deeply thatched roof, a roof that curves closely over the small, diamond-paned windows set high in the upper part of the façade so that they appear to have beetling brows. The iron-hard beams reinforce cob walls: a combination that is eloquent of its age. The inn was originally a hostelry dedicated to pilgrims making their way to and from the ancient priory at Christchurch. It was also for centuries a refuge for wayfarers overtaken by night while attempting to find their way through the New Forest, which in those days reached almost to Christchurch Bay. It is so ancient that it is mentioned in Domesday—the ultimate arbiter when questions of true antiquity are raised.

Later, though still remote, records give the name of the place as the house of Caterine la Fidèle; strangely enough, it is not explained who this lady was, or why she acquired the sobriquet. Was she some medieval Penelope, ever-faithful to her sailor-warrior husband, perhaps? It is unlikely that we shall ever know. It is pleasant to sit at a table in front of the inn and speculate. Inevitably, the name suffered a sea-change. The signboard portrays a cat on its hind legs, merrily playing the fiddle, a cow jumping over the moon, a little dog laughing and, of course, a dish making off with a spoon. Every child—at least, perhaps, until the current sophisticated age—knows the nursery-rhyme that is commemorated here, even though none of its parents can say who Caterine la Fidèle was.

Ten miles to the north, just off the main road to Salisbury, are the twin hamlets of North and South Gorley. Between them stands the *Royal Oak*, named after the centuries-old tree whose enormous limbs—suffering, one might say, from elephantiasis—rise immediately in front of it, survivor of that portion of the New Forest which formerly covered all this south-western corner of the county. Its encroachment has been checked, just here, and there is an open space in front of the inn: a pond, with pastureland all round it; half a hundred New Forest ponies were grazing here as I sat and ate my ploughman's lunch, an enterprise sponsored, I suspect, by the Cheese Marketing Board and now the almost universal offering at these rural inns. They nuzzled so close over my shoulder that it was almost literally impossible to obey the many notices forbidding the feeding of these ponies under the wholly justifiable threat of heavy penalties. It would seem that the New Forest pony has as well developed a taste for crusty bread, a hunk of cheese and smear of sweet pickle (if not, perhaps, the accompanying beer, though I cannot swear to this) as have those of us who have come to possess it in recent years.

The *Royal Oak* is a true forest inn. It started life as a pair of foresters' cottages, like the *Woodman* at Hammerpot. It was also, for a while, a hunting-lodge. Some two hundred years ago its then owner obtained an ale-licence. With shipwrights eternally in search of the right types of timber for their yards, it experienced no lack of customers, remote as it is from any highway. It retains to this day its air of having as it were 'grown' from the forest that still surrounds it: deep thatch lying low over it and, curiously enough, forming a split-level roof as well as a roof for each of its twin small porches.

Two or three miles farther north, on the south side of Fording-bridge (a name that bespeaks its origin if ever a place-name did!), you will come to the *George Inn*. Like the better-known *Rose Revived*, it immediately overlooks a medieval bridge that carries the road across the Avon, though in the case of the first-named it is the Thames. It is not a pretentious inn, but it possesses a proud tradition nevertheless. One of the delights of going about in search of the country's smaller inns is the oft-repeated surprise of the discovery of an unlikely looking inn that has, in fact, something about it that raises it above the level of more immediately striking ones.

In medieval times, as indeed to this day, the bridge carried the main road that leads northwards out of the New Forest to all points north. It has been in use for centuries. The New Forest, to the south of the Avon, was the property of the reigning monarch, who of course had the hunting-rights in an area where deer proliferated. So, successive Lords of the Manor of Fordingbridge were officially designated responsible for guarding this northwards route during what was known as 'Fence Month'—the breeding season of the New Forest deer. This inn, whose windows look due south across the water which flows directly beneath them and on to the forest beyond, was the obvious strategic look-out post, even before the bridge replaced the ford.

There is, of course, no such problem today. The huge bay-window that almost literally overhangs the water, here very wide and shallow, so that it must have been easily fordable in the old days, holds customers drinking at their ease, not keen-eyed men watching for transgressors, poachers on a large scale. But a figure standing in the water-meadow almost immediately opposite caught my eye, and I went to see who he might be. My stroll was rewarding. Poised on the river bank is a statue of that larger-than-life, flamboyant, unforgettable man, the painter and President of the Gipsy Lore Society, Augustus John, the centenary of whose birth is almost due.

22 The Abinger Hatch, Abinger Common

23 The Withies Inn, Compton

24   Kings Head, North Weald Bassett

25   Coach & Horses, Newport

He lived for many years not far from Fordingbridge, and in fact died here.

There is something in the pose in which he was sculpted that instantly reminded me of Bastelica, a village in the heart of Corsica, that loveliest of Mediterranean islands about which I had recently written a book. It had the same air of splendid braggadocio, of sheer defiance, that characterises the statue of Sampiero, '*Le Plus Corse des Corses*', sixteenth-century patriot, whose memory is cherished not only in Bastelica, where he was born in the year that Columbus 'discovered' America, but throughout that proud island. The likeness between the two statues is uncanny. Those who have read the painter's autobiography, *Chiaroscuro*, even if they never had the good fortune to encounter—and encounter, rather than meet, is the appropriate word!—him in the flesh will know what to expect.

Last of the tally of Hampshire inns is the lovely *Tudor Rose*, at Upper Burgate, a couple of miles to the north of Fordingbridge and only three miles or so from the Wiltshire border. 'Olde-Worlde' is an epithet to avoid at all costs, but it must be used here. For this glorious specimen of a half-timbered building, dating back at least to the early sixteenth century, bespeaks its age in every line of its façade; its roof, its pattern of rectangles of whitened brick or wattle-and-daub within huge oak beams, and its thatched roof, impressive in its quality and craftsmanship even in a county renowned for such work. The building has been privately owned for most of its four centuries and more of life, and most obviously cherished by its long succession of owners. That, no doubt, is why it has been so beautifully maintained. It has been an inn for only a very brief portion of its life-span.

Whoever laid the thatch that now forms its roof had obviously been told 'expense is no object'. It extends along a spacious roof, rising over one section, curving deeply over the flattened gable at one end as a mother curves her cherishing arm about her baby, spreading downwards over two a-symmetrical porches. The decorative 'sculpturing' along the ridge is duplicated in miniature over the porches; all is perfectly integrated, most satisfying to the eye. From the windows of the bar and the upstair rooms you look out over an ornamental water-garden, imaginatively planned, containing well-filled rockeries, shrubs of many kinds and a wealth of variegated flowers: a matured garden, the perfect setting for a house of such character. The lesser details are memorable, too. For example, the fluted millstone set in the flagstones that constitute the terrace running the full length of the building, and a curious stone-and-timber structure that seems a cross between a disused well-head and a cider-press; no one in the inn could tell me what it was. A bright-eyed—but clearly unobservant—girl behind one of the bars said she had worked throughout the season and never even noticed it!

As at the *Woodman*, Hammerpot, and *The Trusty Servant*, Minstead, Fate had one more frustrating little ploy, here in the forecourt of the *Tudor Rose*. The morning was one in which brief bursts of sunshine alternated with longish spells of grey sky. I was particularly anxious to obtain my photographs and, since this was to be my last call before I crossed into Dorset, I prepared to linger and catch one of those all-too-rare breaks in the cloud. I picked the most suitable stance—on a low wall by the roadside from which I might include the whole of this long, low building at the most satisfactory angle. I was prepared to wait, keeping meanwhile a wary eye for the moment when the sun might emerge from the scurrying cloud.

At the very moment when it did at last do so, a huge Rolls-Bentley pulled into the courtyard and came to a halt immediately between my stance and my objective, almost completely blocking this from view. In desperation I hopped down, pointed to my camera, and begged the woman at the wheel to move on into one of the many available car spaces farther on. 'I'm desperate for a drink,' she said, somewhat stiffly. 'I'll only be a minute.' That 'minute', I strongly suspected, was likely to last much longer than sixty seconds. 'Be a sweetie!' I said, cajolingly; in her mid-seventies, my appeal was irresistible. She moved her dreadnought of a car. I took two quick photographs; within seconds, literally, and before I could take a third, the cloud had obscured the sun and, in fact, there was no more sunshine all that day. I sat in the car-park and ate my sandwiches, wondering whether perhaps I ought to stand her a drink. I heard the one o'clock BBC News right through; and 'The World at One' thereafter. When I drove off, the woman's Rolls-Bentley was still in the car-park, her sixty seconds already extended to thirty-odd minutes; it was as well that I had succeeded in cajoling her. Temporarily the victor over Fate, I drove on, heading south-westwards across the border into Dorset.

Dorset

There is no county in all England where I am happier to wander, foot-loose and fancy-free, than Dorset; no county which, save for some caravan-camping-site stretches of its eighty-mile coastline, remains more unspoiled. Had I had the time, and no deadline to meet, I could have stayed here indefinitely. As it was, I sternly restricted myself to two or three days and a bare dozen of its innumerable inns. Possibly this deliberate restriction was due to a subconscious desire to avoid making this county seem too delectable and attract so many visitors as to violate its innocence?

In the north-eastern part is the village of Holt and, on its outskirts, a long, low-white-painted inn, its window-frames and doors picked out in the green favoured by the brewery that owns it, with an undulating roof of thatch beautifully arched over the upper windows. It is some three hundred years old. Beside the prominent porch there is a pair of stocks, and these, of course, give the inn its name. The *Stocks Inn* stands facing the road, itself an offshoot of the B3078, at the foot of a narrow, twisting lane still called Smugglers' Lane which climbs away from it towards the village green on which the sturdy rogues and vagabonds used to be punished. Possibly when they were at length released they would make their way down the lane and beg a drink of slops before going on their way out of reach of the authorities. Certainly the lane was used by smugglers, and there is every indication in the cellars beneath the inn that there was at one time an escape-tunnel of which they could avail themselves when word went round that the Preventive Men were close on their heels.

Ten miles away, on the opposite side of Wimborne, is the oddly named *St Peter's Finger*, at Lytchett Minster. Less old by a couple of centuries at least, it makes no claim to antiquity. Nor is it particularly picturesque, though its wealth of creeper spreading over its façade and twin porches does much to enhance its appearance. But, as so often, a dull-looking inn houses something of interest. Here for generations the tenants of the farms and cottages of the district have paid, and continue to pay, their annual rents to the Lord of the Manor, and always on the Feast Day of St Peter, 29th June.

But why the word 'finger' in the name of the inn? As is so often the case—at the *Cat & Fiddle*, for instance, or the *Goat & Compasses* (? 'God Encompasseth All')—it is a corruption of an older form. Originally this was *St Peter ad Vincula*, or St Peter in Chains. The saint appears on the admirably painted signboard by the roadside. True, he is not enchained; there is no chain anywhere in the composition. A golden halo encircles his head; he wears a red robe, across which is draped a sort of plaid in bright green; in his right hand he holds a massive gold object, unmistakably the Key of Heaven. His left hand is raised, forefinger (St Peter's Finger) pointing heavenwards to encourage those enjoying a glass or two at his feet to turn their thoughts to more spiritual matters, to strive to reach the pearly gates of which he alone holds the vital key.

As different an inn as you could well imagine is to be found, if you take the trouble to go and search for it, in that odd misnomer the 'Isle of Purbeck', immediately to the south of Wareham. Here, of course, are the Purbeck Hills; it was of the noble stone of this region that Eric Benfield wrote so illuminatingly. Here are the awe-inspiring ruins of Corfe Castle. Behind the castle there winds a narrow, close-hedged, tree-embowered lane that leads to the stone-built hamlet of Church Knowle and its *New Inn*. Not new at all, of course, any more than most others with that name. But buildings of Purbeck stone are inevitably so beautiful in their hue and texture —rivalled only by those of the Cotswold oolitic limestone, and not always even then!—that they can be of almost any age without giving their secrets away.

Rather more than half the inn is thatched; the remainder is slab-roofed. The two small dormer windows are similarly distinguished. Two gabled porches give access to the interior. You must duck your head to pass beneath their lintels, and you step down as you do so. Set deep in the thickness of the wall are two windows; each contains a perfect scale-model of a gipsy caravan, one English, the other Irish. Each is perhaps four feet long, perfectly proportioned down to the last small detail and painted in the traditional colours peculiar to the place of origin. I asked the landlord about them, to be told that they were the work of a friend of his, a joiner from Kent. He added that he had lost count of the number of offers he had had for them, naming his own price; shaking his head as he poured another pint for an urgent customer, he made it clear that for him the caravans were beyond all price.

Looking about the interior, it is not difficult to see what the building had originally been: either a pair of cottages or a small farmhouse. What had originally been the dairy is now the Public Bar, appropriately ornamented with country-style artefacts; a former cheese store is to be seen just beyond. In the Saloon Bar there can be seen, skilfully rehabilitated, the all-important ham-curing cupboard, and also a bread-oven that was in use until comparatively recently, this part of the house having been the farm kitchen for the greater part of its centuries of existence. While admitting that he had no evidence in support of the claim, the landlord said that there was a strong local tradition that the *New Inn* had at one time been a guest house for pilgrims journeying between the various shrines in the region.

Purbeck stone of course dominates the scene at Corfe Castle, midway along the Purbeck Hills; it was used for the great castle built by the Normans on the natural mound immediately behind the village. This is now in utter ruins, but the ruins are so spectacular that it is hard to think of any others in the country that offer a real parallel. It is a miracle that they still stand; if they fell, the immediate victim would be *The Greyhound*, crouching below it on a sloping road, built of the same stone—some of it, more than likely, taken from the fabric of the castle after it had been abandoned. Unhappily, the inn has had white paint spread over most of its façade, but the true Purbeck quality shows in the untreated roof and the beautifully proportioned dormer windows.

The Greyhound is more than three hundred years old, and probably reached its zenith in the coaching days. Its most pleasing feature is undoubtedly the group of three finely proportioned pillars that form the porch to the main entrance and at the same time support a small square room with a slabstone gable that echoes the gabled dormers above. The signboard portrays, not, as you would expect, a greyhound, but St Edward the Martyr, King of Wessex, 'Treacherously Stabbed at Corves Gate [Corfe] in A.D. 878 by His Stepmother, Elfrida'. He is flanked by a chalice and by the dagger that slew him almost exactly eleven centuries ago. He holds on a leash a dog that could, with a good deal of artistic licence, be termed a greyhound, and so justify the name. The inn has an additional claim to distinction in that Thomas Hardy, who changed the placenames of his native Dorset ('Casterbridge' for Dorchester, for example), referred to this particular one by its real name; it is thus one of the very few to achieve this form of immortality.

The gipsy caravan motif is repeated at the *Scott Arms*, Kingston, on a spur of the Purbeck Hills to the south of Corfe. But this time it is a full-size, genuine caravan, gaily painted in colours as traditional as those of the narrow-boats that once plied our canals. It stands out well against the creeper-clad wall of the inn, which occupies a corner site exposed to the four winds, almost certainly a cottage to begin with, perhaps two centuries ago. The 'feel' is right, as you set your feet on the stone-flagged floor. From its windows you can obtain magnificent views in all directions: southwards to St Aldhem's Head; eastwards to Swanage Bay and the impressive cliff formations at Durlston Head; north-eastwards to Poole Harbour; north-westward to the superbly sited landmark, the Hardy Memorial—the monument commemorating not the Dorset poet and novelist but the man in whose arms Horatio Lord Nelson died after his victory at Trafalgar.

Much of the open country to the west of Wareham is the 'Egdon

Heath' of which Thomas Hardy wrote so memorably in the opening pages of *The Mayor of Casterbridge*—surely one of the most outstanding opening paragraphs to any novel, and comparable (though so different) with that of Dickens's *Bleak House*. All too much of this has been monopolised by the armed services, whose ruthless tentacles reach out almost to the coast at Lulworth Cove. Here and there a village has contrived to maintain itself as *virgo intacta*, undefiled, and one of these is West Lulworth, whose charming *Castle Inn* immediately holds the eye. It stands alongside a climbing road: a long, low façade with deep thatch overhanging it, enshrouding the upper windows and beautifully finished off along the ridge. The lower windows are almost at ground level; a lavish creeper climbs purposefully up the wall, intent on reaching the eaves. Less impressive, admittedly, than the *Tudor Rose* at Upper Burgate, it could perhaps be called its 'country cousin', and it can match it in respect of age. It takes its name from Lulworth Castle, the remains of which stand near the road linking the Lulworths.

Thence, a succession of minor roads will lead you to one of the county's most attractive and least-known hamlets, West Stafford; considering that it is only a mile or two from the county town it is remarkable that it has not become spoiled. In the heart of it, facing a well-cropped turf bank which serves as a plinth to a row of stone-built cottages, stands *The Wise Man*, as perfect an example of a near-West Country inn as you could hope to find. The thatched roof is the work of an artist-craftsman and is its dominant feature. Not only is the thatch beautifully moulded over the supporting rafters and round the end gable, through which the main chimney-stack protrudes, but it carries along its ridge and elsewhere on its surface a succession of small creatures fashioned in straw but disconcertingly lifelike. I refer to them as creatures since it is not easy to define them more exactly. I overheard a woman telling her husband, as they stared up at them, that they were snails, and she based her statement on the fact that they had 'eyes on stalks'. (At least she did not suggest that they were lobsters!) In fact they are birds: probably cock pheasants. since this is a favourite choice among Dorset thatchers of the old school.

The white front of the inn is ornamented also with a wide variety of implements of the type in use until very recently and, in rare instances, to this day: milkmaids' yokes; eel-spears; shepherds' crooks; hay-rakes; flails; miniature cider-barrels and flasks. I was reminded of the indoor display of such objects at the *Queen's Head*, Icklesham, and still more, perhaps, of the magnificent, unmatched display on the walls of the *New Inn* at Sampford Courtenay. Standing out boldly amid these country relics is the signboard that gives point to the name of the inn. It portrays a judge, in full-bottomed wig, chin on hands, deep in thought, epitomising the wise man, confronted perhaps with a decision that demanded the legendary wisdom of Solomon himself.

Nearby, printed boldly on a panel reminiscent of the one at *The Trusty Servant*, Minstead, are the following verses:

> I trust no Wise Man will Condemn
> A Cup of Genuine, now and then.
>> When you're faint, your spirits low,
>> Your String relaxed will Bend the Bow,
> Brace your Drum-head, make you Tight,
> Wind up your Watch and put you 'Right'.
>> But then acquire, thro' too much Use
>> Of all Strong liquors, 'tis th'Abuse;
>> 'Tis Liquid makes the Solid loose;
>>> The Texture and whole Frame destroys:
>>> HEALTH lies—in the EQUIPOISE!

There is obviously significance in the distribution of the capital letters; there is almost certainly an intentional pun in the sixth line, and a probably unintentional pun in the line that precedes it. Sententiousness makes itself apparent midway through the doggerel, which is as enigmatic in parts as that of the curious Trusty Servant. The final line is presumably the poet's version of 'Moderation in all things'. Who penned these lines? Astonishingly, it is claimed that Thomas Hardy—author of *The Dynasts*, no less—was responsible for them. This is impossible to believe. Even at his clumsiest stylistically (and

he could be clumsy on occasion) he could surely never have perpe-
trated this set of verses; and as for their sentiment: could that be
attributed to him either? Perhaps some wise man will one day throw
light on the problem.

On the other side of Dorchester, far to the south and within sound
of the sea rolling the graduated pebbles that constitute Chesil Bank,
is the 'lost' hamlet of Langton Herring. On the edge of it is the *Elm
Tree*, a four-centuries-old inn, give or take a few decades, that
does not look its age. The slabstone floor, however hints strongly
at it, and the capacious bread-oven is a reminder that such houses,
public or private, large or small, used to be self-sufficient in that as
in so many other respects. This feature came to light only quite
recently when the fireplace was being renovated, plasterwork being
removed and the ingle-nook laid bare. Beneath the flagstones the
entrance to an unmistakable smugglers' bolt-hole was also revealed,
but so far it has not been explored. Quite possibly it ends in the tiny
and very ancient Church of St Peter, the apse of which practically
abuts on to the rear wall of the inn. Langton Herring offers a good
example of the fact that the twin focal points of almost every village
in England have always been the church and the pub.

Inside, there is of course the usual beamed ceiling. If you give this
more than a cursory glance you should spot an unusual beam, different from the customary adze-squared oak timber. In fact, it is a
section of a ship's mast, and it has a sinister association as well as
the element of the unusual and unexpected. Some two hundred
years ago rough justice was carried out beneath this roof. A man
who had duped a number of people in the district and thought to
get away with it was captured in flight, brought to the *Elm Tree*,
summarily convicted and strung up to an iron hook in that very
beam, to hang there by the neck until he was dead. It is not recorded
whether his captors drank their pints of ale or cider as his body
hung and twitched there amongst them, its feet just clear of the
slabstone floor. I was reminded of the hook in the beam at the
Jamaica Inn, Bolventor.

Follow the line of Chesil Bank north-westwards to Bridport and
Chideock and then turn inland into the heart of Marshwood Vale.

Here you will come to a minuscule hamlet with the splendidly ecclesi-astical name of Whitchurch Canonicorum. (The county abounds in places whose size is in emphatic contrast to the promise of such resounding names: Toller Fratrum and Toller Porcorum, Stoke Abbott, Wynford Eagle and Ryme Intrinseca, and many more besides. As often as not there is a strong odour of sanctity about them.) Just beyond Whitchurch Canonicorum, tucked away in a narrow lane, is the thatched and cob-walled inn, the *Shave Cross*. Like the much better known *Shaven Crown* at Shipton-under-Wychwood in the Cotswolds, this little inn, much less imposing, served pilgrims to and from the various shrines in the region, notably that of St Wita, one of the most ancient minor shrines in the whole of England.

This shrine is unusual in being what is technically known as an 'embodied shrine', the only other one in the country being in no less a setting than Westminster Abbey. Shaven, as an outward sign of humility, the pilgrims would pause at this inn for the last time, if they were journeying to the sacred site from the north, to refresh themselves and snatch a few hours' sleep before continuing on their way down the narrow, twisting lane to their destination. Between its high hedges, it is probably today much as it was when it was being beaten out by their sandalled feet centuries ago. Today those who pause here are more likely to avail themselves of the skittle-alley—one of the oldest in the country—than sleep off their weari-ness before making for the shrine of St Wita.

Better known by far, if only because it can easily substantiate its claim to be the smallest inn in England, is the *Smith's Arms*, Godman-stone, in the lovely Cerne Valley to the north of Dorchester. The walls, of mingled cob and flint, are hardly more than five feet high to the thatched eaves; the peak of the thatch is perhaps twelve feet from ground level. Inside, two men with outstretched arms, finger-tips to finger-tips, could just about span the length and breadth from wall to wall, the inn being almost exactly square. As its name suggests, it used to be a smithy, a succession of several generations of farriers serving the needs of the local farmers and the packhorse-trains north-wards and southwards bound between the coast and the market towns. Then, as the result of a chance and, as it was to prove momentous call, the smith's whole life-style changed: Charles II halted here to have a horseshoe replaced.

He demanded a glass of ale. The farrier was unable to oblige. Thereupon the monarch granted him a licence to sell liquor as from that day onwards. But there is more to the story than just that. Because of the cramped space, it was impossible to install more than one bar. So, a special charter was duly brought into operation, permitting the licensee to function 'in perpetuity' with only a single bar, though normally licences are granted only when it is possible to have both a public and a saloon bar for the accommodation of customers.

It is an attractive little place, within as well as without. Immediately over your head a cartwheel is suspended from the ceiling, equipped with mellow electric bulbs. The first time I called there, the seating accommodation consisted of a scatter of discarded bus seats. That was more than ten years ago. They have now been replaced by more modern seating, and I for one regret this, for to my knowledge the *Smith's Arms* was the only inn in the country so equipped. Talking to the landlord, a bearded giant of a man, I said as much. He looked quite hurt. 'These days,' he said, reprovingly, you've got to keep up with modern trends if you want to satisfy your customers'.

I asked him to stand in his doorway so that I could take a photograph in such a way as to indicate the smallness of the inn. He did so cheerfully enough, his huge frame dwarfing the doorway. He held a pint mug in his fist, containing not beer, or even cider, but—milk! Talking to him afterwards, I spotted a book I recognised, on a shelf beside the bar. It was one about exploring Britain's byways that I had written some years before. While finishing my drink, I reached for it, took out a pen, and inscribed it. 'What—?' he challenged me, for a moment looking as though he might thump me for interference with his property. I showed him my name on my driving-licence. He grinned. 'Well, well!' he said; and added generously, 'I may say I enjoyed that book.' 'And I may say,' I remarked, 'that I shall probably be placing on record in due course that you are the only inn-keeper I've ever encountered who drinks milk from a beer-mug beneath his own roof!'

Less than five miles up the A352 you will come to Cerne Abbas, one of Dorset's loveliest villages, in which every house is built of stone that has mellowed with age until the place has the integrated perfection of, say, Coln St Aldwyns, or Stanton, or Snowshill, in the Cotswolds. In the heart of it, close to the Abbey Gate House, practically all that remains of the ancient Benedictine Abbey, stands the *Royal Oak*. It has stood there for some four centuries, and though there seems hardly to be a true horizontal or vertical line about its stonework, it looks good for as long again.

The stonework is notably fine both in quality and in composition; the individual quoins, in particular, have a sort of distinction about them that you do not expect to find in such buildings—though there are of course many exceptions. There is a good reason in this case: much of the stone came from the abbey itself, which was so grossly vandalised, or cannibalised, after the Dissolution of the Monasteries on the orders of Henry VIII. That stone had of course been quarried and shaped with more than ordinary skill, in view of the purpose for which it was originally intended. Within, too, there is evidence of the link with the now vanished abbey. Look up at the low ceiling and you will immediately be struck by the quality as well as the ancientness of the beams that support the floor above. Many of these are objects of beauty as well as being functional, moulded by expert craftsmen whose handiwork was designed for a sacred, not a secular, building. Like much of the stonework here, those beams came from the abbey four centuries ago.

The *Royal Oak* was already two hundred years old when, in 1773, the premises changed hands between 'a Gentleman' and 'a Butcher' for the sum of five shillings in coin and 'an annual rent of One Peppercorn'. The circumstances and conditions are recorded in a framed 'Indenture' on the wall, inscribed in intricate Gothic lettering. The inn is a focal point in a village that, like Whitchurch Canonicorum, bespeaks its ecclesiastical associations: Cerne Abbas. Immediately above it, however, within a stone's throw, carved out of the chalk summit of the hill, sprawls the enormous outline of the

'Cerne Giant', a figure belonging to an age, a tradition, a way of life older perhaps by a thousand years than that of the Benedictines who established themselves at his feet in the tenth century of the Christian era.

And so to the *Brace of Pheasants* at Plush, just to the east of this main road, one of a trio of hamlets whose names run trippingly off the tongue: Folly, Mappowder, and Plush. The main fabric of this inn is not stone, as at Cerne Abbas, but of cob, the walls topped by a thatched roof unadorned but curving gracefully over no fewer than five small, high-set windows, so that it looks not unlike a slanting field of dark, windswept corn, or a shadowed expanse of billowing sea. It was originally a row of cottages, the end one of which incorporated a smithy, beneath one continuous roof.

Suspended from a neat wrought-ironwork bracket over the trio of steps that lead up to the single entrance is a bunch of grapes in moulded glass that can be illuminated from within; a bit chi-chi, perhaps; but it represents in contemporary language one of the two oldest signs in the world for a place where a man may quench his thirst—the other, and probably the older, being a representation of a bush, as at the inn of that name at Morwenstow. More impressive, and attractive, by far, however, is a glass case near by containing a stuffed cock and hen pheasant skilfully and most realistically perched on a small branch; in many thousands of miles travelled during past years I do not recall having seen its like elsewhere.

Within, the oak beams that support the low ceiling are decorated, unusually, with a sequence of racing-plates, each inscribed with the name of its bearer and the race for which he was entered, with the date. The party-walls that originally divided one cottage from the next are now represented only by vertical oak beams reinforcing the plasterwork. Behind these, a spiral staircase in one corner gives access to the upper floor, close beneath the thatch. Happily, the open fireplaces of the cottages, together with their bread-ovens, have been retained intact.

I slept at this inn once, many, many years ago, when I first set about discovering this least spoiled of counties. I wish I could have done so on this return visit, but it was still early in the day when I

'Plague Village', but this whole-ox roasting spit certainly sounded arrived and I had many more miles to do. It did not seem to me that anything had changed in the intervening years, save that there is now a large car park. At the smithy end there is still the scarlet letter-box inset in the cob wall, just as I remembered it. In the early thirties it still bore the initials 'V.R.'; now, however, it is 'E II R'. *Sic transit*. . . . As the landlord of the *Smith's Arms*, Godmanstone, had said: 'You've got to keep up with modern trends.'

Wiltshire

'You must,' said a chance-met customer at an inn, 'take a look at the *Swan Inn* at Enford, since you're so obviously interested in out-of-the-way features at these places. There's a spit outside the door on which a whole ox can be roasted. They roasted one on it on Coronation Day, 1953. You may know the sheep-roasting spit at Eyam, in Derbyshire? Well, believe me, that's just a toy compared with the *Swan*.' I did know the sheep-roasting spit at the Derbyshire worth a visit. Enford was not among the places I had intended to visit, but I could take it in, I saw from my road map, without going very far off my proposed itinerary.

My immediate objective, however, was Hindon, a few miles east of Mere on a secondary road to Salisbury. *The Lamb* dominates the corner where the road branches: most obviously a former posting-house, stone-built and creeper-clad, it has a fine pillared porch at one end and a flat-fronted porch at the other, with a display of lofty windows separating them, including what I consider one of the most beautifully proportioned bow-windows I have ever seen in any house, public or private. It is the main window of the tap-room, which contains a huge fireplace at which generations of travellers across the barren wastes of Salisbury Plain must have warmed themselves while quaffing hot punch. It had no fire burning in it the day I was there, but I could well imagine the reflections of the flames from the great logs in the hearth glowing in the copperware which is so notable a feature of the room. Today the inn carries the insignia of both the motoring organisations, but it has not, as it might so well have done, tacked the word 'Hotel' on to its name; *The Lamb, tout court*, it has been for some four centuries, and happily remains to this day.

Just short of Wilton, on a branch road, I looked in at the *Victoria & Albert*, Netherhampton. Outwardly, this thatched and whitewashed inn, secluded, like the *Blue Bell* at Beltring, behind a row of tall trees, is about as ordinary looking a place as you could find. It is worth a visit, however, for one most unusual interior feature. This is a tall, narrow, indeed coffin-like cupboard immediately to the left of the fireplace, with a door hardly more than a foot wide but a good six feet in height. Open this cautiously. When your eyes have become accustomed to the gloom within, or better still, if you borrow a torch from the landlord and switch it on, you will see that it is almost entirely filled to its four-foot depth with, of all things, a closeknit fabric of—cobweb!

This spider's web at the *Victoria & Albert* (would the Queen have been amused?) is no filmy, gauze-like fabric but thick as woven cloth, grey, opaque, resistant to the touch—if you have the nerve to put your fingers to it, as *I* have not! It is the end-product of count-less generations of spiders occupying themselves, as Ulysses' Penelope did during her husband's ten-year long absence from Ithaca, unceasingly spinning. Unlike her, however, they did not spend each night unspinning what their busy spinnerets had achieved during the preceding day. The landlord told me that it was generally believed that this had been going on for at least a hundred years. Ten years or so ago, some of it was inadvertently destroyed (he must have been a bold man who intruded into their lair!), but there was a sufficiency of spinners in reserve, and the destruction was soon made good. You might refer to the contents of this cup-board as a Matto Grosso in miniature; it would not be all that much of an exaggeration. I was reminded of that hideous inn at Boscastle; but here everything was highly concentrated. And as I departed, a thought struck me: in that virtually hermetically sealed cupboard, what did those busy spiders subsist on? Was cannibalism rife among them?

Just north of Netherhampton is the hamlet of Burcombe, with its *Ship Inn*. It has been an ale-house for some four centuries and stands on the site of an even older building. An old drove road runs past it, and its original and more appropriate name was *Sheepe Inn*; here generations of shepherds and drovers, en route from the pastures of Dorset to the markets at Salisbury and elsewhere to the east, slaked their thirst. The landlord could not tell me just when the name was changed, but he drew my attention to some unusual marks on vertical posts in the interior that were proved to have been former ships' timbers, not only because of their shapes and proportions but because they bore the inscribed marks that were commonly placed on such timbers by certain shipwrights. Clearly he himself prefers the new name, for he has decorated his bar with objects that catch the marine flavour: ship's riding-lights, life-belts, binnacles and other such hardware more usually found in seaport inns.

On my way to Enford I lingered at the *Bell Inn*, Wylye, one of Wiltshire's most charming villages. Like the other houses large and small, the inn is built of the somewhat cold grey stone characteristic of the region and capped with a steeply-pitched roof that gives it an impressive gable-end. It is sufficiently distinguished to have been officially designated as 'of Historical Interest'. Among its many historic records is the fact that the first bell to be installed in the twelfth-century Church of St Mary the Virgin, whose graveyard merges with the garden at the rear, was cast by a team of itinerant bell-founders in the actual inn yard. The façade carries a pleasing signboard of a swinging bell mounted in a wrought-iron frame topped by a weathervane; the bell motif is repeated in the bar by an array of horse and cattle bells and a set of hand-ringing bells such as are all too rarely heard today.

Close to the end wall of the inn there is an old bridge spanning the Wylye at an awkward turn and replacing the ford that used to be the only means of access to the village from the north. In stage-coach days, when this was a posting-inn, a coach overturned on the bend at a time when the river was in spate. The postilion, a mere boy, made a gallant attempt to rescue one of the trapped passengers, and was himself drowned. His act of devotion is commemorated in

26 The Ferry, Horning

27 Three Horseshoes, Roydon

28 Trouble House Inn, near Tetbury

29 The Lamb, Filkins

a neat statue erected to his memory by the stream. He may have been buried, as would have been appropriate, in the graveyard close behind the inn; but if he was, I looked in vain for his headstone.

Enford lies just off the main A345 linking Amesbury with Marlborough. There is too much evidence of military occupation—Bulford, Larkhill, Tidworth and other Services bases—for my liking; had it not been for the recommendation to go and have a look at the *Swan Inn* I would have hurried through the region, looking neither to right nor to left. In the event, it proved to be a profitless journey, at least in so far as my objective was concerned. It did, however, prove the wisdom of seeing things for oneself and not merely accepting hearsay. I have rarely, in a long succession of travel and topographical books, amounting now to something over fifty in all, succumbed to the temptation not to bother to check information from others; on those rare occasions I have more than once been caught out. It would certainly have been the case here at Enford.

The *Swan Inn* is a pleasant enough little place: L-shaped, with a neat porch set in the angle overlooking a tiny garden; part of the mellow brickwork has been left in its natural state, part, unhappily, has been whitewashed; the signboard hangs from a white-painted gantry that reaches outward over the lane that runs through the hamlet; the thatch is typical Wiltshire in style, nicely formed but lacking the 'class' that distinguishes the thatch of, say, Dorset or Hampshire. But of the promised ox-roasting spit—nary a sign!

It was not opening-time, so I went round to the back of the inn to see if I could find the landlord; perhaps he was preserving this interesting relic in some outhouse? Perhaps, then, I could have a look at it, take a photograph of it? He answered me off-handedly: 'You've passed what's left of it. It broke up, oh, years ago. Proper mess it became, so we scrapped it. Good riddance to old rubbish, that's what the wife said at the time.'

I had in fact passed it on my way round to the back of the inn, but a casual glance had suggested that it was just a pile of builders' scrap left there for collection in due course, and long since forgotten. The man sensed my disappointment and invited me inside to have a look around. It would have been churlish to refuse. He had a number of bygones; horse-brasses (of course), an old shotgun or two, some minor farm implements; I had seen this sort of thing a hundred times already, and there was nothing outstanding among this lot. All I had gained from going out of my way was the satisfaction of knowing that my instinct for always checking personally had once again proved to be sound. Not quite all, however. I was offered one fragment of information that gave me food for speculation during the next mile or two. Some time in the last century the inn had been run by a landlord who was also the village constable. Had he, I wondered, first had to give the order, 'Time, gentlemen, please!' and then slip away from the bar, don his uniform and then come in through the front door to see that his customers were obeying the order he had just given?

The *Crown Inn*, Everleigh, lies only a few miles away, just beyond a huge R.A.F. station. It occupies a site once owned by Sir Ralph Sadler, who was Lord of Everleigh Manor and, more important, Chief Falconer to Elizabeth I. The tradition is maintained in a fine series of falconry prints to be seen on the walls of the Falcon Room. Two centuries later, the notorious 'Hanging Judge', Judge Jeffreys, held his Court of Assizes beneath this roof, a tradition towards which the landlord preserves a somewhat ambivalent attitude. The same attitude is held in respect of another tradition, which as yet I have been unable to prove or disprove. This is that the first murderer ever to be convicted through means of a fingerprint test was tried and condemned here. But—why here, in this out-of-the-way corner, rather than in London? No one has been able to tell me the answer. Certainly there is no connection with the Hanging Judge, for Judge Jeffreys died (oddly enough) in the Tower of London in 1689, whereas finger-printing as a means of police identification did not operate in this country before the early years of the present century. Was it some genius's shot-in-the-dark that, miraculously, paid off? Once again I had something to speculate about.

The *Waggon & Horses*, Beckhampton, stands at the crossroads of two major routes running east-west and north-south, on the lower edge of the Marlborough Downs and a dozen or so miles to the north of Stonehenge on Salisbury Plain. This is ancient ground: a landscape of Long Barrows and Round Barrows, relics of Megalithic Man, of sarsens, the scattered 'Grey Wethers' for which the county is noted above all others. Even the most cursory glance reveals that this four-centuries-old inn is constructed of this stone. It looks its age, even if additions have been made to it over the years for the convenience of those using it. It has been a staging-post not only for the coaches travelling between London and Bath but for the massive, slow-moving freight wagons with their broad-tyred wheels lumbering by.

Much of the stonework, overhung by heavy thatch, was cannibalised from the great boulders that form the Stone Circle at Avebury, a mile to the north, broken down into pieces that could be handled by men four hundred rather than four thousand years ago, or from the lesser boulders that constitute the Stone Avenue running south-eastwards in the direction of West Kennett and Silbury Hill. Two well-proportioned bay-windows break the frontage, part of this spreading outwards over a porch with a room built over it that is reminiscent of the porch room at *The Greyhound* at Corfe Castle.

Many of the wagons that pulled up on the cobbled forecourt carried valuable freight. Sometimes they were accompanied by merchants or couriers on horseback, with money-bags suspended from their saddles. It was a much-frequented route, and Beckhampton, like certain points on other major routes—particularly the Great North Road—was a target for the highwaymen who proliferated in the region. Until comparatively recently there was a gibbet, one of the few to survive alongside a highway into the last century or early in the present one, from which a highwayman would be hanged and his corpse left to rot as a warning to his fellows of the fate awaiting them if and when they were caught and convicted. It has gone now; but there is still one to be seen not many miles away at Inkpen Beacon, almost within view from the windows of this inn.

A mile to the north of Beckhampton, at Avebury, is the *Red Lion*. It is L-shaped, like the *Swan Inn*, Enford, of disappointing memory, but on a much more ambitious scale. The quality of its thatch is outstanding, roofing a structure that is partly half-timbered and reaching downwards to form a semi-circular roof to a neat and inviting porch set in the angle below. More interesting, however, than its pleasant appearance is the fact that it is set in the heart of the largest Stone Circle known in the world, that of Avebury, and the almost equally famous Stone Avenue commences virtually on its doorstep.

If its site is unique, so too is a feature in its dining-room. This is the raised stone rim of a well, somewhat smaller in diameter than the conventional size. The well was dug here some three hundred years ago and there is water in it to this day; it glints mysteriously part-way down when, as is always the case when the room is in use, it is imaginatively illuminated by floodlighting from within the concave stonework. The stones that cap the well and continue downwards some eighty feet below the surface of the water, are shaped fragments of the ubiquitous sarsens that proliferate here-abouts. Somewhere amid the foundations of the inn, though not within view, is believed to be the popularly named 'Altar Stone', the focal point of the Stone Circle that was a centre for religious (or pagan-superstitious, if you prefer it that way) rites practised by Megalithic Man. The well behind the bar in the *Fox & Hounds*, Beauworth, Hampshire, is wider, deeper by far, and older by a great deal; but its site is merely historic, whereas that of the well at the *Red Lion*, Avebury, goes back into pre-history—a very different matter.

Berkshire

Long Wittenham lies on the Berkshire bank of the Thames which separates it from Clifton Hampden a hundred yards to the north. Facing the bridge between the two hamlets is the remarkable cruck-end gable of the *Barley Mow*, as snugly thatched an inn as any in the country. Jerome K. Jerome, whose Three Men in a Boat tied up here, accurately described it in 1889 as 'without exception the quaintest, most old-world inn up the river, its low-pitched gables and thatched roof and latticed windows giving it a story-book appearance'; it has not basically changed in the eighty-odd years that have since elapsed. The heavy ceiling beams make it almost impossible to stand upright; one bar is fashioned from half a row-boat—one would like to think it was the boat in which George, Harris, and 'I' (and of course Montmorency the dog) made the classic river trip. There is a groove in the mantelpiece cut by the ferryman who operated there before the bridge was built; a hollow in one ceiling beam, tradition has it, was carved out to accommodate the head of an unusually tall 'regular'. Outside the inn a plaque records the level to which in 1894 the Thames in flood filled the cellar and washed two-foot-deep through the whole of the ground floor.

A dozen winding miles to the south, just beyond Pangbourne, is the *Greyhound Inn*, Tidmarsh. No cruck-built inn, this, but an admirable example of cottage-style half-timbering of much the same size as the *Barley Mow*. Cottage-style rather than anything more ambitious; the work of the local joiner rather than a team of known craftsmen working to the order of an affluent house owner. Short upright beams are butt-ended on to a longish lateral beam to form irregular rectangles in-filled with wattle-and-daub. Here and there a cross-brace was slipped in to buttress a corner. One gable-end is continued downwards almost to ground level and the heavily thatched roof practically reaches the ground in the garden behind the inn. Hardly two of the many-paned small windows are of the same size or on the same level. Beneath the heavily timbered end gable stands the fore-carriage of a Berkshire wagon, tilted at an angle to the ground and used as an elaborate framework for a display of multi-coloured flowers that stand out vividly against the white paintwork.

The inn stands on foundations said to date back as far as the thirteenth century. In its earlier days it served as a home for the priest in charge of the little church close by, but two and a half centuries ago it was taken over by one of his parishioners and he obtained a licence to sell ale on the premises. Records show that at that time it was known as the *Grid Iron*, as that is the emblem of the saint to whom the church is dedicated, St Lawrence. With so many inns called *The Greyhound*, it is a pity that the older name was abandoned; it might be a good thing to re-establish it.

Farther downstream from Pangbourne, close to the Thames at Sonning, stands the *Bull Inn*, dating from the early sixteenth or perhaps late fifteenth century. Its courtyard abuts on to the grave-yard of the part-Norman Church of St Andrew : as with the *Bell Inn*, Wylye, only a low hedge separates them. Half-timbered, white-painted, tile-roofed, its neat upper-floor windows capped by trim gables give it the impression of looking out wide-eyed over court-yard and graveyard and their respective occupants, either drinking out of doors or asleep beneath the sod.

The doors are low-lintelled and the ceiling almost as low. Until comparatively recently the ceiling beams were plastered over, but a chance fall of plaster revealed that the beams were of exceptional quality and they have now been deliberately exposed. The marks of the carpenters' adzes, no two identical, catch the light from the fire and individual lamps like some roughly faceted semi-precious black stones or hand-worked jet. The old fireplace, too, was dis-covered some time ago behind an ugly Victorian cast-iron grate; in the stonework of its jambs there are recesses carved out for the mulling of ale. There is a touch of interest, too, in the name of the inn. Queen Elizabeth I appointed as Steward-in-Chief to her proper-ties in the district one Sir Henry Nevil; his family coat-of-arms included a bull, so this was transferred to the inn and has been its sign for some four hundred years.

Ye Olde Bell, Hurley, was originally built as the Guest House for visitors to the neighbouring twelfth-century Benedictine Priory of St Mary, of which today such remnants as survive are largely incor-porated in a large private house. The Guest House, however, survives appropriately enough as a hostelry. As might be expected in view of its original function, like that of *The Star*, Alfriston, this is a building of some distinction. The main structure is composed of very heavy moulded beams framing a variety of types of window, some of which project boldly from the façade, others of which are flush with it and can be covered in inclement weather with heavy yet handsome shutters. The doorway is more than ordinarily impressive: a massive structure of heavy timbers supporting an overhanging upper storey which itself is capped by a steeply-pitched gable.

Not surprisingly, as is so often the case with buildings of this age, particularly when they are associated with some other building only a hundred yards distant, there is a tradition that an underground passageway links the inn with the priory to which it belonged; its sealed entrance, you will be assured, is close to the fireplace. But why should such an underground passage be required, if this was the official Guest House for the priory? Perhaps it was constructed later, you may suggest. But again, if so—why? The alternative traditional explanation, of course, is that it was a smugglers' escape-route, or at least hide-out; but here, within a few yards of the wide-flowing Thames ('Sweete Themmes! runne softly till I end my song'), smuggling can hardly have been on a scale to justify this sort of undertaking.

There is a keen sense of antiquity explicit in both the exterior and the interior of this lovely old inn. It has literary associations too. Within its walls, beneath its noble roof, the Cavalier courtier, soldier and poet Richard Lovelace wrote some of his memorable and often melancholy verses before dying in abject poverty towards the end of the seventeenth century. If only, as was sometimes the case, he had thought to inscribe but just one single line on a window-pane—his 'Amarantha, Sweet and Fair', for example—what a treasure that would be!

Smaller, less ancient by a century or two and certainly less ambitious in style, is the *Bell Inn*, Waltham St Lawrence, on the south side of the Thames a few miles short of Maidenhead. Its frontage is most unusual: two halves of its upper storey project well beyond the lower, carried on the butt-ends of no fewer than two dozen massive beams, black with age, in the manner of the *Plume of Feathers* at Crondall in Hampshire. They are not gables, but simply portions of the frontage, each with a window set high beneath the eaves. Between them there is a recessed portion, inset between a pair of perfectly matched curved oak timbers that support the overhang of the eaves and are reminiscent, though on a more impressive scale, of the same feature at the *Red Lion*, Hernhill, in Kent. Below this, a modestly proportioned bay-window juts forward to pick up the main lines of the façade. From one of the many beams, at head height, there hangs a small but heavy bronze bell; you may draw attention to your needs by striking it with its clapper. With two other bells in evidence, painted in gold-bronze on an ebony background, there is no doubt as you wind your way into this small hamlet that you have arrived at the objective of your journey.

Surrey

With the restless tentacles of Greater London reaching ever outwards, octopus-like, in all directions, seeking to engulf the adjacent areas of Surrey and Buckinghamshire, Hertfordshire, Essex and Kent, the true country inn becomes increasingly difficult to find. They tend to lie in obscure corners, keeping their distance from threats as long as they are able to do so. But a handful deserve mention before it is too late, and one of these is the *White Hart* at Witley; it is well worth looking at.

Its exterior is white-painted and tile-hung as to its upper floor in such a way that the tile-hanging curves attractively outwards like a mini-mini-skirt extended downwards to form unequal porches for the two doorways. One diamond-paned window hides half beneath the eaves of the roof, which itself is higher from the eaves to ridge-pole than the façade; another and smaller diamond-paned window breaks the line of the eaves and has its own small tiled gable; yet another is a genuine dormer, projecting from the long forward slope of the roof. A massive grouped chimney-stack lifts boldly from the ridge.

Outwardly, you might guess the age of the inn to be perhaps a hundred years or maybe a little more. There are no exterior ancient beams, and the tiles that cover the upper half of the frontage are too ornamental in design to be anything other than, say, mid- or late-Victorian. Once across the threshold, however, and it is a very different story indeed; you will not be at all surprised to learn that you are standing between walls erected on foundations that are a full six hundred years old. Originally it was a barn-like structure of heavy timbering with a slabstone floor on which, as careful research has revealed, there burned in medieval times an open central hearth, the smoke from which rose through a hole in the roof immediately above. The smoke, in fact, has helped to preserve rather than destroy the beams in the roof. It was used, in the days of Richard II, as a hunting-lodge. In due course the open fire was replaced by a hearth fashioned in one of the main walls; it is there to this day. You can see by the hearth a series of blackened hooks from which great hams were hung, to cure in the smoke. Behind the ingle-nooks is a bar which, centuries ago, was used for stabling the horses while the monarch and his favourites relaxed after stag-hunting in what was then a huge beech forest, only parts of which survive.

On the upper floor, lit by lead-paned windows, there is a whole labyrinth of small rooms and corridors, intersected by ancient timbers, iron-hard. They are, the majority of them, survivors from the original fabric. They will have been known to innumerable customers, for an ale-licence was granted to this inn four hundred years ago and it was about the date the licence was granted that the famous Witley Friday Market was instituted; throughout the centuries of its vigorous life it was held in the cobbled courtyard of the *White Hart*.

The *Crown Inn*, Chiddingfold, is one of the most beautiful specimens of medieval half-timbering, not only in the county but in the whole of England. It was built some time towards the end of the thirteenth century as a guest house for pilgrims of the less humble sort making their way between Canterbury and Winchester, and for the occasional use, too, of Cistercian monks in need of temporary relief from the austerities of the life their Order imposed on them. As at the *Bell Inn* at Waltham St Lawrence, there is a recessed section between the two main portions of the façade, withdrawn behind as well as beneath the eaves of the splendid roof with its ornate chimneys. The fabric is enhanced by the skilful use of finely matched curved timbers linking one rectangle of plasterwork in its oak-timbered frame with another, buttressing the corners and gable-ends. The lead-paned windows, no two of them the same either in size or in proportion, give an individual, even personal, touch to the whole. One vast beam lies slightly aslant over the main entrance, as though the builder had left his level at home when he came to work the day he inserted it into the main fabric. Unusually, the timbers are of light oak rather than the more traditional black oak, and merge with the plasterwork in-filling the irregular spaces between them.

Within, even before you look about you at the great wealth of timbering of the interior, your eye will certainly be caught by one rare feature. The public telephone has been installed, not in the usual kiosk or glass-fronted cabinet but in an eighteenth-century sedan-chair, its brocade upholstery in a remarkable state of preservation. Beyond is a great stone fireplace, such as was so characteristic a feature of these hostelries; it bears the date 1584, so is obviously later by a good deal than the building itself. Inscribed in its upper stonework is the name JHON KNIGHT—a mis-spelling that was not infrequent in those days and for many years afterwards

The main room, like the *King's Head*, North Weald, in Essex, rises through both storeys, its ceiling, therefore, being part of the heavily beamed roof. An ancient Deed to be seen here records that an ale-licence was granted to the inn in the mid-fourteenth century, when its annual rent was fixed at the sum of 4 shillings. This might suggest that it was a place of no great note. But a century or two later, Edward VI and his Court stayed beneath this roof, and not for one night only but for several. He was travelling with a retinue of no fewer than 4,000 attendant knights and servants, the vast majority of whom camped in tents on the spacious green surrounding the village pond almost immediately opposite, below the windows of the inn. You may linger on that same green today, resting on the rail that part-surrounds the pond, and speculate as to how these thousands of men were fed in a village as small as Chiddingfold. They must, surely, have brought their own provender with them. Few, if any, one would guess, dared to enter the *Crown Inn* and call for a 'stoup of ale', since their lord and master, the monarch himself, had taken up residence there.

Another Surrey inn, but on a very much smaller scale, also facing the village green, is the quite charmingly unpretentious *Abinger*

Hatch, on Abinger Common. A white-painted gable with a diminutive window in its peak rises on either side of the middle portion, which, small as it is, possesses two miniature gables of its own, one spanning the doorway, the other a window. It is a secretive looking place, half hidden at both ends by spreading trees; indeed, it has the air of a place unwilling to be noticed, retiring into itself. Do not, however, be misled by this impression: the signboard bears a charming portrayal of an old-time serving maid busy waiting on her customers, and the names of the man and wife who run the inn are there as well, to emphasise the personal touch. As I walked away, I noticed a 'personal touch' of a very different kind, a few yards across the village green just opposite: a set of stocks that offered a less welcome type of accommodation to its patrons.

Ye Old Six Bells at Horley is very much more prominent: an L-shaped inn, the upper part of one arm tile-hung more than half-way down, above brick-and-timber, the other arm being brickwork with half-timbering above; the whole is covered with a heavy roof of the famous Horsham slate, including the two trim gabled dormer windows.

Its really unusual, possibly unique, feature, however, is not actually to be seen. The inn was built very close indeed to the River Mole, a tributary of the Thames which has always had a tendency to flood. There is believed to have been a building here as long ago as the ninth century; certainly those responsible for its replacement some time in the fifteenth century should have had the wit to find another site for it. Instead, they retained the site, but for foundations constructed an elaborate framework of massive timbers. There may have been a reason for retaining the site, for all its perennial hazards: the building, now designated as 'of Historic Interest', was intended as a Guest House for Dorking Monastery, some ten miles to the north-west. So sound was the timber framework that, in spite of countless successive annual floodings, the inn stands firm and secure to this day, even if one or two sections of its outer walling tend to bulge slightly.

Inside, you will see at once a large refectory-type table, reminiscent of the one at *Ye Olde King's Arms* in Litton, Somerset, for it is marked out obviously for some elaborate form of the once-popular game of shove-ha'penny, in which coins or counters had to be propelled towards a six-inch nail inset in the solid table-top, the stub of which may still be seen. The table-top has been worn smooth by generations of beer drinkers, and is still in use today; but during the long years prior to the Dissolution of the Monasteries this room, now the bar, was the chapel at which some brother from Dorking would lead the visiting pilgrims in their devotions before they continued on their way next morning to worship at the monastery itself.

In strong contrast to this inn is *Ye Old Bell* at Oxted. No tile-hung walls here; instead, an intricate pattern of half-timbering on main wall and gable-ends. Black oak beams, too—very different from those at the *Crown Inn*, Chiddingfold. The upper storey projects a little beyond the lower, carried on a large number of oak butt-ends supporting a vast lateral beam. Below and above, the white-painted plasterwork is framed in a pattern of horizontal and vertical beams buttressed by diagonal cross-members. Fitted ingeniously into these are a number of lead-paned windows of diamond shape, no two alike in size, in level or in positioning, yet—as always seems to be the case in medieval buildings where rule-of-thumb has been the only rule—harmoniously and most pleasingly distributed.

There is an obvious explanation for this wealth of timbers in so modestly sized an inn. It stands close enough to the old Pilgrims' Way to have been an obvious rest house for wayfarers bound to and from the shrine of St Thomas à Becket at Canterbury, sixty miles to the east. But the ground slopes steeply downwards away from the road, now the A25, and the fifteenth-century builders recognised its vulnerability and compensated for this with their many cross-braces. They built with artistry as well as with understanding: witness the beautiful proportions of the moulded beam at the corner where Sandy Lane dips so steeply away from the road. Above this, suspended from a fine wrought-iron bracket, is the swinging inn sign in the form of a curiously moulded bell; the motif is echoed in a charming little half-bell inset in the plasterwork of another, smaller gable.

And so to the last couple of Surrey inns for which space can be found. In the 'ear' of the county that sticks out a mile or two, south of Farnham and almost on the Hampshire border, tucked away off a small road that leads to Farnham near the village of Compton, is the *Withies Inn*. Here, obviously, is an amalgam of two former cottages beneath one roof. Its white façade has four or five neat windows, each with its gay window-box; its brightness is alleviated by a doorway at one end beneath an extension of the original roof; at the other end, roses climb riotously. Somewhat oddly, a row of old-time coach-lamps adorn the façade—not where you would expect to find them, on either side of the doors, but high up beneath the eaves. Well, at least the colony of house-martins who obviously know a good home when they find one will have house-lighting for free during the summer occupation of their homestead! The interior is exactly what you would anticipate in a place of this kind: a beamed ceiling so low that you can hardly stand upright once you have crossed the threshold, a cosy air that is all you could ask for.

The *Withies Inn* is close to the Hampshire border. Close to the Sussex border, just north of East Grinstead, is the *Fox & Hounds*, South Godstone. It is set back from the road, at the foot of the long, tree-clad hill that climbs up and over the North Downs. The lower part of its attractive frontage is square, no-nonsense half-timbering, with two little porches and unevenly spaced windows too small, one would have thought, to admit any light whatsoever, inset in the brickwork and peeping out through the tile-hung upper storey. The little inn has its feet set deep in a generous plinth of flowers and small shrubs; a wagon wheel nicely occupies the frame of one section of the half-timbering. In addition, a number of essentially rural objects are scattered about the façade of the inn, among them a besom that might well have been the property of some local witch whose night-riding days had come to an end. It lies across the tiles just below the name of the inn, which is set out in bold (? too bold) white lettering. Below the tiles, again framed by the oak timbers, are some horseshoes, carefully placed with their points upwards so that the good luck they are supposed to ensure shall not run out, down and away.

CHAPTER THREE

East Anglia

Essex

Place one point of a pair of compasses on the border between Norfolk
and Suffolk, a little to the south-west of Thetford, and the other point
just off Hunstanton, to the north, or Chelmsford to the south; the
arc it will describe will follow the coastline pretty closely round
from one to the other, give or take a few inconsequential miles, and
the segment formed will include the whole of those two named
counties—which to most of us *are* East Anglia. It will include also
the truly rural part of Essex, the county with the most substantial
claim for inclusion in this region, some 5,000 square miles, more
unspoiled, less exploited, than perhaps any other region of comparable extent, at least in the southern half of England.

East Anglia is great corn-growing land. Travel about it during
harvest time and the huge combine harvesters are ploughing their
way through the wheatfields that seem to stretch to the horizon in
every direction. Throughout the long, hot summers thirst is a
constant companion; and not always a welcome one at that, unless
it can be handily controlled. Does this fact perhaps partly explain
the proliferation of homely rural inns? Statistics are notoriously
suspect, and it would be a bold man who stated categorically that
there are more of these inns in this region than in any other of
comparable area. But certainly they do exist in abundance, and often
in what seem the unlikeliest places. The thirsty farm-labourer, as
Spike Mays has shown in his book, *Five Miles from Bunkum*, slaked
his thirst in the field from home-made wines—often from quite

startling recipes; but he also gravitated to the nearest inn to cap his intake with something less exotic, less potent, and more lastingly refreshing.

The inns in which he did so are mostly unpretentious and small. It is probably true that they are on the whole less immediately attractive than those to be found in some other parts of the country (though there are exceptions); but it has to be said that this is the over-all impression as you wander about the network of minor roads that interconnect the tiny hamlets of these three counties. I started in Essex, worked my way northwards through Suffolk into Norfolk, and returned to my starting-point touching on a western corner of both Suffolk and Essex that I had missed on my outward journey. Though generally northwards to begin with, it was a zigzag journey, inevitably, and counter-clockwise from start to finish.

Ye Olde White Harte at Burnham-on-Crouch is as attractive looking a waterside inn as you are likely to find, at least until you come to those scattered about the Norfolk Broads. The dazzling white of the paintwork round the large windows of this Georgian, or perhaps Queen Anne, building contrasts beautifully with the mellow red brickwork. The windows stare boldly across the water, only a few yards away, reached by a private wicket-gate if you are a member and have a boat tied to a buoy within view; it is clearly so marked.

Curiously, the landlord had little information to offer me when I asked him about the house he runs. There were no stories of rum-runners' activities, of fights between the Excise Men and the small-boat sailers bringing in illicit brandy for the parson, baccy for the clerk, or of hauntings by characters long since drowned in the wide waters of the Crouch on which now the pleasure-boats sail or idle above their own reflections. He did tell me, however, that not so long ago the then Prime Minister, having cast off his Common Market problems, the worry about the prison riots in the Isle of Wight, the country's mixed reactions to the arrival of several thousand Ugandan Asians (this had all been some time before, in fact), and doubtless a score of other matters that had not so far hit the headlines, had snatched time for a day or two's sailing here; the arrival of *Morning Cloud* among the lesser fry had been something of an event.

My guess is that, if he had eaten ashore, it would have been in the nicely appointed dining-room. As for me, I ordered a beer and sat down on a scarlet wooden-slatted seat beside the door, in the blazing sunshine, to eat my sandwiches. A wasp joined me, and was my sole company for a while. It then felt thirsty, and decided to sample my beer. The bouquet went to its head and it tumbled in and swam disconsolately round the periphery of the mug until I rescued it and laid it on the flagstones at my feet to dry out. Whirring its wings busily and turning this way and that to obtain the maximum benefit of the sun, it eventually dried out and, casting an ungrateful look in my direction, shot off to tell its family what had befallen it. The beer tasted neither better nor worse for the temporary presence of the wasp.

Less than a hundred yards along the quay there is a humbler looking inn altogether, *The Anchor*. It was obviously the place for the locals to relax in, and also no doubt for the owners of the smaller boats. A young couple with a baby in a pram and a two-year-old toddling beside it went by me. They came to a halt outside the inn and the young man went in, to return with two glasses of lager. The toddler objected strongly to seeing his parents enjoying their drink, and burst into a storm of protest. Father went inside again, and returned this time with an iced lolly, which he crammed into the small boy's mouth; it proved an effective stopper, and peace reigned once more. All pretty irrelevant, you may reasonably object. But somehow it set the pace, as it were, for the days I was to spend in East Anglia, where time seems to run more slowly than elsewhere and nothing much happens, or matters. I had written of this part of England long, long ago, in a section of a book that I headed 'Delay in the Sun'; as I was about to find out, precious little had changed during the intervening years.

Extremely low-lying terrain extends all about you here; it is a region of marshland, in places not more than twenty feet above sea level, like the Romney Marshes in Kent. Somehow, minute hamlets have contrived to maintain a footing here, though they are often in isolated groups, visible to one another yet separated by wide estuaries. The shallow Roach flows into the Crouch almost opposite

30 The Wagon Wheel, Grimley

31 The Whittington Inn, Kinver

32   The Pound Inn, Leebotwood

33   The Nags Head, Pontesbury

Ye Olde White Harte and *The Anchor;* to approach *The Hope*, at Tollesbury, you must travel inland to Maldon and on to Tolleshunt d'Arcy. The inn, though its exterior is not particularly attractive, is very truly *au bout du monde*: a few hundred yards at most, and you are on the water's edge, though the road that has led you as far as the inn gives up the effort long before. It is not surprising that *The Hope* claims a long association with smuggling, for there can surely be few lonelier spots anywhere along this coastline and there is little or no cover for the Preventive Men. The estuary of the Blackwater offers side creeks in plenty, and doubtless these were as familiar to the smugglers as any along the whole coastline.

Beyond the Blackwater and its tributaries, the Colne, Brightling-sea Reach (how gaily the name trips off the tongue!), the labyrinth of creeks that enmesh Horsey Isle, the estuaries of the Stour, and, just beyond that, the Orwell and the Deben, you have crossed the border into Suffolk. But before doing so, you may care to turn aside by way of Manningtree to Dedham, and take a look at *The Sun*, a posting-house that dates back to the fifteenth century. Though it has been modernised to meet modern requirements, you find that you have stepped back more than a pace or two into history when you pass through its high archway into the courtyard behind, on which horses' hooves have struck sparks from the cobbles for three centuries and more, and iron-shod wheels have rumbled and shaken. You are about to leave Essex, but will be back in the county again before you have seen the last of East Anglia's inns.

Suffolk

North by west from Dedham you come to Lavenham, the glory of whose 'Wool' church is matched only by that of its half-timbering. Here *The Swan* must rank among the most perfect examples of this style of building in all England. It is perhaps too large to be included in a book concerned with small country inns; indeed, it has recently been very considerably enlarged (and most skilfully, too) by the incorporation of the fifteenth-century Wool Hall immediately adjacent. I remember it best from my first visit there, nearly thirty years ago, when it was of a size that would certainly have made its inclusion permissible here. I was exploring East Anglia on foot.

Having sat down to a meal, I was astonished to be offered a large plateful of meat, unmistakably a thick steak. Astonished because this was very soon after the war and rationing was still in force, I dug my knife in, prepared to enjoy a steak such as I had not seen for six years and more. My fellow diners, most of them with their eyebrows raised, did likewise. But our knives bounced off those steaks; impossible even to slice a flake off a single corner, try as we might. One by one, we sat back, disappointed, to await developments.

The truth emerged. Someone had summoned the manager. In silence, and without the sort of protest we might have anticipated, he and his small staff removed our plates; when they returned, each had a portion of Spam on it instead of the steak. One of us asked what it was all about. The answer came pat, if ruefully: what we had been offered was—whale steak, something he had believed would prove more than welcome. There must be some special art in making whale steak palatable, or even eatable; he had not discovered it. It probably takes a whaler to relish, or even tackle, such meat; we were not whalers but English folk with shrunken stomachs after years of rationing. We felt as sorry for him as we did for ourselves. I have eaten many times since at *The Swan*; indeed, I ate and slept there the night after I had shared my lunch with that wasp; and I have never been disappointed at the fare again.

You do not need to go as far as Lavenham to find an inn built of the sort of timber that is traditional in oak-growing country—as the heavy clay of Essex is, to the west, and from undoubtedly that of which *The Crown* at Bildeston is built. It is an altogether more modest establishment than *The Swan* at Lavenham, and less often written-up in the guide-books. But here is oak a-plenty: massive blackened beams intersecting the off-white plaster that sets them off so well, and a kind of craziness about the whole building—tip-tilted, cock-eyed, what you will—that is most satisfying to the eye even if it may have been something of a nightmare to fit out and furnish. Its substantial timberwork, for a building so relatively small, is perhaps explained by the fact that it was built for one of the wealthy merchants who had made their fortunes out of the sheep and the vast quantities of wool that they yielded here five hundred years ago. His date is known, and that of the house he became affluent enough to have built for himself, in the last decade of the fifteenth century:

The lure of oak may well tempt you farther inland. It is probably true to say that no one style of building catches and fires the imagination quite as half-timbering does. The *elegance* of Georgian, Regency, Queen Anne: yes; the classic grace, yes. But half-timbering: this stands in a class of its own, whether you think of it in the context of Suffolk and Essex—from the clay of which latter county came the best of the oak when it was the building material *par excellence* of both dwellings and ships—or in that of the Welsh Border country northwards through Herefordshire and Shropshire into Cheshire and rural Lancashire, where are to be found such outstanding examples as Little Moreton Hall and Rufford Old Hall.

You will come upon more half-timbering when you round the corner into the beautiful village of Clare. Immediately on your left, in the angle of the road, stands *The Bell*, overlooking what could be a small market-place but is in fact hardly more than an upward-sloping extension of the main through-road, with a shop or two beyond. A finely tiled roof overhangs a beamed exterior and the plasterwork typical of the region, though unlike some of the smaller houses in the narrow side streets it has none of the pargetting for which Clare is famous. The oak beams have not darkened to pitch-black, as they have at most such inns; here they have remained pale, as at the *Crown Inn*, Chiddingfold, and, for that matter, at *The Swan*, Lavenham, *The Bull* at Long Melford, in the same county, and at the *Coach & Horses* at Newport, in Essex.

There is no question that *The Bell* is of fifteenth-century origin—as a true inn. Equally, there is no question that the boldly curved window that bulges outwards on the corner is of later date. It is almost equally certain that the origins of the building, as such, date much further back in time than the fifteenth century, possibly as far back as the twelfth. For records reveal that the garrison of the castle built by one of William the Conqueror's knights, one Richard de Clare, used a building on this site for relaxation—which included the consumption of enormous quantities of mead. The approximate date of the castle is 1078, so that it is not surprising that none of the fabric of that original building can be identified today; it was only the castles of that remote period that were built strongly enough to outlast nine centuries of wear and tear and weather.

In the heyday of the wool trade, when Suffolk 'wool men' were among the most prosperous in the country, Clare as a market town came into her own. (Somehow one must write 'her' rather than 'its' in this context, and with such a name.) The inn, such as it had been, was enlarged; it came into use not only for pack-trains but as a posting-house; around its spacious courtyard there was stabling for a score and more horses, and room, too, for the wagons they hauled. One odd fact, however, no historical records seem able to explain: for many years it was known, not as *The Bell* but as the *Green Dragon*. Neither name has any relevance today, but of the two, the first seems perhaps the more suitable.

Few of the inns I visited in this county were roofed with thatch—possibly on account of the very high rate of fire insurance for such buildings; this fact seems all the more odd since the finest examples of the thatcher's art are to be found in East Anglia, with rivals only, perhaps, in Hampshire, Dorset and Devon. Most of the inns are roofed with ordinary tiles, or with the more attractive pantiles. But there are exceptions, and I came upon one of these at Stowupland. *The Crown* is a homely, retiring sort of an inn, lying back off the A1120 so that you will have passed it without noticing it if you were speeding—something you should never do in this county, whose whole tempo belongs to a more leisurely age. It is part-embowered with trees behind its small courtyard, longish, low, white-painted. But its thatch is the work of a true craftsman. Because it is now so weathered, it is difficult, unless you are a professional, to be sure whether it is of reed or rye-straw; probably it is of the latter, for reed thatch is extremely expensive, even though it has perhaps twice the life of straw thatch. Though I did not actually see it, my guess is that somewhere beneath the low eaves, probably at the back, would be found the traditional long-stemmed iron 'claw', kept in readiness to tear burning thatch away when it has caught fire so that the remainder, and the rafters beneath, may be spared destruction. Such long-handled 'claws' have been a feature of buildings in 'thatch country' for centuries, and are the immediate resort in emergency until the arrival of the fire brigade.

There is no thatch on *Ye Old Bell & Steelyard* at Woodbridge, however. Indeed, it would seem wholly out of place here. The second half of the inn's name is excuse enough for a diversion eastwards, and it will not surprise you to find here all the heavy oak beams that you have been looking for in so many of Suffolk's smaller inns. For the main structure of this fifteenth-century inn had to be strong enough to resist the pull not only of the enormous beam outthrust across the road in front of it but of a three-ton wagon-load of grain while it was checked by the authorities before being permitted to pass through to the maltster's warehouse. Three tons was the maximum weight, wagon included, that could be accepted; this was checked by the enormous steelyard that still dominates the road, as it has done for most of the four centuries and more since the inn was built.

A steelyard, of course, was one of the oldest, and incidentally most accurate, types of weighing-machine ever devised; its origins go back into the mists of time, but you will still see fishwives in small Spanish and other seaports weighing their fish with them beneath the keen glance of their prospective customers, miniature steelyards held aloft in the hand. The weights that are moved along the scale are, in those cases, minute; but the weight used on this Woodbridge steelyard during the centuries must weigh more than a hundred pounds; it may still be seen in the fireplace of one of the inn's rooms.

Norfolk

Some of the best known inns in this county are to be found among the Norfolk Broads, frequented mainly, of course, by small-boat sailers out in their pleasure-craft, whether under sail or with out-board or diesel engines; once they served the wherry-men, the reed-cutters and other labourers who earned their living in this well-watered corner of East Anglia. The *Ferry Inn* at Horning is as good an example as any. It overlooks the Bure, a stream that links one open stretch of water with another. Wroxham, that paradise of yachtsmen, is only a mile or two away; Potter Heigham only a mile or two in the opposite direction, and Hickling Broad, where the *Pleasure Boat* is popular with the more sophisticated, though I found it just a little off-putting since I arrived by road instead of under sail and was immediately recognised (but not welcomed) as a mere motorist.

The *Ferry Inn* does not claim to be ancient, or even very old; certainly if there is anything that would justify such a claim it would seem to have been well concealed, for with its lightly timbered and plastered walls beneath a smartly thatched roof, and its thrusting bow-windows, it looks quite modern. There is a story told of it that monks from a monastery not far away used to fish here, and stored their liquor in cellars. The heady brew inflamed some of them so that one day a mass rape of a local girl took place among the casks. It is not easy to accept such a story as you look at the gay scene presented by the sunshades on the smooth lawns and the yachts-men tying-up alongside. Nevertheless the story is believed by the older inhabitants hereabouts, and they will tell you, in proof of it, that once in every second decade, and always on 25th September, the ghost of the village girl is to be seen fleeing across the turf from a door that is never unlocked and plunging into the Bure in which on some distant 25th September, in a year unspecified, she drowned herself in her youthful agony.

Horning village, a mile from *The Ferry*, lies on the B354, five miles north of Acle; the same distance to the south of Acle, on the B1140, you will find another ferry, at Reedham. Give yourself plenty of time, if your way lies along this road, for the ferry here is the only means of crossing the Yare at this point, some ten winding miles inland from Yarmouth. Here you have no option but to accept the traditional tempo of East Anglia : the slow, deliberate, unhurried tempo which pervades this corner of England as it has done for centuries past and will, one dares to hope, continue to do for many years to come. Why have you no option here? Because you cross by a square-ended chain-ferry that can carry only two cars at a time and shuttles to and fro across the water, slightly crabwise, between its two sloping termini from dawn to dusk. It must surely be the slowest ferry of its kind in the land; I was reminded of the King Harry ferry near Philleigh, in far-off Cornwall. Small craft dodge up and downstream, just clearing the chains that sag below the surface and momentarily rise to run over the ferry-boat's guiding-wheels, ignoring at their peril the peremptory blast from the miniature siren.

On the north side, almost entirely screened by trees, is *The Ferry*, its glass-fronted façade overlooking a small timber-built quay at which yachts and power-boats of a much humbler type than those at Horning and Wroxham tie-up. But at holiday-times at any rate the inn itself is practically cut off from the waterside by an unbroken stream of stationary traffic facing in both directions awaiting their turn to cross by the ferry northwards to Acle, southwards to Beccles, ten miles away in Suffolk. The inn seems to have withdrawn into itself, as though despairing of custom, aware that no motorist in the queue waiting to cross will risk losing his place just for a drink, while those in the other queue will be hastening to make up for lost time.

The probable gainer from all this is the pleasant *Lord Nelson*, in the village of Reedham, a mile beyond the ferry. The inn shares something with *Ye Olde White Harte*, far to the south at Burnham-on-Crouch, though everything about it, including its setting, is on a more modest scale. The Yare is wider here than it is at the chain-ferry crossing; indeed, you must have your own boat to cross from one side to the other. Craft lie peacefully at anchor off the long quay-side overlooked by the *Lord Nelson*; here men and girls, once again, are 'messing about in boats' to their hearts' content; but these are unpretentious craft, small sailing-dinghies, low-powered motor-boats, even rowing-boats and skiffs. The grander yachts are far to the north, at Wroxham and Horning, Hickling and Potter Heigham.

There is the same contrast, here, as there is between, say, Villefranche on the one hand and Nice and Cannes on the other. This is no place for the counterparts of Aristotle Onassis!

The inn itself makes up for its comparative lack of picturesqueness as a building in the warmth and friendliness of its welcome. But this would seem to be a characteristic of such inns, both large and small, and it is revealed in both those who make use of them and those who serve their needs. There must be something in the air that breeds companionship and conviviality. Certainly this is true at the *Lord Nelson*.

There was accommodation available at the time at neither of these inns, at both of which I should have been happy enough to stay. I had however to remain in the district, because the photographs I wanted of *The Ferry* inn at Horning could only be taken satisfactorily when the light had worked round far enough to the south. So, reluctantly, I stayed overnight at the only inn that seemed to have a bed to spare; reluctantly, because it overlooks the main A47 midway between Norwich and Yarmouth. *The Globe*, at Blofield, could put on a satisfying meal, and offered a comfortable enough bed—though it was on the side facing the road, and it seemed to me that traffic on that road never ceased. And there was noise within, also; not that of men drinking, for that can be pleasant enough; rather, it was Charlie-the-Parrot, who never let up. He was a permanent resident there, with a range of vocabulary that I have rarely heard equalled, never surpassed; and a stridency certainly unparalleled. I hurried through my meal, and spent the balmy evening in the forecourt, reading by an immensely powerful floodlight overhead that cast its rays down on me rather than on the inn sign, as though anxious to make amends for my having been driven out into the open. The air was balmy; I read until closing-time; it was closing-time for Charlie, too, and his cage was covered by a dark cloth. He was, however, in full cry next morning, and I ate my eggs and bacon to a cacophony that suggested a larynx of hardened steel, and stainless at that.

So, next morning, my photographs taken, I set off north-westwards by way of Little Walsingham, along minor roads, till I came

close to the coast at Brancaster Staithe. It is not an impressive village
in spite of the implicit dignity and promise of its name. Was there
anything of particular interest in the tiny *White Horse* inn, I asked
while my tank was being filled at a petrol station. The lad shook his
head. 'Not as I knows of,' was his answer; and it did not surprise
me, for there was nothing particularly promising about the inn. I
was about to drive on when an ancient who had been squatting on
an upturned box close by gave utterance. 'There's always the ould
flying horse,' he observed, briefly.

'I thought it was called the *White Horse*,' I said. But there was
something in the manner in which he corrected me that made me
switch off the engine and give ear.

It was a somewhat garbled tale that he told me, and made no
easier to comprehend by the strong Norfolk accent, but one thing
was certainly clear: he firmly believed what he was telling me.
This was no story of a headless coachman such as the one that
haunts the Bolney crossroads near the *Eight Bells* inn; no boggart,
wailing woman-in-white, pot-bellied monk with shaven crown,
phantom butcher with blood-stained cleaver at the ready, or moaning ravished maiden in dripping weeds, was to be seen in the vicinity
of Brancaster Staithe's small inn. But a *flying* horse assuredly there
was. If the old man himself had never encountered it, he knew
plenty of people who had. It is neither black nor brown nor roan
nor chestnut; indeed (if he was to be believed) it is virtually invisible,
taking on the colour of the road or hedgerow or wherever you may
chance to meet it. And always, it seems, galloping fast and free.
'That'll do you a mischief if you chance to meet it, bor,' he ended,
and I heard for the first time on that trip that word, peculiar to East
Anglia, once familiar enough but today used only by ancients like
himself. I thanked him, concealing my disbelief, and went on my
way.

There followed, within seconds, what with hindsight seems truly
to belong to the supernatural, though at the time it was real and
startling enough in all conscience. I had not driven a hundred yards,
was still on the outskirts of the village, still within sight of the *White
Horse*, which I had so deliberately ignored. Suddenly there was a

CRACK! like a pistol shot at closest quarters, and my windscreen exploded within inches of my face, fractured into a myriad small rectangles, many of which, before I could bring the car to a halt, had blown back on to my face, into my open-necked shirt and into my hair. Had I not been wearing glasses I might have been injured. Now, there was no car in sight on the road, either ahead of me or behind. To what, then, did I owe this mischance? There was but one answer: the invisible 'flying horse' about whose existence the ancient on the upturned box had been so positive, while I had been so disbelieving.

I pulled on to the side of the road, and knocked out the remainder of the shattered windscreen. Two small boys appeared from no-where, and one of them volunteered to fetch a brush and pan to sweep up the fragments. The garage boy told me it was twenty-five miles to the nearest agent who could fit a windscreen. Between Brancaster Staithe and King's Lynn there was a handful of small inns that I had it in my mind to visit. I gave the boy with the pan and brush the wherewithal to buy some ice-cream, exchanged a silent glance with the ancient, who may or may not have attributed my mishap to the mythical creature about which he had spoken with such conviction, and drove slowly, thoughtfully, away. Mythical....?

Three miles along the road I came upon the *King's Head*, at Thornham. I remember it as perhaps the most picturesque of all the East Anglian inns I had seen: a pantiled roof hung low over a white-painted façade, the whole backed by trees, and with shrubs and banks of bright flowers set about its feet. A tall pole stood isolated in front of it, its sign enclosed within a wrought-iron frame that could have been the work of some local smith. There were flowers planted at its feet, too. The interior wholly matched the inviting quality of its exterior: a low ceiling and a pleasant ambience gener-ally. That this was in part contrived was suggested by the wording of a notice which informed the customer that 'Pat and John offer you comfort and good fare in congenial surroundings'; it reminded me of the welcome by 'Jock and Jenny' at Abinger Common. The welcome, felt rather than obviously expressed, did much to restore my spirits as I looked about me at the gleaming copper and brass utensils hanging on the walls and displayed on the shelves, including harnesswork and a notable array of horseshoes ranging from those worn by Suffolk Punches and Shires to those of a child's cob.

An old man was drinking at the bar. He might have been a twin brother of the man at Brancaster Staithe who had just seen his unwitting prophecy come true. He was more articulate, and easier to comprehend. In answer to my inquiry as to the age of the inn he said with conviction, 1720. I asked him how he could be so positive, and his brisk answer left me with no reply possible that would not be offensive: 'I was born here,' he said, 'so I ought to know. I've lived in Thornham all my life.' He went on to tell me that on the green immediately opposite the inn, where now only a telephone-kiosk stands, there used to be stabling to accommodate the horses that drew the post-coaches and other long-distance vehicles. He spoke as though he himself remembered the day, had perhaps served as a postilion, or an ostler working at the *King's Head*.

I went out to my car, with more than twenty miles still to go. A small boy, with a diminutive puppy on a piece of twine, was staring wide-eyed at the damage. 'Your window's broke,' he observed. I fixed him with a stern eye: 'Your puppy must have barked too loudly!' I said, accusingly. He blanched, and withdrew a step or two. 'He didn't, *really*, mister!' he protested. 'He hasn't learned to bark yet.' And with that, he shot off at high speed, dragging the poor little thing at the end of his makeshift lead, before worse could befall either of them.

The *Rose & Crown* at Snettisham claims to date back to the fourteenth century. Maybe; but few houses can substantiate this sort of claim, and I should be surprised indeed if this one could. But its atmosphere is pleasant, though the peacefulness of its tap-room was interrupted at irregular intervals by the screech of a parrot that was, surely own cousin to Charlie, at *The Globe*, Blofield. I did not linger long, since my presence obviously disturbed the bird, but continued on my way towards Castle Rising, where some years before I had happened on the inmates of the quiet almshouses wearing their most unusual and charming old-world 'Sunday-best', assembling for worship in their little private chapel.

Castle Rising is one of the most exquisite of all Norfolk's tiny hamlets, set about by stands of trees, accessible only by a crazy spider's-web of narrow lanes, with its small church and its inn, the *Black Horse*. This stands back behind its own spacious courtyard, part-screened from the road by tall, well-grown trees. It was the wife and joint proprietor of the inn who informed me as I entered that I had no windscreen. After some twenty miles of driving in those conditions, I did not really need to be apprised of the fact.

The inn, built of darkish stone, has a substantial rather than an immediately inviting air. Its large gables crush between them a small dormer window recessed into the roof, and the four large windows stare out at you, somehow challenging rather than welcoming. Immediately inside there is the seventy-five-year old inn sign. Until comparatively recently it stood outside, exposed to the weather. Happily, it has now been brought in under cover and may be looked at as it stands preserved in a large glass case. It merits close inspection.

It is three-dimensional (like the charming *Brace of Pheasants* at Plush, in Dorset). Fittingly, here it is a black horse, carved in wood, with a gaily-coloured pack laid across its back. Its elaborately bushy tail flares upwards to merge with a framing of vine leaves and tendrils and carved bunches of grapes that curves upwards on each side and meets overhead; the horse's mane, too, flares upwards and becomes enmeshed with the branches and leaves: black amid vine-green and purple. The whole conception is at once artistic—and a reminder of one of the oldest of hostelry symbols as well as of the days when packhorse-trains threaded the countryside, linking one small community with another, carrying the gossip of one county to another in addition to their wares.

A door on the left admits you to the Stable Grill, aptly named. The old dining-room has been remodelled so that it consists of a series of tables each standing in its own individual 'stall'; on the corner of each is a head-height wrought-iron lamp-standard. The far end of the room consists in the main of the simulated end of a vast barrel—a tun, surely, which would have contained at least the imperial measure of 252 gallons of good liquor had it been filled.

But the upper semi-circle of the barrel-end has been cut away so that it now serves as a hatchway into the kitchen on the other side. Neat, effective, and original too.

I was about to turn away when, on glancing upwards, I caught sight of something which is surely not just original but unique. An area of the ceiling perhaps twenty feet long by rather more than half that in width represents a map of Scotland, complete with the majority of its islands. It is composed of more than eighty of the One-inch Ordnance Survey series of maps expertly set edge to edge from John O'Groats and Cape Wrath southwards to the Cheviots. They have been varnished over to preserve them against the smoke of diners' tobacco, the chafing-dishes of the serving staff and such fumes as might escape through the hatchway from the kitchen stoves. Clearly this is an expert's work: the ceiling is low enough for it to be possible to note the skill with which the maps have been laid edge to edge, their margins trimmed away so that every road-end meets its opposite number on the adjoining map and the complex coastline runs round Scotland without any unnatural break. The surrounding sea has been cleverly indicated in faintly-tinted plasterwork.

The proprietor's wife glanced at me, a quizzical look in her eye. 'You're probably thinking we're mad, aren't you?' she asked. 'My husband's crazy about maps. Until he left his job they were an essential part of his everyday work, and he still likes to have them within view.' I told her that I did not think him mad at all; indeed, far from it. We have one wall at home almost completely covered with maps of European countries on which the roads we have driven over, and our innumerable stopping places, are inked-in and ringed round. 'Well,' she commented, 'at least you don't have to crick your neck to look at them! But we've no wall at the *Black Horse* large enough to take the full set, so this was the only solution. Between you and me,' she added confidentially, 'more than once when business has been slack I've come in and found my husband lying flat on his back, staring reminiscently up at them!'

I myself had a slight crick in the neck by the time I left; but I felt it was worth it, as I drove on the last few miles to King's Lynn. I went by way of Roydon in order to avoid using the main road and the heavy holiday traffic it was carrying. Just outside the village I came upon the *Three Horseshoes*, an unpretentious inn if ever there was one but the epitome, I think, of the smaller Norfolk inns. It is built neither wholly of brick nor wholly of stone, but of an odd and apparently haphazard mixture of the two, the in-filling mortar varying in thickness from half an inch to three or even four times as much to accommodate the inevitable irregularities. And in the mortar there is an element that I do not remember having seen before, though surely I must have done so without taking particular notice of it; indeed, I have seen it once or twice since, notably in the older part of a friend's house in Surrey. It consists of an infinite number of what appear at a little distance to be small raisins, dark, irregularly shaped fragments of a flint-like substance contrasting strongly with the mortar in which they are embedded. They are, in fact, stone-masons' chippings, or sometimes actual fragments of flint, inserted to strengthen the mortar; it is a practice that dates back to medieval times, known as 'garneting'.

Unusual as it might be, I did not feel that it was an attractive feature. But it was amply compensated for by the general appearance of the inn as a whole: long and low, rising from a plinth of bright flowers in full bloom. It was closed, but a peep through more than one of the windows showed that whoever owned the inn was a flower lover. This is no inn such as might expect the patronage of what used to be known as 'the quality'; it is unlikely that it has any bedrooms to let. But it exudes a curiously strong aura of self-sufficiency and contentment. This may have been in part due to the fact that one end of it, a continuation of the building itself, consists of the village general store.

The whole region is good nursery-garden country. As I went back to my car I saw one of the best-tended vegetable gardens I have ever seen. Rows of scarlet runners in full flower; tomatoes in a small greenhouse; bed after bed peopled by a diversity of vegetables of whose condition nonagenarian Fred ('Cheerio-everyone-cheerio!') Streeter would have heartily approved. As I put away my camera I commented on the perfection displayed, deploring the fact that my own garden was so poor by contrast. The woman who was tending some plants in it switched off her spray. 'Perhaps,' she said, deliberately, 'you don't love your plants as my husband and I do. Plants need cherishing, just as human beings do.' Then having said her say, she resumed her task.

Essex (again)

It is a hundred-odd miles from the *Three Horseshoes* at Roydon to London. The first sixty miles run across some of the lowest-lying ground in the whole country; not since I had left *The Hope*, at Tollesbury, had I been on land so near to sea level. The contour-lines drop to an all-time low of five feet near Welney; every other name on the map, hereabouts. seems designed to emphasise that this is fen country. Even in such low-lying terrain, I told myself, there must be a few inns worth a visit. But, to be honest, I found such terrain dispiriting, and I drove on southwards, skirting the western edge of Suffolk, into that part of Essex which I had not visited when I set out for East Anglia, though I knew it well enough from the past.

A succession of minor roads led me to Clare and a second look at the beautiful inn there of which I have already written. Here is the border with Essex, and just over the border one of the finest specimens of heavily oak-timbered building in the county. The *White Hart* faces eastwards across the A604 near Great Yeldham, standing fair and square behind its ample courtyard. Two high gables, one at each end, are linked by a vast spread of tiled roof topped by a quartet and a triplet of linked ornate chimneys. They must have been noble Essex oaks from which these timbers were hewn, in Tudor times, for they are straight rather than, as is more usually the case, curving this way and that. Perhaps fifty vertical beams, no less, with a diagonal or two here and there beneath the gables for additional rigidity beneath the heavy roof.

Fewer, but of course heavier, beams run laterally to carry the overhanging storey, from which baskets amply filled with flowers enliven the dark oak and enrich the contrasting plasterwork between beam and beam. Appropriately, the windows are square lead-paned; the upper ones are considerably smaller than those on the ground floor. Inside, below ground level, there may be seen a feature more commonly found in medieval castles than elsewhere: a dungeon. I asked the landlord whether the place, being so obviously old (though skilled restoration is evident here and there), is haunted. 'Well,' he replied, 'we certainly do have spirits here. We store them in the dungeon, where the temperature is just right all the year round.'

Midway between Great Yeldham (much smaller than its name suggests!) and Saffron Walden lies the hamlet of Hempstead. Until a hundred years ago, its inn was named *The Bell*; no one could tell me why, towards the end of last century, it changed to the *Rose & Crown*. But everyone in the village will be quick to assure you that Dick Turpin, legendary highwayman, was born in this inn, even if few can give the date of his birth, 1705, without a glance at his birth certificate which hangs on the low-ceilinged wall of the bar. Turpin's father was landlord here. Whatever he may have thought about the misdeeds of his wayward son, he 'looked after his own'. Peer upwards and you will spot a small aperture in one of the wide, shallow beams. In the floorboard of the small room immediately above it is a little hole that corresponds with the one in the beam. Through this, it is said, when he had taken refuge here the highwayman watched and listened. Malefactors are more sophisticated these days, and the last place they make for when on the run is 'home'; Dick Turpin was an exception to this rule, if the story is to be credited—as I think it should be.

Opposite the inn is a cluster of elms linked by heavy chains to enclose a thirty-foot cock-pit. Owners of the birds, the men who staked money on the fights organised between them, and the mere onlookers, too impoverished, many of them, to lay bets, drank at the *Rose & Crown* before and after each 'main', to the landlord's profit. It is odd that this small inn, so closely linked with this brutal blood-sport, did not take the appropriate name, but remained *The Bell* for most of its life, until it took its present name. Incidentally, it has

34 The Mother Huff Cap, Great Alne

35 The Old Bull, Inkberrow

36 The Old Nag's Head, Edale

37 The Peacock, Rowsley

another claim to fame, and one truly linked with blood. It was owned, a hundred years before Dick Turpin was born, by the parents of one William Harvey, discoverer of the principle of the circulation of the blood; he was born in a cottage immediately behind the inn.

Three or four miles south of Saffron Walden is the village of Newport, astride the busy A11 road to London and urgently in need of a by-pass. Just short of it, on the left-hand side going south and only a few hundred yards beyond the 'leper-stone' inset in the brick wall bordering the road, is the *Coach & Horses*, with a white-painted gallows-type signboard swinging in front of its porched entrance. It overlooks what has been the major road between London and Norwich for many centuries and, since it has held a licence for selling liquor for well over two hundred years, was an obvious port-of-call for long-distance travellers. Yet, strangely, it has no arched entrance, so it was perhaps not used by the stage-coaches, as were so many, such as *The George* at Dorchester-on-Thames in Oxfordshire and the *George & Dragon* at Westerham, Kent.

It has an unassuming look about it. But for its sign you might almost think it just a dwelling-house. Its exterior timbers support a lengthy spread of roof though it lacks the twin gables that lend distinction to Great Yeldham's *White Hart*. It has lattice windows, lead-paned, in its upper storey, and larger, sixteen-paned bay-windows along its frontage, overhung by window-boxes, flower-filled and interspersed with hanging baskets no less gay. But its cherished record states that it belongs to the second half of the sixteenth century, and was subsequently enlarged. Certainly care has been taken over its preservation as well as its building. There are some good moulded ceiling beams, and the arched fireplace with its elegantly chamfered jambs is worth more than just a second glance. The impression of its being more private than public—though of course it has always been the latter—is borne out by the pride with which the claim is made that George Villiers, Duke of Buckingham, who sold his London residence, now Buckingham Palace, to George III in 1762, regularly used the *Coach & Horses* as a private staging-post. On his way between his London residence and East Anglia he may

first have broken his journeys from time to time at the *King's Head*
North Weald Bassett, which lies just off the main road and, in his
day, would have been almost completely surrounded by Epping
Forest. This is an older inn by far than his known posting-house at
Newport, twenty miles to the north. It lies just midway between
that township and London, and is one of the finest examples of an
Essex half-timbered hostelry you can hope to find. Indeed, it matches
in calibre, as in age, the perhaps better known *King's Head* at Chigwell, on the southern fringe of Epping Forest and only ten miles
from the centre of the metropolis.

It was already well established in Elizabethan times but, strangely
enough, as the landlord told me with a sort of inverted pride, 'We
believe this is about the only inn in the country where Queen
Elizabeth did *not* sleep'. He offered no explanation for this; probably
it was simply because it was too near to her London home to be of
any use to her. I suggested that perhaps she usually set her sights on
the comfort of the great house twenty-five miles farther on, Audley
End. He looked at me somewhat coldly, as a historian might do at a
nitwit who appeared not to know, say, the date of the Battle of
Hastings. 'Audley End', he observed, 'was only beginning to be
built in 1603, in which year, you may remember, Elizabeth I died.'
Conscious, perhaps, that he had been a little harsh in thus drawing
attention to my ignorance, he added a titbit that amused me: 'The
original Audley End was so gigantic in conception that James I
rebuked the 1st Earl of Suffolk for commissioning a residence larger
even than Hampton Court Palace, remarking acidly that it was "too
large for a monarch, though probably well enough suited to the
needs of his Lord Treasurer".'

This inn has two large gables linking a fine spread of roof supported on an array of vertical timbers. There is a lopsidedness about
some of these that emphasises the building's age. There are more
diagonal beams than at the *White Hart* at Great Yeldham, those at
each corner possessing the natural curve that suggests that the builders had something of the skill of the Hampshire shipwrights who
chose their timbers from the New Forest with specific purposes in
view. The walls of the structure between the gables tilt forward a

little; no two of the diamond-paned windows are identical in size or shape, and that goes for the massive oak doors too.

If the exterior is impressive, it is the interior that makes the greatest impact. You must duck your head beneath every lintel, for the doorways linking room with room are as they were originally constructed four centuries and more ago when, as is proved by tests with medieval armour, man's average stature was considerably less than it is today. With one exception, all the heavily beamed ceilings are low to match. The exception is the curious chamber long known as the Squire's Room. It is of a type very rare among inns. At some time, the ground-floor ceiling of this room was removed, so that it gained an additional storey in height. The effect is of a medieval baronial hall-in-miniature; it would not be difficult to imagine the smoke from a central hearth rising to the distant rafters overhead to escape through the roof.

To look at the timbers today you would find it hard to believe that during World War Two a bomb that fell nearby blew out much of the wattle-and-plaster in-filling of the façade. But the massive timbers never budged—proof both of their iron constitution and of the skill with which they had been mortised and tenoned by the men who worked on them in Tudor times. Their shape, and the manner of their fixing, when thus exposed by the bomb damage, confirmed the opinion long held that actual ships' timbers could well have been used in the construction of this inn. For some time after the bomb fell, because of shortage of labour and scarcity of materials, the *King's Head* remained in its skeleton state and, the landlord told me as we chatted at my table in the Squire's Room, it was known locally as *The Filleted Inn*.

Ten miles to the south, on the A113, an offshoot of the London to Norwich main road, is that better-known *King's Head*, at Chigwell. It is more ornate than its opposite number at North Weald Bassett: five small gables, no two of the same size, instead of the two large, well-matched ones. It was of these gables that Dickens wrote, in *Barnaby Rudge* (where he calls the inn *The Maypole*), 'more gable-ends than a lazy man would care to count'. He commented, too, on the 'huge zigzag chimneys, out of which it seemed that even smoke could not choose to come in more than naturally fantastic shapes, imparted to it in its tortuous progress'.

There is a curious variety of styles in the façade of this inn. Part of its ground floor is weather-boarded—a very characteristic feature of Essex inns, though more usually found in the smaller ones, as in Kent. The square, diamond-paned bay-windows of the upper floor project beyond the ones below, and one large bay-window in the floor above projects even farther. One of the entrances has twin white-painted pillars which certainly belong to a much later period than that of the main structure, as does the charming little oriel window above it. The half-timbering of the upper floors is less massive than that at North Weald Bassett, and there is some delicately beautiful moulding along one of the main lateral timbers. If there really are attic rooms behind the small windows in those gables—and I was too lazy to go and check for myself—then they must have been constructed for occupation by dwarfs!

Certainly Chigwell's *King's Head* was an important posting-house on the alternative route north-eastwards from London to Norwich, developed perhaps because of the conditions once obtaining in the Epping Forest area. During the reign of Elizabeth I, who certainly slept here, and James I, the 'Forty Day Courts' were held beneath this roof. Dickens used this as the setting in his novel for the famous meeting between Sir John Chester and Geoffrey Haredale, and the room has been known ever since as the 'Chester Room'. Another link with the novelist to be seen here is a replica of the life insurance policy that he took out when he was at the height of his fame. Indeed, the reminders of the novelist and his *Barnaby Rudge* are as strong here as those to be felt at the *Leather Bottle* at Cobham, Kent, some twenty miles distant across the Thames Estuary as it would have been flown by Barnaby's beloved raven, Grip.

It is a far cry, in more senses than one, from the riverside inns of Burnham-on-Crouch and Tollesbury to North Weald Bassett and Chigwell: a counter-clockwise journey that I had found most rewarding. But now the north-eastern tentacles of London had reached out so far that traffic was thickening appreciably, ribbon-development had blurred the boundary outlines; it was impossible

for anyone but a resident to know where Woodford and Snares-
brook, Walthamstow and Wanstead—one-time villages I had known
so well as a boy—began or ended. So far as was practicable, therefore,
I put on speed in order to pass through them, into the heart of
London and out again on the other side to what is now my home,
on the Kent and Sussex border.

CHAPTER FOUR

The Home Counties and Midlands

Hertfordshire

It may be reasonably objected that in a book on the country inns of England, an inn that lies within the boundary of a city should not be permitted to appear. Nevertheless I am including *Ye Old Fighting Cocks*, St Albans. My justification—slender, I agree—is that it is not so much an urban pub as an inn that stands close to the little River Ver from which some two thousand years ago the Romans gave today's city the name Verulamium; or at any rate, Verulamium lies not so far distant from the city that one sees today, its museum and excavating under the aegis of the city authorities. The inn is tucked away, far from the traffic that streams through St Albans, whether on the A6 to Manchester or the A5, Watling Street, which the Romans themselves planned and largely built as a through-way between Dover and the north-west.

Ye Old Fighting Cocks claims to be 'The Oldest Inhabited Licensed House in England', justifying this claim—surely tongue-in-cheek?—on the uncompromising statement that it was 'Built Before the Flood'. True enough; it was. But the flood referred to was not the one over which Noah & Co. sailed until the Ark grounded on Mt Ararat; it was the somewhat less spectacular flooding of the Ver at the close of the sixteenth century; the inn was already old, even then.

It was originally a dove-cote such as most large manor houses and monasteries possessed. In this particular case it was the property of the Abbey of St Albans, hard by, providing meat for the monks when other sources of supply ran short. It was re-erected on its present site some time in the fifteenth century, enlarged sufficiently to make it habitable for featherless rather than feathered bipeds, given a tall, buttressed chimney and duly named *The Rounde House*, a name which, curiously enough, it still bears as an alternative, one of the very few inns in the country to have two distinct and unrelated names. But—*are* they entirely unrelated? *The Rounde House* (it is in fact octagonal rather than circular) very soon became the venue for cock-fighting, and remained as such until 1894 when a law was enacted prohibiting the so-called sport. The name was changed to *The Fisherman*, the allusion being to the amenities provided by the stripling Ver. Close by are the fish-ponds from which the monks of the abbey each week took their Friday fare.

Though it is small, it is rich in history. Oliver Cromwell is known to have sought seclusion here; as was his custom, he stabled his horse beneath the same roof. There is a secretive look about the small windows, as though they have much to hide. From them you can look up, beneath the eaves supported by the crooked oak beams, at the abbey towering on the height above. It is interesting that today, as indeed for many years past, the old name, *The Rounde House*, superseded more than a century ago by *The Fisherman*, should have been replaced by the name under which it became notorious: *Ye Old Fighting Cocks*. Doubtless its 'promotional' value was a consideration. As for the claim that it is the oldest inhabited licensed house in England, there are a good many houses that would stoutly challenge it.

Buckinghamshire

Westwards across the Hertfordshire-Buckinghamshire border, on the outskirts of the hamlet of Penn Street, near Amersham, is an inn about as different as any could well be. It is younger by a good many centuries, though it has been in the hands of the same family for no less than five generations. This is the oddly named *Hit or Miss Inn*, a name readily explained by its signboard, which portrays cricketers of former times wielding (like their contemporaries at Broadhalf-penny Down) the old-fashioned curved bat. Here too the inn over-looks a cricket-field, owned by the landlord; and here matches are played throughout the season between visiting teams and the appro-priately named 'Hit or Miss' team: country cricket at its best, so much more acceptable to many of us than the turbulence and 'politics' and 'win-at-all-costs' of Test cricket.

The interior of this mellow russet-brick-wisteria-clad inn, formerly no doubt a pair of cottages, is even more attractive than the exterior might lead you to expect. There is an open log hearth; there are blunderbusses on the low-ceilinged walls; there are country tools and implements such as those used by the Chiltern 'bodgers' who worked in the beechwoods turning chair legs, struts and rails on their home-made pole-lathes until the day-before-yesterday (and some may be working there still). A reminder that this has been chair-making country, a rural industry until very recently indeed, for many generations may be seen on one wall of the bar: here a 'dismantled' Windsor chair—elm seat, beech hoop frame, splats, rails, stretchers and so forth—is most attractively displayed, an object of beauty in itself quite apart from being an example of true rural craftsman-ship at its best.

Ten miles to the west, in the very heart of the South Chilterns, is the hamlet of Turville; to enter it you must pass the *Bull and Butcher* on your left, a straight-fronted brick and up-and-down-half-timbered inn with two small dormer windows breaking the slope of its roof, one on either side of the prominent central chimney. It was a cottage four hundred years ago at least, and more probably five hundred. Nearby is the very ancient church, some parts of which date back to late Norman times. When it became necessary to restore the oldest parts of the church, masons were called in and they refused to work until facilities were provided for them to refresh themselves. The owner of the cottage saw his chance and applied for a licence to sell ale; the licence was granted, and from that time onwards this has been an inn.

Much of it, notably the vertical timbers carried by one very long, lateral beam, and the in-filling of wattle-and-daub of the upper storey, is obviously very old; but the roof and the chimney-stack are certainly less old, though they have settled down nicely to blend with the remainder of the fabric. It is the sort of inn that you might safely expect to find quite unchanged were you to visit it a century or two or three hence. Its name suggests that at one time it served also as a butcher's shop, and perhaps also a slaughterhouse, but no one I met in Turville could confirm this.

Oxfordshire

Still on the South Chilterns, a mile or two from Turville and so close to the border with Oxfordshire that you need a large-scale map to establish the fact that it is in fact just over the border, is a hamlet with an unfortunate name, Pishill. It nestles in a hollow beneath the high ridge that carried Cockley Green. Here you will find what appears, even after a searching glance, to be a small, private house. It is almost completely creeper-clad, but from one angle at any rate you can read its name: *Crown Inn*. Like the *Bull and Butcher*, it was formerly a private dwelling; it is, however, very much less old, and quite obviously the property of someone of higher standing than a labourer. No half-timbering here; so far as you can tell through the somewhat overwhelming luxuriance of the creeper, brick-built throughout. One large gable reaches outwards to the road; below and to one side of it, a most attractively proportioned porch with a Gothic-arched doorway set in it, its point reaching almost to the tip of the gable, at once catches the eye.

No one can say for certain in what year its then owner obtained a licence not only to sell but to brew ale on the premises. But it is known that at one period, when there was much persecution of the Jesuits, one unhappy priest, Father Dominique by name, sought refuge here. During his spell of sanctuary he so far forgot his religious vows as to seduce (or permit himself to be seduced by: the full circumstances are not on record) a buxom serving-girl. Realising too late that he had committed an unpardonable sin, he proceeded to commit another, equally unpardonable: he hanged himself from an oak beam in the gabled room. His ghost, they will tell you in the bar, is still to be encountered; or at least his moaning presence felt, once every year on the anniversary of his suicide. An echo here of the story associated with the monks and the girl at the *Ferry Inn*, Horning, though the story evokes perhaps compassion rather than horror.

Westwards from the rolling Chilterns the ground drops progressively towards the Thames Valley and the 'tail' of the county to the south of Oxford. At the same time, a spur of Berkshire thrusts northwards into the wide bulge of the county, and just here, where the river forms the actual dividing-line between the two, you will come to one of the most beautifully named of all our inns: the *Rose Revived*.

There was a bridge here in the twelfth century. After some three hundred years it had fallen into disrepair and money had to be found for its rebuilding. On the river bank, on the Oxfordshire side, there stood a stone cottage variously referred to in old documents as 'an hermytage' and as 'a pettie inn'. In return for an annual rental of '3 shyllings and 1 groat' the owner was granted an ale-licence and permitted to demand a toll from every person, and every four-footed beast, that took the risk of crossing the bridge during a makeshift repair to it. The major proportion of the toll money, however, was to be devoted to the full restoration of the structure. It is not recorded just how a check was kept on the moneys received so that the stipulated proportion went towards the restoration fund, and no doubt the toll money was fiddled then as it has always been fiddled, and is still fiddled at toll-bridges to this day.

The cottager-turned-toll-keeper-and-inn-keeper named his place the *Chequer Inn*; as long ago as the seventeenth century the Oxford historian, Anthony à Wood, wrote that the place 'hath been, beyond the memorie of man, an ale house, *id est Chequers*.' In due course sufficient money had been raised for the old bridge to be made fully safe even for heavy horse-drawn traffic. Its six beautifully proportioned arches, with their cut-waters and V-shaped recesses for pedestrians above them, its parapets and approaches: all were put in order. So well pleased were the authorities with the result that they named the cluster of houses nearby, Newbridge. It does not seem to have been established, however, at what point in time the old name of the inn was changed to its present one. This may well have been when the original structure was enlarged to something like the condition in which it is to be seen today.

Here at Newbridge you are of course on the eastern edge of the Cotswolds. The stone of which the *Rose Revived* is built is Cotswold stone, with roof to match. Its longer side, with its trio of porches, faces the road as it approaches the bridge; the side at right angles to this, with its bow-window, overlooks the river, separated from it only by terraced lawns. Within, you step on to a floor of cardinal-red tiles and walk beneath great oak beams. An enormous stone fireplace confronts you, and there are ingle-nooks spanned by one huge, irregularly shaped beam. A brass-and-iron mechanical turnspit dangles from the beam, while malt-shovels and other such implements emphasise the essentially rural atmosphere of the house. From any one of its many windows you look straight out over the downstream side of this medieval bridge.

The *Trout Inn*, Godstow, barely three miles to the north of Oxford, is perhaps even more beautifully sited than is the *Rose Revived*, for it fronts right on to the river, so close to it that there is room only for a narrow terrace with a stone wall against which swans nuzzle for crumbs thrown from the tables above. It is a neat, smallish building, with four lead-paned windows to its upper storey and one on either side of its twin doorways contained within a single small porch. Of grey stone, with a finely pitched roof of the famous Stonesfield slate (which is not, of course, slate at all but slabs of stone), it was originally the Guest House of Godstow Nunnery, which was founded by the pious Ediva on a site 'on which the Light of Heaven had fallen during a Vision that was vouchsafed to me'. After the Dissolution, much of the stonework from the nunnery was salvaged and used to enlarge the Guest House.

It is, of course, best approached by water, so that you can tie-up alongside or, better still, opposite, and so take your fill of the cool beauty confronting you before you cross the threshold. Inside you will find a massive fireplace that dates from Tudor times; impressive ceiling beams; a display of cartoons by the inimitable 'Phiz'; another display, this time of engravings of the University City by no less an artist than J. M. W. Turner himself.

Here I would say that it is the site that is even more memorable than the interior of the inn. Standing on the terrace or lawn, you can look across towards the ruins of the nunnery where there once lived for a while that tragic figure, Rosamunde, mistress of King Henry II. And close by, too, is the spot where, a century or so ago, a don of Christchurch College named Charles Lutwidge Dodgson 'took three children on a river picnic; we rowed up to Godstow and had tea beside a haystack, and there I told them the story of *Alice in Wonderland*'. We know him better as Lewis Carroll.

Westwards from Godstow, beyond Witney, there stands the lovely *Old Swan*, at Minster Lovell. You are now coming into the heart of the Oxfordshire Cotswolds, with the Gloucester half still to come. It is perhaps surprising to find here a building that is a blend of the essential Cotswold style and of half-timbering. The main body of this beautiful inn is of Cotswold stone with traditional roof steeply pitched over a small gable as well as the main one. But the framing of the main gable is of heavy oak beams, vertical and transverse alike, inset with wattle-and-daub, which carry it forward until it overhangs the main façade below, giving it the true medieval appearance. It claims to be between five and six hundred years old, and the claim is less open to doubt than many of the kind. Until little more than a century ago, ale was brewed as well as sold beneath this splendid roof, and the water for the brewing was obtained from a well that still exists beneath the tap-room floor, though it is no longer used.

Ale here will have had plenty of demand, for the inn stands alongside one of the old drove roads, as does the inn at Fulking, in Sussex, and also the one at Burcombe, in Wiltshire, among many others. Along these routes, whether Downland tracks or valley tracks, enormous flocks of sheep were driven, not only from the Southern Midlands but from far-distant Wales. Here at Minster Lovell, the sheep drank from the stream nearby, while the drovers slaked their thirst at the *Old Swan*. There was a granary, too, in olden times, now adapted to contemporary needs. It was during one stage of conversion and renovation that the discovery was made that Richard III had once stayed beneath this roof. When some thick plaster was stripped away, a mural that still retained much of its original colour was laid bare: it was of the Sun in Splendour—the crest of that monarch. The crest is to be seen also on the fireplace of what was for so many generations the brew-house. On every hand there are relics of former use and occupation, small items as often as not, but interesting for all that: some hand-forged nails, a pair of wrought-iron hinges, some old coins picked up by chance from cracks that had developed in the floor-boards, and so on.

Five miles to the north, on higher ground, is the *Shaven Crown*, Shipton-under-Wychwood. It is, without question, the most beautiful of all the country inns in Oxfordshire, at any rate as a building, even if it is not as perfectly sited as, say, the *Rose Revived*, the *Trout Inn*, or Minster Lovell's *Old Swan*. It is the epitome of Cotswold building at its absolute best: perfection in choice of stone; perfection in the proportions and distribution of its lead-paned, mullioned windows, in the moulding of its characteristic dripstones, the angle of its sills, the ornamentation of its arched doorway, the slope of its roof and inter-relationship of its gables.

Nor is this surprising. For it was designed as the Guest House for the neighbouring Bruern Abbey and as an occasional Rest House for its brethren, as was *Ye Olde Bell* at Hurley, in Berkshire, among so many others. Its very name, of course, implies relationship with a monastic institution, as does the *Shave Cross* near Whitchurch Canonicorum, Dorset.

The outstandingly beautiful Tudor doorway, with its massive nail-studded door, leads directly into the rear courtyard. Immediately on the left when you have crossed the paved threshold is the magnificent two-storey Great Chamber, with stone-flagged floor and glorious timbers supporting the lofty roof. From this chamber a staircase sweeps upwards to the upper floors, and here are the rooms lit by windows which are not only mullioned and transomed but elaborately carved with trefoils.

As in other cases throughout the country, the *Shaven Crown* has had a varied history. What had been designed as the Guest House for an abbey in due course became a hunting-lodge, for it then stood in the heart of an extensive forest, of which only a few stands of beech trees now remain, though the place-name is evidence of what used to be; at that time, as amid the beechwoods then surrounding the *White Hart* at Witley, in Surrey, game was plentiful. Later on, the building was donated to the parish of Shipton-under-Wychwood, with a proviso interesting because it recaptured the essence of the function for which it was originally designed: this was that its owner must provide free accommodation for any wayfarer who was too poor to pay for it. Curiously, and pleasingly too, that proviso obtains to this day; but it is hard to believe that any of today's motor-borne wayfarers would not be prevented by innate pride from insisting on their right to accommodation 'for free', particularly when standing on the threshold of an inn of such manifest distinction.

Gloucestershire

The *Lamb Inn*, Filkins, a hamlet a few miles south of Burford and just over the border from Oxfordshire, is as unassuming an inn as you can imagine. Its name is printed so small (there is no signboard, just a little plaque immediately below the porch to the small door) that you must look closely to make sure that it is not someone's private dwelling. The Cotswold stone is almost completely clad in Virginia creeper, which engulfs the small windows and reaches to the tip of the gable; the roof is outstandingly good, especially for a building of such modest pretensions, for it is made of the famous Stonesfield slates such as we have already seen at Godstow and which are more often found on the manor houses and other and larger Cotswold buildings in which no expense was spared. The creeper-clad façade, the half-hidden windows, the modestly proportioned doorway, give the whole place a secretive air, that of a house-that-does-not-wish-to-be-visited; that it is, in fact, asleep, and does not wish to be disturbed.

Visit it, nevertheless: it is well worth your while, and you will be warmly welcomed. Here you will find one of the most notable collections of corn-dollies anywhere in the country, all of them the work of a local craftsman. There are the traditional tasselled, spiralling scrolls, of course; but there are also shepherds' crooks and other artefacts associated with the rural scene, objects that you might well have thought beyond the imagination and skill of even the most expert craftsman. Outstanding among these is a beautifully fashioned ship's anchor and stock—a masterpiece amid a display of smaller masterpieces. There are other unusual objects of particular interest, too. These include a number of the old Fire Insurance Plaques, reminders of the days when only the wealthy householder could take out any form of insurance and a cast-iron plaque had to be displayed on his outer wall so that he received priority in the event of a conflagration. These are collectors' items today. Other unexpected objects include two 'Cricketers' Plates' of Worcester porcelain that bear the signatures of Australian touring sides.

Lechlade, five or six miles to the south and only twenty miles from the source of the stripling Thames on whose right bank it stands, also has a *Trout Inn*. Superficially it has not a great deal to commend it, and certainly it cannot begin to compare with the one at Godstow of the same name. Its stonework is surprisingly cold-looking for the Cotswolds and its windows are not beautified by mullions and dripstones, as are those notably of the *Shaven Crown* and indeed many much less pretentious buildings hereabouts. Yet, though its appearance may be said to lack character, its story, as well as its site, offers some compensation; indeed, it has parallels with that of the beautiful *Rose Revived*.

More than seven centuries ago a bridge was built here to replace the near-derelict one that stood alongside the ford, which was too deep to cross in times of heavy rain. There was no accommodation for the men who were called in to build the new bridge, so a rough stone cottage was erected on this site, and dedicated to St John the Baptist to whom, as was the custom in medieval times, bridges were often dedicated. The bridge was built under the auspices of a priory not far away. Disaster befell the priory in the late fifteenth century, but the building that had been constructed for the use of the masons survived. For a century or two it served as an alms-house for the poor and needy and also as a rest house for the chance wayfarer. In due course the building reverted to private ownership and the new owner applied for an ale-licence. This was granted, and he very naturally gave his premises the name, *St John Baptist Head*. A later owner obtained the fishing-rights along this reach of the Thames and, with an eye to self-promotion, sensibly changed the name of the inn to the one it bears today, and indeed has borne for some two hundred years. Nor, so long as trout are to be taken from the waters that slide quietly past the door of the inn, is that name likely to be changed yet again. Why should it?

Very few inns achieve the distinction of being mentioned by name on any but the larger-scale maps. There is the *Castle of Comfort*, on the Mendips; there is the *Saltersgate Inn* on the road that skirts Pickering Moor to the east, in the North Riding of Yorkshire; not surprisingly, there are a number of *Moorcock Inns* scattered about the moors of the North Country: all these appear on the usual 5-miles-to-the-inch motorists' maps. You could not find an inn with a name in stronger contrast with the first of those named above than one by the roadside near Tetbury, in the southern part of Gloucestershire: *Trouble House*. The name appears, uncompromisingly, on the road map, and may well pull you up with a jerk, not so much to have a look at it, for it is not particularly photogenic, as to find out if possible how it came to possess so unusual a name. If there is another inn so named, I have yet to find it.

It is a long, low building right on the roadside, stucco-faced, heavily roofed, with a number of chimneys; its only noticeable feature is a flight of stone steps leading up the outer wall to a blue-painted door at one end. Inside it is certainly cosy enough, low-ceilinged, darkish and snug. Until nearly the end of the seventeenth century it bore the very common name, the *Wagon & Horses*; its most regular customers, like those of the inn with the same name at Beckhampton, were drivers of the heavy wagons trundling between one market and another. Apparently either one landlord became unpopular, or another inconveniently near set up in opposition, perhaps offering a better brew of ale or cider: whichever was

38 Ye Horn's Inn, near Goosnargh

39 White Bull, Ribchester

40 The Blacksmiths Arms, Hartoft End

41 The Crown, Helmsley

the case, trade slackened off and in due course the house was abandoned and fell into disrepair. In the early eighteenth century someone bought it and set about renovating it. Before the work was completed he ran out of cash, borrowed money and found himself unable to repay his creditors; one night he threw a noose of rope over a beam in his own roof and hanged himself.

The place remained empty for a period, and then a second speculator took a chance, ignoring the common belief in the district that it was now haunted by its previous owner. Perhaps there was something in that belief, however, for this man also ran into trouble, borrowed money, failed to repay it, failed to complete the restoration too, and in a similar mood of despair, being harried by his creditors and threatened with the prospect of languishing in a debtors' prison, went out one night and drowned himself in a pond near by.

Again the place stood empty for a while; there were those who alleged that it was now doubly haunted; it came to be known in the district as 'Trouble House'. In spite of that, a third speculator came along, with enough money to renovate the place completely and set up in business. He must have been a brave—or a foolhardy—man, for he tempted Providence and actually put up a signboard: *Trouble House*. But Fate had not yet done with the inn. About the middle of the nineteenth century there was a revolt among farmworkers in the district, the men objecting to the installation of farm machinery by some of their more progressive employers. There were hints of imminent violence and troops were summoned as a precaution. A few miles to the north-east of Tetbury they came upon an ugly scene. The labourers had set fire to a wagon carrying a hay-making machine. While the driver was desperately trying to free his horses, he was set upon by the infuriated men and badly mauled. The site of the ugly episode? You have guessed it: it was outside the *Trouble House*.

The labourers' womenfolk had by now appeared on the scene, and the officer in charge told his men to fire over their heads. As this had no effect, he gave the order to fire into the milling crowd. In time the men and women dispersed, dragging away the injured.

Some arrests were made, and those arrested carried off to Gloucester gaol. Meanwhile—and no one noticed this until it was too late—sparks from the burning wagon had set fire to the thatched roof of the inn. Within minutes it was ablaze from end to end, the rafters collapsed one after another and by nightfall the place was reduced to a shell. The inn had certainly lived up to its name!

And it lives to this day. For in spite of all, yet another owner came along. The rafters were renewed, tiles were laid in place of the thatch—the only concession to Fate—and the signboard boldly, challengingly, repainted. 'Aren't you superstitious?' I asked the landlord over a pint. He grinned. 'Not me! I'm often asked why I don't revert to the old *Wagon & Horses* name for fear something happens. But there ain't any wagons and horses these days, or hardly any. And the name is one that strikes the fancy. It brings me more passing trade than probably there was in the bad old days, which some folks *will* call the good old days!'

Tetbury is well off the Cotswolds, but the road past the *Trouble House* runs on north-eastwards to Cirencester and thence to a covey of perfect Cotswold hamlets, the first of which is Coln St Aldwyns, where the *New Inn* is a perfect example of the smaller inn to be found in this delectable region. Built of the local oolitic limestone, creamy-grey, rough-textured, mellowed with the passing of the years, changing delicately in hue according to the strength and direction of the light and shadow falling on it, it blends naturally and quite perfectly with all the other buildings, most of them of modest pretensions, that constitute this hamlet, one of a group taking their name from the little river that meanders among them.

A low stone terrace runs along the full length of its façade, with the staddle-stones characteristic of this region spaced out at intervals, alternating with tubs of gay flowers according to the season. A slabstone roof of perfectly graduated slates, the smallest along the ridge, the largest at the eaves, incorporates inset dormer windows towards which roses and Virginia creeper climb purposefully, adding a natural dimension to the man-made stonework. Step inside, and you find yourself on a flagstoned floor that has acquired a satin-like patina through generations of use and care. There are two large open fireplaces, and on the walls copperware and brass, harness-ware and yokes and other items of equipment that always seem so essentially right in a truly rural setting such as this.

Northwards beyond these Coln villages is Northleach, with its *Red Lion*, four hundred years old at least and, like the *Old Swan* at Minster Lovell, interesting because it is a mixture of two styles of building. The ground floor, and the great roof, are both of Cotswold stone, but the upper storey is of half-timbering: a series of close-set verticals carried on an immense lateral beam running the full length of the building. Some of these have been truncated so that a row of windows could be inset beneath the spreading eaves. At the right-hand end there is an archway through which wagons and coaches passed to the enclosed rear courtyard. Standing as it does close to the Roman-built Fosse Way at its junction with an almost equally important, if less ancient, east-west running main road between the Welsh Border and London, it has always been an important stopping-place. The low-ceilinged interior reminds one (sometimes painfully, for there is no 'Duck-or-Growse' warning on view) that four centuries ago men were very much smaller of stature than we are today.

On the western slopes of the Cotswolds, between Winchcombe and Broadway, is the village of Stanton: one straight street climbing steeply towards the height on which is the *Mount Inn* (well named, too, if you have to approach it on foot!). Here the site is more memorable than the appearance of the inn. It is built in the local stone, of course, but is almost permanently shadowed by the close-set yews that grow along its frontage, so that it is only to be seen effectively when the sun shines briefly between one tree and its neighbour. It is worth a visit if only for the magnificent view to be obtained from the high terrace on which it stands. From this you look out southwards across low-lying ground to a range of the wolds rising to well over 800 feet, among which are to be found such perfect Cotswold villages as Temple Guiting and Guiting Power to the immediate south-east; Snowshill (Sno'zl to the initiated) a mile or two to the east of Stanton; and northwards, just over the Worcester border, even better known Broadway, with its famous *Lygon*

Arms—emphatically hotel rather than inn, so not included here. But the *Mount Inn* sits on its mound at the steep upper end of the village, remote from the rest of Stanton almost to the extent of aloofness, its roots deep in the stone from which its fabric was hewn.

One more (though so many others really call for mention) Gloucestershire inn remains to be visited. *Ye Hobnails Inn* at Little Washbourne, five miles or so to the west. No Cotswold stone here, but white-painted brickwork beneath warm russet tiles, the building L-shaped and, as is so often the case with buildings shaped thus, its welcome more explicit than that offered by the more usual flat-fronted inn. If, as its present owners claim, it really dates back to the late fifteenth century it has, as they say, worn very well! But at least one other claim can be easily verified: it has been in the hands of the same family for well over two hundred years, and it bears every sign of having been cherished during that long period, and is cherished still.

Noteworthy in the two bars, one of them very snug indeed, is the collection of corn-dollies in many forms and sizes, comparable with those at the *Lamb Inn*, Filkins, and also a variegated assembly of rural bygones. More unusual, however, is the skittle-alley. This one instead of being outside the inn is to be found installed along one side of the dining-room, contained within the outer wall. It has been cleverly designed on a gentle upward slope so that the balls, after knocking down the skittles (or failing to do so in the hands of the less practised player) automatically run back to the players for the succeeding round. As for the name: a gaily painted signboard on a tall post stands against a shapely tree; it portrays a box from which a great spillage of assorted hobnails large and small scatters down to the bold lettering beneath.

Herefordshire

Herefordshire is so very much the westernmost of this group of counties that it is perhaps inviting trouble to include it here. Nevertheless mention must be made of what is unquestionably its most noteworthy rural inn : the *New Inn*, Pembridge. Like most inns bearing this name, it is anything but new; every square foot of this inn bespeaks its age. It is one of the finest examples of half-timbering in a region notable for this particular style. Apart from a short, naturally-curved ornamental timber or two in the peak of the twin gables, every oak beam is short, squat, dividing up the impressive façade, both ground and projecting upper storey, into relatively small rectangles and occasional exact squares, though no two of them are identical in size, so that the overall effect is of variety rather than of duplication. A dozen or so windows are interposed amid these beams and cross-beams, the majority of them lighting the upper storey, whose gables are carried on massive lateral timbers.

The *New Inn* is at least five hundred years old—and looks it. In the early centuries of its long life it was curiously known as *The Inn Without a Name*, though the lack of a name certainly did not prevent sheep drovers and others on the move in and out of Wales across the border five miles or so to the west from making use of it. Having started life as a farm, it early on obtained a licence to sell ale and became a hostelry of some note as the years went by. Evidence of its farmhouse origin, however, has been deliberately maintained to this day. There are mangers on the inner walls of what was once stabling, and these are kept filled as long as possible with sweet-smelling hay. Some of the stalls themselves from the original accommodation for animals such as the pack-ponies working along this route have been retained, as at the *Black Horse*, Castle Rising, and elsewhere, so that small parties of diners have a sense of seclusion as they sit at table. To complete this aspect of the scene, the kitchen now occupies what was originally the cow byre or shippen. Perhaps more interesting still : for a century or so the *New Inn* served as the local Court House at which the magistrates dispensed summary justice (and doubtless not a little injustice too). Tradition has it, also, that the treaty which eventually brought the Wars of the Roses to an end was actually signed beneath this roof; if this is really so, and not mere legend, then there was certainly a well-established building of some sort here as long ago as 1497, by whatever name it may have been known.

Worcestershire/Staffordshire

An unexpected dual heading, for which I hope the following explanation will suffice. The village of Kinver is an oddity among English villages in that half of it stands in one county, the other half in another; local residents, whether shopkeepers or house-holders, are very particular indeed as to whether they are 'Stafford-shire' or 'Worcestershire'; I found out when I went to make inquiries and establish the facts that confusion reigns even behind the counter of the little post-office in the main street. One assistant said one thing, the other raised an eyebrow but forbore to comment as she was serving a customer not only with stamps but with a packet of cornflakes. I retired to a snack-bar to take a closer look at my map and have some sandwiches made up for my lunch while drinking a cup of coffee. I happened to mention to the proprietor that I usually ate sandwiches, with a glass of lager, when on safari in this way.

'I recommend the *Whittington Inn*,' he said helpfully, 'unless you want to go a good deal further before lunch time. It's worth looking at anyway, and it's only a mile or two from Kinver.'

'In Staffordshire, or in Worcestershire?' I asked, peering at my map. His reply was prompt: 'You pays your money and you takes your choice. Whoever drew the county boundaries hereabouts must have been drunk at the time!' He sliced some tomatoes, and went on talking. 'You know it's haunted, of course?' This was more of a statement than an inquiry. I told him that I'd heard that sort of yarn in half the inns I'd visited so far, from Cornwall and Kent northwards, zigzagging up the country. 'Maybe,' he retorted, 'but the *Whittington* is. I know it for a *fact*.'

The bare outlines are straightforward enough. The building, which I had yet to see for myself, and did not already have on my itinerary, was some four hundred years old when Queen Anne stayed beneath its roof in 1711: a plaque inscribed ANNE R. 1711 by the door, which I was to see in due course, is proof of the fact that she did sleep there, for it was her practice to have her iron seal fixed to the walls of houses which she had graced with her presence. It was built by Sir William de Whittenton—grandfather of the better known Dick Whittington, 'Thrice Lord Mayor of London'—as his Manor House, in the year 1310; built, indeed, of timbers from his own oak forests, for he was a major landowner on the Worcestershire-Staffordshire border. Over succeeding centuries the house changed hands, one of its owners being outlawed by Edward III. In the fifteenth century it passed into the hands of the Grey family, and Lady Jane Grey, who attempted to succeed Edward VI on the throne of England in 1553 and was executed on Tower Green a year later, spent much of her childhood beneath this roof. It is her ghost which is believed to haunt the *Whittington Inn*, as it had now become.

'I'll tell you something,' the café-proprietor said as he packaged my sandwiches. 'A party of six of us went there a year or two ago for a celebration dinner. They have a special room there for private parties, on the upper floor, called the "Lady Jane Room". We'd only just started our meal—I mention this in case you may think we'd been drinking heavily and had come to the end of the meal—when one of us saw the door-handle move. It went down, then up. The door didn't open, you understand, but immediately afterwards the temperature of the room dropped—well, ten or twenty degrees, I'd say. We all felt it. None of us spoke. But as the cold air passed us we all turned to the other door, at the far end of the room. We all saw the door-handle there go down, then up again. The door itself didn't open. Immediately afterwards, the temperature was back again to what it had been before. Now, say what you like! Remember, there were six of us, and the meal was only just beginning. That's not imagination; that's for real!' He twirled the paper bag with my sandwiches in it, and looked me straight in the eye. 'If you go for a drink there, you won't meet her; she only walks *upstairs*.'

My curiosity whetted, I set off. Certainly, as he had remarked, the boundary between the northernmost tip of Worcestershire and the extreme 'tail' of Staffordshire must have constituted a cartographer's nightmare. The *Whittington Inn* is, in fact, by a hundred yards or so in the latter county, but its address is 'nr Stourbridge, Worcestershire', so make of that what you will! It stands back from the A499

Stourbridge road, screened by a high bank of trees; travelling in one direction you could easily miss it altogether. I am glad that I did not.

Certainly it is one of the finest, as well as the oldest, specimens of a truly medieval half-timbered building anywhere in the country; among public as opposed to private houses it would be hard indeed to surpass. Two huge gables, each with a window in its peak, break the line of the roof, each a complex of bold oak-beamed rectangles with wattle-and-daub in-filling. Between them, a smaller gable thrusts outwards over the round-arched stone entrance, which has a small room built over it, topped by the gable, its window-frame braced by two of the many diagonal cross-members. William de Whittenton's early-fourteenth-century builders certainly built to last.

I went inside. The feel of antiquity is there immediately you cross the threshold; it is emphasised by the splendid panelling to be seen in such profusion on the walls, and it comes through the soles of your shoes from the floor-boards, which, if they are not the original ones, certainly date back centuries, as their beautiful patina makes evident. The upper floor is reached by a notable oak staircase, lined with panelling placed there in Tudor times. It was in Tudor times that some Jesuits related to the Greys took refuge there, and still to be seen is a secret staircase that leads to a hiding-place in the roof. There is also a Priest's Room and Chapel, complete with small font and piscina. Beneath the ground floor there are cellars concealing the entrance to an underground tunnel that has been explored for some thirty yards or so, but at that point the roof caved in and no further exploration has yet proved to be practicable.

Some time towards the end of the eighteenth century the manor house passed into the hands of a man named Dunn; he obtained a licence for it, which it has held ever since. Among other activities that went on here in his day and for some time afterwards was the once popular 'sport' of bull-baiting, and the stout post, ring and chain used for this still survive. It was in a room in this inn that, early in the nineteenth century, one William Howe sought refuge after perpetrating a murder in the vicinity. Clues led the officers of justice to the *Whittington Inn*; he was found, apprehended, accused and tried, and subsequently hanged in a wood still marked on the larger-scale maps as Gallows Wood—the last man in England, it is said, to be thus gibbeted.

So far as I know, his ghost does not share with that of the unhappy Lady Jane Grey the haunting of the inn. But as to *her* ghost, one member of the staff is in no doubt whatsoever. I was being shown round the corridors and various rooms on the upper floor by a pleasant teen-age girl, who had been polishing copperware in the bar when I arrived, and started to make inquiries. I mentioned the tradition that the place was haunted. Her retort was swift, contemptuous. 'There's nothing in the story,' she said. 'And even if there had been—which there wasn't—the renovations that have been going on here would have driven Lady Jane away.'

Within a yard or two of where we were standing at the time there was an elderly woman polishing the banister-rail. She bridled instantly. Looking up from her work, one hand on the rail, she declared her own belief in no uncertain terms. 'I've been working here, Miss, nearly as long as you've been alive, and there's been some strange goings-on, whatever *you* may think.' There was an edge of scorn in her voice. 'P'raps you've forgotten, or weren't here at the time, but it's not so long since we got up one morning to find that all the brickwork in the big hearth by the Priest's Room had been spilled out on to the carpet. It had been all right the evening before and none of us sleeping in the house heard anything in the night. But it *happened*. I saw it next morning with my own eyes.' She bent down again to her polishing, grimly silent under the mocking glance of the girl. I asked the girl: 'Would you be willing to sleep beneath this roof, alone?' Her reply came swift as a flash: 'Not on your nelly!' Thoughtfully, I went on my way.

Worcestershire

On the outskirts of the hamlet of Great Witley, overlooking the busy A451 running southwards from the industrial Midlands, stands an impressive looking inn which has, among others already mentioned

in various counties, the same tradition as Pembridge's *New Inn*. Here
for much of its three centuries of life was held the County Court,
or Petty Sessions, functioning under the name of 'The Hundred',
from which derives the inn's name: *Hundred House*. It is an impressive building with two large bow-windows that rise through
two of its storeys, one on each side of the white-pillared porch.

It was also a posting-house in the heyday of the long-distance
stage-coaches plying to and from the growing Midlands towns to the
north and such towns to the south and west as Gloucester, Bristol
and Bath. But it is the dignity of the County Court association that
impresses here, rather than the bustle of changing horses, feeding
drivers and passengers, off-loading baggage and so forth; the place
has the air of being the private property of some affluent gentleman
rather than of some inn-keeper selling ale. There is something
splendid even in its rather colourless name, echoing the term
'Chiltern Hundreds' without necessarily explaining itself.

Tucked away in the secretive, even 'lost', hamlet of Grimley, very
much off the beaten track near Ombersley, is the *Wagon Wheel*, an
inn which could hardly offer a stronger contrast. To begin with, it
is very small; it is also thatched—a comparative rarity in this district
nowadays. Its thatching is obviously the work of a true craftsman,
indeed it is something of a show-piece; it has been designed and
carried out so as to curve exquisitely, like superciliously raised eyebrows, over the lintels of its three upper-floor windows and forward
too, more boldly, over the protruding gabled porch, itself as large
as a small room. The motif of clear-cut triangles projecting downwards from the ridge line is repeated along the thatch of the gable,
integrating the whole. The signboard itself is of course of a wagon
wheel, tilted to one side rather than full-face; it is matched by a real
wagon wheel braced against the side of the porch. Only here has
imagination fallen short of what might have been expected in so
obviously a cared-for building: like the wall itself, the wagon wheel
has been painted white instead of the traditional vermilion, and small
pink roses have been painted round its rim to complement those that
climb the wall alongside. This is altogether too 'pretty-pretty', altogether *wrong*!

Again right off the beaten track, but on the opposite side of the A449 that runs south through Ombersley, is the *Bowling Green Inn*, just outside the village of Hadley. It looks what it may well have been: a pair of cottages or a smallish farmhouse. As so often hereabouts, its brickwork has been painted white and its six windows, in exact pairs, 'three-up-three-down' beneath three roof dormers, stare out somewhat starkly from such a background, though their diamond-paned glass softens the impact. There was once a much older building than this on the site, and the owner makes no claim to the contrary. What he does claim, and probably with justification, is that the bowling-green that occupies the ground to the right of the inn, shaded by a fine stand of Scots pines, is one of the oldest in the country to have been in continuous use to this day. A plaque referring to the green bears the date 1572; this is sixteen years earlier than the green on Plymouth Hoe on which Sir Francis Drake was playing when the Spanish Armada was sighted. Certainly the game has not been played continuously on *that* green ever since!

On the outskirts of Bewdley stands the *Black Boy*, white-painted brickwork again, interspersed with black window-frames, one side of the inn overlooking a snug courtyard dominated by one large tree, like that of *Ye Hobnails Inn* at Little Washbourne. Oddly enough, the inn-sign on the corner depicts, not a black boy but the bewigged head of King Charles II, though no one seemed prepared to state that the monarch had slept here or otherwise established some intimate connection with the place. 'Which Charles would that be?' inquired the girl behind the bar, and stayed not for an answer.

The interior blends the deliberately olde-worlde and the pseudo-sophisticated. Some good pewterware hangs from the beams overhead; brass and copperware adorn shelves over a modern-ish fireplace; a heavy Jacobean upright, high-backed chair faces a much less old Chiltern-built Windsor splay-back; and so on. Most intriguing—indeed aggravatingly so to one who has long relished the work of A. E. Housman, for all his pessimism—is a framed set of verses on the wall decorated with entertaining cartoon-like painted figures and scenes. These are ascribed to that poet. Well, the inn, which has

held an ale-licence for some four centuries, does indeed stand on
the edge of what is loosely referred to as the 'Housman country'—
Shropshire's Bredon and Clee Hills, and so on. Whoever in fact
penned these verses undoubtedly knew his *The Shropshire Lad* and
Last Poems, and had certainly assimilated the clipped style of the
quatrains with their regular and fixed rhythms, and had even grasped
tions, could A. E. Housman ever have written, for example:

I asked myself as I scanned the verses threaded among the illustra-
    Why, if 'tis dancing you would be,
something of the ironic vein in which the poet tended to write. But,
    There's brisker pipes than poetry.

     Say, for what were hop-yards meant,
     Or why was Burton built on Trent?

     Ale, man, ale's the stuff to drink
     For fellows whom it hurts to think:
     The Home Counties and Midlands
     Look into the pewter pot
     To see the world as the world is not!

Or:

     And down in lovely muck I've lain,
     Happy till I woke again
      And then I saw the morning sky—
     Heigh-ho, the tale was all a lie!

There were other couplets and quatrains. One such, I must admit,
came near to persuading me that Housman might indeed have composed these verses:

     Malt does more than liquor can
     To justify God's ways to man.

For it was so strongly reminiscent of the ironic lines that he really
did write, in *Last Poems*:

     The Laws of God, the laws of man,
     He may keep that will and can . . .
     . . . Keep we must, if keep we can,
     These foreign laws of God and man.

But I remain unconvinced, nevertheless. Is there perhaps some collection of Housmaniana unknown to me that reveals him as ribald rather than ironic-pessimistic?

The *Bell Inn* at Bell End near Kidderminster is built of mellow red-russet brick, creeper-clad. Its interior is more sophisticated than that of Bewdley's *Black Boy*. If it really is as old as it claims to be—dating from 1577—then that date can surely be no more than that of the original building on this site. Its most striking feature is a bell executed in very elaborate mosaic work; it catches and holds the eye immediately you enter from the forecourt after climbing a short flight of steps. It stands so close to the border of Worcestershire that some maps actually place it in the adjacent county, though the more carefully drawn maps locate it correctly. The matter of the inn's 'nationality', so to speak, is further complicated by the fact that its landlord's name, at the time of writing, is—Adnad Hakki!

Farther to the south, very close to the Warwickshire border, is the charming little hamlet of Inkberrow, a congeries of small and for the most part half-timbered dwellings. Standing back from the A422, towards the foot of a slope that leads to the church and partly screened by a huge sycamore, is *The Old Bull*. It is any one of the smaller timber-framed houses, as it were, writ large: a three-storeyed building of impressive as well as distinguished aspect. The main structure consists of innumerable panels of wattle-and-daub inset in square oak frames black with age. In the two main gables this rectangularity is relieved by cross-braces and diagonals. Since the inn dates back to the sixteenth century, and stands on a slanting site, it is not surprising that its builders, like those responsible for *Ye Old Bell* at Oxted, Surrey, also on a slope, saw fit to insert these diagonals as a precaution.

The whole place certainly looks its age, save perhaps for the roof, which has certainly been renewed, probably several times, though some of the beams supporting it may well be the original ones; the fact that the present roof has a slightly undulating character suggests this. Unlike so many inns built about this period, *The Old Bull* does not have those cramped ceilings that force a man to duck when walking beneath them; there is in fact ample head-room, and one of the bars is even vaulted.

You will be surprised to learn of the well-established tradition that King Charles II spent a night or two beneath this roof immediately before the Battle of Evesham, for the battlefield is only about ten miles to the south of Inkberrow. The tradition adds that the monarch departed in such haste that he left behind him his battle plans. If so, they have never come to light; perhaps some opportunist of his day slipped in through a window and filched them. History books, however, make a ruin of that comfortable little story—though it would have seemed a shame to have cast doubts upon it as recounted over beer mugs in the inn that evening. Was not the Battle of Evesham in fact fought between Edward, Prince of Wales, and Simon de Montfort, as long ago as 1265—some three centuries before the inn was even built? A much more tenable 'tradition', and one that is easy enough to substantiate, is that *The Old Bull* is the inn that has so long served as prototype for '*The Bull*' of the everlastingly popular BBC radio series, 'The Archers'.

Warwickshire

Any building, whether inn or private house, fortunate enough to be set close to running water starts off with an immediate advantage; the *Old Mill*, on the outskirts of Shipston-on-Stour, in the extreme south of Warwickshire, is a perfect example of this. Its many-windowed white façade overlooks an old-fashioned garden enclosed by a wall of mellow brickwork beneath which flows the little River Stour. One small dormer window in the tiled roof is matched by another and much larger one that has been modified from the original gabled projection into which sacks of grain were hoisted by pulley tackle—for this was built as a watermill. Its origins date back to the twelfth century, possibly even to the late eleventh century; this is shown by the fact that there is a reference to it in Domesday, where the parish church is stated to own 'a mill worth ten shillings and 16 acres of meadowland adjoining'. Today, the

Stour, and the actual mill-stream, virtually enclose the property, which is as picturesque and as modestly tuneful as any that you are likely to find in a county as generally delightful (at least in its southern parts) as this.

The College Arms, Quinton, south of Stratford-upon-Avon, is an unusual name for any inn located outside the limits of a university town. Though it lies well outside the limestone belt of the Cotswolds, it is fortunate in having been built of the beautiful stone for which that whole region is famed, its special and deserved pride. L-shaped, it part-surrounds a small paved courtyard, and roses climb lavishly up the wall of the gable-end that faces on to the village green. On that green, close by, stands a tall oaken post bearing the signboard, one which most Oxford men, and especially those from Magdalen College, will be quick to recognise. It portrays the college arms: 'Lozengry Sable and Ermine and a chief Sable charged with three garden lillies Proper', as the official heraldic rendering is worded. In fact, the site on which this attractive small inn stands, together with the building, was a gift to that Oxford college some four hundred years ago from no less a patron than King Henry VIII. It certainly is attractive, and satisfying to look upon: mullioned windows (again in the Cotswold style) filled with lead-paned glass, and a tile-gabled porch set in the right angle facing into the little courtyard. Within, a huge hearth at one end of the low-ceilinged bar gives the impression of having been scooped out of the thickness of the wall, its ingle-nooks curving round and outwards most invitingly.

At a road junction a few miles to the north-east of Alcester, close to the Worcestershire border at Great Alne, stands the oddly named *Mother Huff Cap*, a tall, white-painted inn whose somewhat cold, even austere, appearance is relieved by five wagon wheels, their spokes picked out in soft blue, spaced out along the main façade and interspersed with baskets of flowers hanging from wrought-iron brackets. Inset in one corner is the local pillar-box, a welcome splash of colour reminiscent of that on the wall of the *Brace of Pheasants* at Plush, in Dorset; against the opposite end is the village post-office. On the outward corner between them, suspended over the junction of the two roads, a main road and a lane, is a bright swinging signboard depicting a very buxom 'Mother Huff' handing over a brimming quart mug of, presumably, the very special brew referred to in the verses associated with the inn. Oddly, though, the quart mug is being handed, not to a regular customer, but—to a bunch of pink flowers! The doggerel verses read:

> Twixt Michaelmas and Martinmas
> Old Dame began to brew; ...
> First she brewed some olde beer,
> Then she brewed some new.

> The first to pour was cloudy beer,
> The next came crystal clear;
> Then she brewed a LOT like THAT:
> And on the top was HUFF the CAP!

Not very distinguished verses, you will agree; but you must allow them a certain olde-worldly charm. At least they are not attributed to A. E. Housman or, as was the case at *The Wise Man* at West Stafford in Dorset, to Thomas Hardy; either of those poets would turn in his grave at the thought!

Five miles north-east of this inn is the much more traditionally named *Bull's Head*, at Wootton Wawen, a notable example of Warwickshire half-timbering. It is an L-shaped inn, its main structure consisting of irregularly arranged vertical and horizontal short, squat, black oak beams with an occasional cross-brace for added strength, reminiscent of *The Old Bull* at Inkberrow, just across the border in Worcestershire. The oak framework is in-filled with wattle-and-daub for the most part, though also here and there with brickwork. Two very tall white-painted chimneys rise prominently from the dark-tiled roof, each between a pair of gabled dormer windows. I came across this inn as evening was coming on; the immediate impression in the half-light was of a boyhood's memory of a picture of Lot's wife, frozen (unfairly, it always seemed to me) into a pillar of salt because she had looked back towards the condemned city from which she was fleeing.

42   Saltersgate Inn, Pickering Moor

43   Tan Hill Inn, near Arkengarthdale

44   Blue Bell, Belford

45   Lord Crewe Arms, Blanchland

In the garden-cum-courtyard formed by the right angle between the two main blocks a number of staddle-stones have been placed at random, almost as though the landlord was deliberately trying to make things difficult for the car-driving customer. They would certainly not have been there in the inn's heyday, when it was a well-known posting-house on an important highway now designated the A34. It claims to date back to the latter end of the fourteenth century, and for once the claim is not one that would be instantly challenged. It bears every mark of real age: the distribution of its main timbers as well as their quality; the type of in-filling; the manner in which the great roof seems to have settled comfortably down upon it, and so on. But one concession to modernity catches the eye: the signboard carries the boldly painted head of a bull. The name of the inn appears beneath this: *Bull's Head*. But it appears there also in translation: *Tête de Boeuf*. Is this, by any chance, a gimmick thought up by an opportunist owner with one eye on customers from the Common Market?

Northamptonshire

The Boat, at Stoke Bruerne, near Towcester, is one of the relatively few canal-side inns that survive today. It stood on this site long, long before it was used by the 'navvies' who built the Grand Junction (now the Grand Union) Canal in the eighteenth century and became a popular port-of-call from the day the first boatmen tied-up by the lock immediately in front of it and went in for a drink while their barge-horses were baited at the trough alongside. The beer they drank beneath that thatched roof, within the shelter of those stone walls, russet rather than creamy-golden because of the ironstone of the quarry from which this stone was taken, was actually brewed here, though it is no longer so today. At one time, too, there was a butchery attached and the boatmen bought the good red beef for use on their slow journey north-westwards into the industrial Midlands or southwards to London.

There are boatmen alive today who remember those days, and the inn has been managed by three generations of the same family. On the outside wall is one of the old Fire Insurance Plaques that are so rarely to be found *in situ* today; at least the firemen would have plenty of water to hand if they were called upon! Inside, as you might expect, there are specimens of the buckets and cans and other metalware painted in the style and colours that have been traditional among canal users for generations. There is also one very odd feature, unique, so far as I know: a very old oak table that can be swivelled round while in use. Beer drinkers have protested—in terms both bitter and mild, though usually the former—about this, declaring that it leads to the spilling of their drink if they fail to snatch up their tankards in time. Wily landlords down the years have found that this is 'good for trade'! When you have quenched your own thirst, and watched a boat or two passing through the lock immediately opposite the inn, it is well worth your while to cross over to the far side and have a look round the Canal Transport Museum in a former warehouse not fifty yards from the inn.

Leicestershire

On a dead straight stretch of the old Great North Road, facing eastwards some eight miles north of Stamford, is the oddly named *Ram Jam Inn*, Stretton. Travelling fast, you are likely to miss it, even though it stands so close to the road; indeed, so narrow is the eastern corner of this smallest of our English counties that you are in and out of it literally in a matter of minutes. Do not, however, ignore this inn, for all that it looks new and relatively lacking in character. There is more to it than immediately meets the eye.

There was an inn on this site five hundred years ago, and by all accounts a busy one at that; for this road, much of it lying on foundations laid by the Romans some two thousand years ago, has been a main highway from London to Scotland ever since wheeled traffic came into use. The original ale-house would no doubt have been a mixture of stone, some timber, and wattle-and-daub in-filling, and of course thatched; it had not changed, though it may have been

enlarged, by the seventeenth century, as you may see from an
engraving in the bar, a copy of a sketch by an artist named Hier-
onymus Grimm which is still in existence. Nothing, however, could
be more unlike that old thatched inn than the long, low, grey stone
building that you see today. It was in fact built round the seventeenth-century inn, absorbing it wholly; as you stand in the bar you
are in the only part of the earlier structure that still survives.

Accounts of how the inn came to have its name are numerous.
One states that it derives from an unusual eighteenth-century 'cock-
tail'; another that it was so named by an army man, son of a Rutland squire, who had fought in India and had his life saved by a
loyal native soldier, whose name he duly gave to the inn as it stood
on land that his father owned and he was to inherit. The most
popular of the various explanations, and certainly the most picturesque (and also improbable!) is as follows. Some two hundred years
ago a customer—some accounts state that he was an off-duty highwayman, though that seems less than likely—came in for a drink
and found that the innkeeper had gone out, leaving his wife, a
notoriously simple-minded woman, temporarily in charge. The man
bet her that he could draw both mild and bitter ale from one and
the same barrel, and simultaneously at that. This was too improbable a claim even for a woman as dim as she was, and she rashly
told him that if he could substantiate his claim he could have a drink
'on the house'.

The man thereupon bored a hole in the barrel and told the woman
to stick her thumb into it for a moment to prevent the ale from
escaping. He then bored a second hole in the barrel, but on the
opposite side, and told her to stick her thumb into that hole, too.
She did so, and thus became 'anchored' to the barrel, flattened up
against it; she dared not remove her thumbs, knowing that if she
did so the ale would spurt out and her husband return to find the
barrel empty and the cellar floor ankle-deep in ale. The man laughed
heartily, then coolly rifled the box in which the takings were kept,
snatched up whatever he could see of value in the place, chucked
her under the chin and went out of the door, mounted his horse and
rode off at full speed, leaving the poor woman with her two thumbs

'rammed' and 'jammed' into the barrel and with no choice but to remain thus until her husband returned. Well, true or false—it is as good an explanation as any!

Nottinghamshire

North-west of Stretton is Nottingham. Strictly speaking, no inn here should be included; but since the rule was broken for *Ye Old Fighting Cocks*, St Albans, it shall be broken once again for a county town: Nottingham's *Ye Olde Trip to Jerusalem* is not only unique but, even though it is located well within the confines of the town, it is 'of the country' rather than truly urban. It crouches low beneath the enormous rock bluff known as Castle Rock, the most impressive natural feature of the town.

It claims to be 'the oldest inn in England', and specifies its date uncompromisingly: A.D. 1189. (It may be remembered that the landlord of the *George & Dragon*, Speldhurst, Kent, had told me that the claim of A.D. 1212 on his signboard was wrong and that it should have been A.D. 1189; why, if he knew of this Nottingham inn, had he at least not suggested 1188?) In 1189 the Crusades were in full swing, and tradition hereabouts has it that the knights bound for battle with the Saracens 'tripped' at this inn on their outward journey and, if they survived their encounters with the infidels, celebrated here on their return. (Again an echo of that Kentish inn where the bowmen are alleged to have celebrated their triumph at the Battle of Agincourt, though this was more than two centuries later.)

The explanation of the name is a romantic one, and you may accept or reject it as you will. Even the most cursory glance at this inn's white-painted brick exterior tends to discredit the claim to nearly eight centuries of life, in spite of an oak beam here and there among the small windows. But if you care to go inside, you may be less sure that the claim is false for the truly ancient part of the inn consists of small rooms literally carved out of the friable sandstone of the huge rock beneath whose shadow it stands.

Some of the natural clefts in the rock have been artificially enlarged; 'faults' in the geological formation have been adapted; the cellars are hewn out of the lower strata of the rock, so you can imagine how excellent is the quality of the beer stored there, as it's been ever since the place first became a brew-house as well as an ale-house. Nor was it only casks of liquor that found shelter in those cellars; smugglers and other men seeking refuge when they were on the run, whether of low degree or high, made use of them. One of them is known to this day as Mortimer's Hole: six centuries ago he was Queen Isabella's lover; fleeing from the wrath of the cuckolded monarch, Edward III, he was tracked down and in due course hanged at Tyburn.

There are many relics of history on view here, among them the famous so-called Armada Chest, enormous padlocks and their complicated, massive keys, some of which were used in connection with the set of stocks which, until comparatively recently, stood outside the inn. One mystery, however, has yet to be solved. It is known that in medieval times there was an almost vertical tunnel, like some primitive lift-shaft, that connected the base of Castle Rock with the castle on the top from which it takes its name. It is believed that the entrance to that shaft lies within the rock-hewn walls of *Ye Olde Trip to Jerusalem*; but unless someone has succeeded since my last call there, that secret remains as impenetrable as ever.

Derbyshire

By the village of Rowsley, just where the road forks, one branch going to Chatsworth Park and the Stately Home of the Duke of Devonshire, the other to Bakewell by way of Haddon Hall, there stands *The Peacock*, one of the most beautiful hostelries to be found anywhere in the vicinity of the Derbyshire Pennines. If it were not for the fact that it is built of the dark grey millstone grit of the region, instead of oolitic limestone, it could be a Cotswold manor house. Its fine mullioned windows are inset with diamond-paned glass; its large twin gables have the same pitch as those that are roofed with the incomparable Stonesfield slate of the Cotswolds, and its chimneys something of the same memorable proportions. Between the two prominent gables is a boldly protruding, castellated porch, with a mullion-windowed room over the actual entrance, topped by battlements. This, emphatically, was never built to be an inn; it was designed for some private and affluent individual who could afford to employ a first-rate architect, skilled masons and the best materials available. We know his name, for he had it inscribed on the massive stone lintel above the doorway. Whoever carved the inscription was a better stone-mason than speller, and it would seem that his employer was either ignorant too, or just plain careless; for the inscription reads:

IOHИSTE

16   52

VEИSON

After some years of occupation by this John Stevenson, the house was sold to the owner of Haddon Hall, the country seat of the Duke of Rutland, two or three miles away, to become the Duke's Dower House. Later on it was relegated to the lowlier status of a mere farmhouse, and it was not until 1820 that its then owner was granted an ale-licence and the lovely old house, by then somewhat neglected, began its century and a half, to date, as a hostelry. It is not surprising, in view of its distinction as a building, that it prefers nowadays to call itself Hotel rather than Inn, though its setting fully justifies its inclusion among rural inns, as does the sense of homeliness, even of intimacy, that shines through its sophistication.

There are, as might be expected from a place of such age and tradition, a good many examples of interesting bygones. One of these, well placed in a window recess, is a particularly fine specimen of an iron-bound coffer. There is a profusion of good copper and brassware; there are pistols of antique design and various periods ornamenting the walls among engravings that have real character. But the most striking feature in the whole of the spacious interior is a beautiful five-foot-high peacock perched on a plinth of stonework and, surprisingly, half hidden from immediate view by one of the pillars that support the ceiling of the vestibule. It is an 'echo', as it were, of the peacock carved in stone that perches on the battlements of the porch, but so much more beautiful that one immediately forgets the older one. It has, too, a strange story attached to it . . .

This Peacock [says a plaque on the wall close by], which is considered to be the most skilful example of ceramic art ever to be made in England, was manufactured by MINTON'S LTD about 1850/51. The modelling was carried out by the celebrated artist and sculptor of Limoges, Paul Comolera, who was employed by Minton's for a period of three years. During this time only about five of these peacocks were in fact produced. The decoration is carried out in the majolica style, being hand painted in soft coloured glazes.

In fact, this is only part of its story; the postscript is far more dramatic. The peacock was sent to Australia for exhibition in 1878, but the ship carrying it, the *Loch Ard*, was wrecked fourteen miles off Moonlight Heads, Victoria. A Mr Miller purchased the wreck for salvage, and it was one of his divers who brought up a cask which, fortunately, had not been broached or stove-in. When it had been hauled to the cliff top it was opened, and the diver and his companion were astonished to find that it contained not, as they may have hoped in view of the name of the vessel, whisky but—the peacock! It was in perfect condition, not a chip anywhere on its finely glazed surface. It remained in the possession of the Miller family for some fifty years, until the daughter who then owned it died, in 1937. There is no statement as to how this rare and beautiful piece of glazed sculpture came into the possession of the owners of *The Peacock*, but surely no inn could have a more perfect emblem than this, a work of art in its own right. As the stone-carved peacock above the porch makes clear, this inn bore the name long, long before the acquisition of the Minton-made ceramic masterpiece which now lends its own particular emphasis to the name. And this Minton peacock is well and safely housed, for *The Peacock*, Rowsley, has, very properly, now been designated a National Monument.

A couple of miles or so to the west of Buxton, very close indeed to the border of Derbyshire and Cheshire on Axe Edge, 1,707 feet above sea level, stands another of that very small handful of inns distinguished by being shown by name even on the smaller-scale road maps: the *Cat & Fiddle*. How different in appearance, though, from its counterpart in Hinton Admiral, Hampshire! Built of sombre stone, which requires strong sunlight to give it any colour, it stands on the roadside overlooking Wildboarclough, exposed to all the winds that blow. In such a setting, it must have proved a haven to untold numbers of wayfarers and others overtaken by night or wild weather down the years.

I remember well the first time I came to it. Still a schoolboy in the last years of World War One, I had set out to cycle by way of all the highest road-summits I could find on the map from Hertfordshire to Edinburgh, a 500-mile solo trip which I wrote-up in an article I dashingly entitled *Per Ardua ad—Edinburgh*. By the time I had pushed my bicycle, complete with lightweight tent and sleeping-bag, to the summit on Axe Edge from Buxton, itself about 1,000 feet above sea level, I felt a sense of achievement very much greater than that which I felt as I sat and looked again at that inn through the windscreen of my car. It was, as it had been on that first occasion, late in July; as on that first visit, the wind was blowing strongly, and coldly; perhaps it always does blow thus, on Axe Edge? This time, however, I could look in comfort at the sign-board: a cat on its hind legs beside a milestone, fiddling away for dear life in the foreground, while the bleak moors stretch away in all directions to remote horizons. *Caton Fidèle* once again? Whether or no matters little. Nor was shelter necessary to me, this time; though it might well have been.

On the other side of Buxton and a little farther to the north at Lanehead, near Tideswell, is the *Anchor Inn*. Whitewashed, black-painted, diamond-paned windows, this inn, too, stands high and isolated, though only at about 1,200 feet instead of 1,707, and amid a network of criss-crossing Pennine drystone walls that likewise reach out in all directions to the horizon. It was originally a farm-house, and still looks like one, apart from its sign; but unhappily its slabstone floor has now been covered with linoleum and its brick walls with panelling not quite in the class of the *Whittington Inn*. Like so many farmhouses that lay on or near established pack-horse routes, its owner obtained a licence to sell ale and, as usual, found this more profitable than farming, especially on such barren ground where only the hardiest of sheep can manage to subsist.

On the oak beams of this building, which is not less than three hundred years old, there are muskets as well as the more familiar brass and copperware. More interesting, and certainly more unusual, is a remarkable display of 'signed' bank-notes, two or three hundred in all, presented by customers over the years. They are of every currency you can think of, including Chinese, Japanese, Peruvian, Russian and other exotica, and of almost every denomination within those currencies. Many of them represent currencies that no longer exist, or are no longer valid, which greatly enhances their value among collectors, and the inn-keeper is constantly asked to part with some of them in particular. He is obviously very trusting, for the beams are low over your head and each bank-note is secured individually with no more than a couple of drawing-pins.

Looking round them, I asked why an inn so very far from the sea in every direction should be named *Anchor Inn*; I was thinking perhaps, of that Warwickshire *Crab Mill*, equally remote from the sea, though it proved to have an easy explanation. Here, according to tradition, came the answer: a sailor who had become disillusioned with life at sea jumped ship and set off inland, to settle down to a landlubber's life as far as possible from Liverpool to the west and Hull to the east. By his reckoning, this was about the midway spot; so, he 'dropped anchor'. But being, like most sailormen, a sentimentalist at heart, he constructed an anchor and set it up as a reminder of the life he had thrown up, as well as a symbol of the new life he was embarking upon. Whether or not the explanation is the true one, it will serve well enough.

A few miles to the north, at Castleton, is *Ye Olde Nag's Head*, a seventeenth-century inn whose entrance is reached by a short flight of railed stone steps from either side. Immediately within, the eye is caught by a row of no fewer than thirteen old-fashioned call-bells on spiral springs running along one wall close beneath the ceiling.

Only five of these now bear numbers, but the long row suggests the busy life of the inn during its heyday, with plenty of servants, from ostlers and grooms to chambermaids and kitchen staff. The interior is snug within its thick gritstone walls, as it needs to be in a region such as this, with Mam Tor ('Shivering Mountain') and the Winnats Pass ('Wind-Gates') hard by and the lofty summits of The Peak and Kinder Scout only two or three miles to the north. Immediately behind the inn, beyond the sombre graveyard of the Church of St Edmund, rises the precipitous rock and turf slope dominated by the ruins of Peveril Castle, to be reached only by a strenuous scramble up a zigzagging pathway—the *Peveril of the Peak* of Scott's novel; you stare straight up at it from the windows of *Ye Olde Nag's Head*.

There is another *Old Nag's Head* (none of your 'Ye Olde' about this one!) only a couple of miles on the other side of the Hope Valley to the north of Castleton, one known to a very different type of clientele. It lies on the outskirts of the minuscule village of Edale; more important, however, it lies on the very doorstep of the 250-mile 'Pennine Way'. The type of customer who makes use of its facilities is the 'hard' man: the type that will be wearing heavy boots, carrying a rucksack, with a compass and whistle in his pocket and, quite possibly, 'iron rations' as a precaution against emergency in the wilds through which so much of this long-distance track runs. Immediately beyond the inn, the track will take him northwards on to Kinder Scout and The Peak—and eventually, if he has the stamina, to Kirk Yetholm on the Cheviots.

Like every other building in this region the inn is built of Derbyshire gritstone; here this somewhat forbidding material is muted by climbing roses (though their season is short); the south-facing windows are painted black and look out over the shallow valley towards Castleton and Mam Tor; the north-facing windows look out and up at the stern and uncompromising slope which walkers bound for the moors must tackle from the outset.

As I stood there on a windswept morning in 1973 I looked back in my memory to just such another morning when I had stood there for the first time, immediately after the last war. At that date the 'Way' was not officially open to the walker; certain illimitable stretches of it were still the monopoly of the owners of the grouse moors over which it passed, and their keepers (as I had found more than once) were themselves hard men who were not easy to persuade to permit one to continue on one's way even with a solemn promise not to trespass unduly. I had walked those two-hundred-and-fifty miles, solo, pack on back; reached Kirk Yetholm, with its age-long tradition as a gipsy base; and I was so exhilarated by having covered the miles that lay behind me that I had walked on across the Lowlands of Scotland and fetched up in Edinburgh, 'Auld Reekie' herself. Today this walk from Edale to the Cheviots is open to all; it is already becoming one of those long-distance walks which successive individuals or groups undertake with, as their main objective, not the unforgettable sense of splendid isolation that I had experienced in those far-off days but, sadly, the knocking of a day, a few hours, even minutes, from the best overall time so far on record. This, I hold, is no way in which to set out to walk the Pennine Way.

I was about to take some photographs of the inn, as a glint of sunshine had at last broken through, when two stoutly booted youths, with rucksacks on their backs, came up from behind me and walked on to the corner of the inn, where a large-scale map is displayed in a waterproof frame. One of them pulled out a map of his own, orientated it, and studied it closely. Meanwhile, two attractive girls, college students to judge by their long scarves, sat down on a seat nearby. They were obviously all together, but the girls were certainly not prepared for long-distance walking. We got into conversation. Yes, they were all from a Midlands University College; one of the lads was a sociology student, his friend was studying physics. The arrangement was that they would set off for Kirk Yetholm that morning, and their girl-friends would be waiting there for them at the end of their walk to drive them home.

I asked how long they anticipated taking over their walk. 'Twelve days, maybe fourteen,' was the answer. 'Not more—we *hope*!' It was just the length of time I myself had taken, nearly thirty years ago. They were proposing to sleep rough. They did not even have a tent, but had waterproof ground-sheeted sleeping-bags and a light-weight waterproof sheet that could be spread over them. I asked them what their rucksacks weighed, with those sleeping-bags slung on them. 'Twenty-eight pounds,' they said. I myself had travelled lighter than that, but then I had always found some sort of over-night shelter, even if it had been no better than the floor of some moorland cottage. I wished them well. They said they were going to wait till the *Old Nag's Head* opened, so that they could have a final beer before setting out, and asked if I would join them. 'Oh, you and your beer!' exploded one of the girls, as I declined the invitation, and the two young men laughed at her and went back to studying their map.

CHAPTER FIVE

The North Country

Lancashire

There is only a handful of truly rural inns to be found in this county, so much of which is heavily industrialised. To the north of Preston, however, you will begin to encounter the odd one here and there. On the outskirts of Goosnargh, for instance, almost within the shadow of beautiful Longridge Fell, is *Ye Horns Inn*. It stands at the junction of two minor roads, the B5269 leading south-west-wards to Preston and Horns Lane itself, a narrow road that climbs fairly steeply northwards on to Beacon Fell. Of bright white-painted rough-cast relieved by black oak beams, you might wonder why it should be standing there at all, in so isolated a spot. The date that it carries may hint at an explanation: 1782. And an old, much weathered milestone furnishes another clue.

From time immemorial this has been a through-route for pack-horse trains passing between the estuary of the Ribble on which Preston is built and Yorkshire, a few miles to the east. Later, wagons used it.

There was a farmhouse on this site long before the present building, which is an extension of the original, made when the owner obtained an ale-licence and increased his income by cater-ing for the needs of thirsty packhorse men, wagon drivers and sheep and cattle drovers. A hint that there was hunting in the region is offered by the fact that pairs of antlers are mounted high on the walls at the corner overlooking the junction of the two routes. Asked how long they had been there, the landlord shrugged: ' A long, long while,' was all he would say, and the answer is obviously open to wide interpretation.

A few miles to the east and very close to the border with the West Riding of Yorkshire there is a hostelry of infinitely older date, and with a history that indirectly goes back to the period of the Roman occupation of Britain eighteen centuries ago, though of course the inn itself does not date back that far. It is the *White Bull* at Ribchester—and the latter part of the place-name reveals its Roman origin as surely as, for example, Chester, Tadcaster and Lancaster. Here, in the earliest years of the Christian era, was a Roman camp, on the bank of the River Ribble; it was of course named Ribchester.

Unlike the white stucco and black beams of *Ye Horns Inn*, the *White Bull* is built of the sombre local gritstone. But at least the model bull, calf-size or thereabouts, being painted white, stands out boldly enough against this background, perched high above the porch and part-sheltered by the gable above. It is a very forthright looking bull, as befits its setting, which is monolithic, stark and unrelieved save by its remarkable and, for an inn of its size and situation, unexpected portico. This consists of four stone columns that support a room topped by a heavy gable, not unlike that of *The Greyhound* at Corfe Castle. The columns themselves are of exceptional interest, even though they may not look so. They had been part of a Roman building when Ribchester was a rest camp for Hadrian's legions. In the year 1700, some thirteen centuries after the departure of the Romans from Britain, a summer of exceptional drought lowered the level of the Ribble to such an extent that these columns, and other remains now to be seen in the local museum, were left high and dry. Someone had the inspiration to salvage the columns and use them to add character to what was a very ordinary, typical gritstone building such as can be multiplied a thousandfold anywhere on this side of the Pennines.

Further evidence of the Roman origin of Ribchester is to be found in the cellarage of the *White Bull*: fragments of pillars and other such stonework, which experts have positively certified as having once formed part of one or more of the edifices that constituted the Roman Camp-on-the-Ribble. There are plans afoot, yet to be put into execution, to excavate more deeply into these cellars, in the hope of revealing yet more evidence of the connection between the inn and those occupants of nearly two thousand years ago.

There is later 'history' , too, associated with the *White Bull*. Like so many rural inns up and down the country which have already been mentioned, and also at Torver, in the Lake District area of this county, the local Justices of the Peace met beneath the roof of this inn to judge and condemn (or occasionally release) felons apprehended in the region. One room was for many years actually used as the local short-term gaol, and comparatively recently some rusted leg-irons were found, still securely attached to an inner wall. Do not, however, be misled by a stone inset in the outer wall close by the portico, which has the date 1705 inscribed on it. The landlord admitted cheerfully enough that it was not 'genuine', but was a stone on which that date had been carved by someone who had then deliberately built it into the wall. Beside the portico, on the other hand, there is something that is quite genuine: a three-step mounting-block worn smooth by the feet of generations of horsemen who had tied their mounts to an iron ring in the wall, enjoyed a leisurely drink and then, refreshed, continued on their way, on business or pleasure bound.

Yorkshire

Just over the border from Lancashire, at a point where the West Riding dips sharply into that county, some three miles north-west of Clitheroe, is *Ye Moorcock Inn*, a large stone-stucco-and-timber building that was formerly a staging-post for traffic passing between industrial Yorkshire and North Lancashire by way of the Trough of Bowland. Over the entrance is a large carved and painted sign of a typical moorland scene with *Ye Moorcock Inn* silhouetted against a rising sun in gold, a nicely carved moorcock in the foreground, the whole enclosed in an ornate wrought-iron frame.

It has been to some extent modernised and brought up to the standards now demanded by a different class of customer, but this has been intelligently done so that the new blends harmoniously with the old. The walls are hung with engravings, only a few of them dated but each one revealing its approximate date by the costumes worn and other details; they are delicately coloured, too. Less welcome perhaps, but possessing a certain macabre interest, is a set of coloured engravings depicting the successive stages of a cock-fight from the start of the 'main' to its bloody and beastly conclusion. This sport continued to flourish in some of the more isolated parts of these northern counties long after it had been officially banned. Indeed, there are rumours, difficult to prove or disprove, that it continues to this day in the remotest, least accessible corners of the region.

There is the usual display of brass and copperware; less usual is an array of burnished breastplates, objects of beauty in themselves, whatever their association, once the prime feature of medieval suits of armour. Among the exhibits is a bill, hand-written in faded ink and carefully framed. It records '12 Dinners, £1-4-0; Liquor etc., £1-9-6; Waiters, 2/6; Total for Twelve Diners, £2-16-0.' The date when the dinner was served was 11th March, 1844. Those were the days! A half-crown tip for waiters serving twelve diners. And as to the ratio of drink to eatables, one is reminded of the piece of paper found by Prince Hal and Peto in Falstaff's pocket. It contained the items 'Sack, two gallons, 5s. 8d.; Bread. ob.' and elicited from Prince Hal the scornful comment: 'O monstrous! But one halfpennyworth of bread to this intolerable deal of sack!'

A much-enlarged framed photograph by the door bears the date 29th June, 1927. As well as the date, the time is recorded: 6.30 a.m. How many people, I wonder, can immediately place that date, that hour? The answer is given in a note attached to the photograph: 'Eclipse Morning'. I had long forgotten that date, but the photograph brought memories flooding back: an uncomfortable train journey to somewhere in the region of Giggleswick where, in a field on a greyish, uneasy early morning, I, with hundreds of others, had stood and waited. The bird-song gradually faded; the morning light subtly dimmed; there came a chill in the air that was 'somehow all wrong'; and then the famous eclipse of the sun, which had not been wit-

essed by people in so many other areas but was seen at its best up
ere. The photograph was of those who had made up a coach
arty—they called them chars-à-bancs in those days—from some
ndustrial town and, having marvelled or shuddered at the phenom-
non, breakfasted heartily soon afterwards at *Ye Moorcock Inn*,
heir ordeal over. I, alas, was not among them, but ate some sand-
viches and made my way back to the station.

As I was leaving the inn a small plaque caught my eye. It informs
ll and sundry that the landlord of an inn, if he wished to be 'The
erfect Landlord', must possess the 'Dignity of an Archbishop;
Geniality of George Robey; Hope of a Company Promoter; Smile of
Film Star; Elastic Conscience of an M.P. (sic!); Voice of a Sergeant-
Major; and Skin of a Rhinoceros.' A footnote adds that if he can say
Time, Gentlemen, Please!' in a voice that combines 'Firmness,
Regret, Condolence, Hope for the Future, Thankfulness for Past
avours, together with the suggestion that This Hurts Me Far More
han its Hurts You', then—he is well and truly set for success.

Many miles to the east and north, at Coxwold, a delightful one-
treet village just beyond Thirsk, you will find the *Fauconberg Arms*.
t is built of good Yorkshire stone, well windowed, with one gable and
t the upper end, a black-and-white painted pillared porch. Boldly set
n its long façade is a huge square plaque carrying the emblem of the
Fauconbergs: the Lion and Unicorn grasping their crest and, below
hem, the enigmatic motto, *Bonne et Belle Assez*. (Now, what *does*
ne make of that fourth word?) The inn's name derives from
Thomas, Earl of Fauconberg, who endowed the place in the mid-
eventeenth century as a home of rest for elderly and infirm men.

The interior is just what you would expect from the exterior:
nug, with massive oak beams, a stone-flagged floor and huge log-
urning fireplaces. From its generous bay-window you look out on
o the original cobblestoned terrace that runs the full length of the
rontage and is some thirty feet wide, composed of quartern-loaf
ized cobbles set apparently at random and haphazard in cement,
which makes walking not merely difficult but potentially painful if
your soles are thin. From the same window you can look right-
andedly up the tree-shaded street towards the fifteenth-century

parish church of which Laurence Sterne was 'curate-in-perpetuity and, between the inn and the church, his vicarage where he wrot parts of his immortal *Tristram Shandy*. From the windows at th rear of the inn you can look out over the low-lying meadowlan graced by the hauntingly beautiful ruins of Byland Abbey.

The *Crown*, Helmsley, is one of the most attractive inns in th North Riding; indeed, it does not have the typical North Countr 'look' about it, but could well have for its setting a Devon villag If in fact it is stone-built, then the stonework has been covered wit stucco, painted dazzlingly white, though the expanse of whitene: is softened to the eye by a mass of climbing roses and even mor rampaging clematis. Between two of the part-overgrown window there is a noble looking gold-and-scarlet Crown, not painted as sign but standing out three-dimensionally from the wall. Thre dormer windows break the long sweep of the pantiled roof.

The fact that it was formerly known as *Cooper's Posting House* i a reminder that in the heyday of coach traffic it was a place of n small importance on the route between Thirsk and Scarborough in fact, however, as its massive oak interior beams confirm, it date from two centuries earlier. Like the *Fauconberg Arms* at Coxwolc eight miles to the south-west, *The Crown* looks out over a cobble terrace. But this one, though it slopes down to the road, is mucl kinder to the feet than the other. Opposite the inn is the beautifull proportioned market-place of this, one of the county's most attract ive smaller towns.

North-east of Helmsley is the *Blacksmith's Arms*, Lastingham Built of rough-hewn stone with staring white-painted windows abov black sills and topped by a pantiled roof, it is not particularly pre possessing—certainly when compared with *The Crown* at Helmsley Its signboard depicts an anvil with a sledge-hammer and a pair o long-handled smith's tongs forming a sort of St Andrew's Cross. / horseshoe has been added to the composition and whoever paintec it appears not to have known that a horseshoe should always be dis played with its points upwards, not downwards, otherwise 'the luck will run out'.

The building itself, originally two cottages, dates back no furthei than to the eighteenth century, or possibly late seventeenth century; but it has been established that there was a building on the site many centuries before that. It stands right opposite the very ancient Church of St Mary's, in the crypt of which lie the remains of St Cedd, a Saxon bishop who founded a small monastery nearby some thirteen centuries ago. To this sacred site, as to the monastery itself, pilgrims journeyed across the moors for many hundreds of years, so that the original building was undoubtedly used to house and refresh them, and other visitors to the monastery.

One odd and rather pleasing touch of more recent history emerged as the landlord and I talked, looking across at the little church on the slope beyond the narrow road. A predecessor of his was the wife of one Jeremiah Carter, who was vicar of the church in the mid-eighteenth century. She had presented him with no fewer than thirteen children in a dozen years of wedded bliss. His annual stipend in 1750 was—£20. His wife, however, in addition to bearing and rearing thirteen children, ran the inn. Unfortunately she was so open-hearted a type that as often as not she refused payment from anyone who seemed impoverished—as all too many of her customers were, or pretended they were. The joint income therefore remained very little more than £20. But happily the vicar was a skilled angler and supplemented this by selling the fish he caught. He also played the fiddle, and made up to some extent for his wife's losses behind the bar by singing and playing to her customers and passing round his hat.

North-eastwards again, a narrow road climbs on to Cropton Moor. This is not so much a moorland road as a dale road; everything about it is on a miniature scale. For much of the way, intermittently sparkling amid the trees runs the little River Seven from its source high on Westerdale Moor to the north. At a point on this road named on the map Hartoft End, just short of Rosedale Abbey, stands another *Blacksmith's Arms*. White-painted rough-cast with glossy jet-black window-frames brightened by yellow-painted sills and lintels, the façade catches the eye and invites inspection.

The name suggests an earlier use; this was in fact a farmhouse with a smithy attached to one end. An extension to the bar that

you enter today was once stabling and the smithy itself; you park
where once the big horses stood and stamped their heavy hooves on
the stony ground. The rough-cast covers solid stonework, much of
it salvaged from the long derelict Rosedale Abbey a mile or two
to the north. The building itself is certainly four hundred years old
and, according to the landlord, nearer five hundred. He emphasised
the claim by talking of 'a scholar who collects old maps of the
North Riding' and who once showed him 'a 500-year-old map on
which the inn is clearly marked'. During the course of my travels
in search of this sort of material for various books I have learned
better than to risk offence to informants by challenging this sort of
claim—at any rate to their faces!

The interior, as you would expect in such a place, is snug and
homely to a degree. In the bar there are a number of locally-caught
pike, each in a curve-fronted glass case that is a work of art in
itself and well worthy of its contents. The largest of the pike is a
28½-pounder caught by a former landlord, one Septimus Bland, in
1887—within two pounds, I was assured, of the record for any pike
ever caught in Yorkshire. Mounted on their heavy black leather
strapping, so much more appropriate than the usual mounting on a
mantelpiece or overhead beam, is an outstanding collection of horse-
brasses, no two of them identical. Some of these were in groups of
four, five, or six, on heavy straps dangling from hooks on the wall.
I asked what part of the harness these would have formed. For a
moment the landlord looked blank. Then he pushed open a door
and called out a question. A youth, long-haired and, to my surprise,
wearing a chef's tall white cap, emerged, and answered promptly:
'It's a farthingale.' He went back to his work. Surprise, surprise!
Perhaps he meant 'martingale'? At any rate that is the only piece
of harness, to my knowledge, that could be confused so charmingly
with a seventeenth-century woman's garment.

It was a blazing hot day and I sat outside the inn with an ice-
cold lager to drink with my sandwiches. Above my head hung the
inn-sign: a gold anvil standing out against a matt black background.
I had wondered why, in so remote a spot as this, there should have
been any need for a smithy. The answer is interesting: at one time

the Rosedale Ironstone Works flourished in this valley, and it was
here that the big horses that drew the heavily loaded wagons were
brought to be shod. An echo of the blacksmith's forge lingers in the
bar, accompanied by the ghostly stamping of those hooves.

Almost due east across Pickering Moor (though you cannot reach
it direct by road but must go down to Pickering and then take the
A169 to reach it) stands the *Saltersgate Inn*, another of that handful
of inns marked by name on the motorist's map. It stands isolated on
Lockton High Moor at about 900 feet above sea level. Approaching
it from the south, which you must do with care, it comes suddenly,
challengingly, into view as you negotiate a particularly dangerous
twist in the road on a steepish gradient. This is known characteristic-
ally as the 'Devil's Elbow'—just one of the many dangerous corners
scattered about the country and inevitably associated with Old
Nick himself.

But in this case the Devil after whose Elbow the treacherous
corner was named did in fact exist. He was, they told me as I
relaxed in the sunshine outside the inn, a recluse who according to
tradition made his home in a cranny of the notorious Hole of
Horcum, a freak geological formation a stone's throw from the
road. He made a practice of descending to the inn and demanding
to sit and warm himself by the fire. Furthermore, he insisted
that the fire should be kept perpetually burning, and threatened that
if ever he should come down to the inn and find its ashes cold,
disaster would befall. One day this recluse, who for more years
than anyone could remember had been known as 'The Owd Devil',
came down as usual to the inn, sat for a while in front of the fire,
and then without warning threw himself into it and vanished up the
chimney amid the flames and smoke.

That was all of two hundred years ago. The fire has been kept
alight ever since, for immediately after The Owd Devil's death the
idea got around that if it were allowed to go out he would be resur-
rected and return to haunt the place—or worse. There is an alternative and much more prosaic explanation of the fact that the fire is
kept perpetually burning, winter and summer alike. It is to the
effect that, by statute, it must be kept alight for the benefit of the

moorland shepherds. This, of course, is paralleled by the fire at the marshland inn, *The Lamb*, at Hooe in Sussex, though that burned only during the winter months, and by order of the Prior of Battle Abbey, You may take your choice as to the explanation; for my own part, I know which one I prefer, improbable as it may seem.

The *Saltersgate Inn* can hardly be called picturesque. It stands four-square: stone-sided, brick-faced and white-painted, with a small porch and a three-step mounting-block alongside. How many thousands of travellers, whether afoot, in the saddle or on the roof of stage-coaches (or even inside), must have made thankfully for that doorway to escape the bitter cold of the winds sweeping in off the North Sea ten miles away across Goathland Moor, Allerton and Wykeham High Moors and Fylingdales Moor (the last-named with its monstrous white 'golf-balls' of the Early Warning System readily visible from the inn's eastwards-facing windows)!

It was originally known as the *Wagon & Horses*. Its more recent name derives from the fact that in the eighteenth century, during the period when there was a crippling tax on salt, that commodity used to be smuggled via the coast between Scarborough and Robin Hood's Bay and carried by pack-animals across one or other of those moors to the inn. Fish caught at Whitby and elsewhere along the coast was brought here too, stored in the stone building on the opposite side of the road and there secretly 'salted' ready for dis-tribution by other pack-horse trains throughout the North Country. You can still see a flight of well-worn stone steps running up the side of what remains of this old building. Here the pack-ponies were stabled and their drivers dossed down while the salting went on. As I was leaving, I asked the landlord whether he himself believed either version of the 'perpetual hearth' story. He grinned: 'Which-ever you believe, it's all good for trade!' The fuel that is burned on this hearth down the centuries has always been peat; it used to be cut on the moors close by, but now, he told me, it comes all the way from distant Somerset: a nice example, this, of 'carrying coals to Newcastle'.

Like some other lowly inns that have already been mentioned, the *King's Head* at Osmotherly, to the north-east of Northallerton, unpretentious as it is, has yet known its moments of history, though t has nothing explicit to show for it. It stands at the junction of wo roads, one of which has long been a high road running roughly parallel with the old Great North Road. Rough-cast, with black-illed windows, a small gabled porch and a pantiled roof, it looks out over a cobblestoned forecourt reminiscent of those at Coxwold nd Helmsley.

It was formerly known as the *Duke William*—William being Butcher' William, Duke of Cumberland, so named because of his brutality towards those he defeated. It was he who destroyed the army of Bonnie Prince Charlie at Culloden on that fateful day in April, 1746, known to all Scotsmen as the day of 'Black Culloden'. And here lies the historical touch: at the end of 1745 Bonnie Prince Charlie marched his victorious army southwards across the Border, heading for what he believed would be victory. He halted at Osmotherly for one night and slept beneath this roof, before marching on to Derby and defeat. On his return march he broke his journey here once again, and slept here a second time, before marching on northwards again to his terrible defeat at Culloden. It is odd that the inn should have been named after so brutal a general as the Duke of Cumberland; how much more appropriate it would have been to name it after the Young Pretender who had crossed its threshold with such high hopes.

Two or three miles to the north-west at Ingleby Cross you will find an inn far more attractive in appearance though it lays no par-ticular claim to historical associations. The *Blue Bell* overlooks a small, square courtyard almost completely shadowed by a huge sycamore; the sense of seclusion is accentuated by the L-shaped plan, and you feel that you are being welcomed with open arms. If you arrive on horseback (unlikely these days!) you can tether your mount, as generations of travellers have done in the past, to the white rail that runs along two sides of the courtyard, nicely con-trasted with the sombre stone. On the corner overlooking the road hangs a blue-and-white painted bell suspended from an ornate wrought-iron bracket; the bell motif is repeated, somewhat un-usually, in a miniature replica carved in a niche in the stone lintel

over the doorway, painted blue with white rings, its small clapper
also picked out in white.

No historical event seems to be commemorated here, though
doubtless the highwaymen frequenting the Great North Road a few
miles away will have used it as a temporary refuge. But there is an
echo of history less than half a mile distant from its windows. For
here is Mount Grace Priory, or such of it as remains after all these
centuries; it is one of the very, very few surviving examples of a
monastery built for the exclusive Carthusian Order. Close by, too,
is the starting-point of the famous Lyke-Wake Walk, a cross-country
route that climbs up and over the Cleveland Hills of the North
Riding, to end at Ravenscar on the North Sea coast some fifty miles
distant.

And so to the last of the Yorkshire inns to be included here—and
how very many still remain, deserving of mention! On the summit
of Arkengarthdale, midway between Bowes and Kirkby Stephen,
is the *Tan Hill*, at 1,732 feet the highest inn in England. The claim is
challenged from time to time by successive landlords of the *Cat &
Fiddle* on Axe Edge, but a glance at the one-inch Ordnance Survey
map shows immediately why the challenge is always ignored
Tan Hill is the highest by twenty-seven feet.

It stands bleak and exposed, with not another building in sight as
far as you can see in every direction to the far horizon. Its stone
walls, as you would expect, are immensely thick, its low porch jutting forwards from its austere façade, you might say more challengingly than welcomingly—though I for one would never say this
I have known this inn for nearly thirty years, and it is today
virtually unchanged in appearance from how it looked when I first
staggered up to that narrow door after walking some twenty-eight
miles along what was in due course to become the Pennine Way—a
long day's walk on terrain such as this, by any standards save perhaps those of the 'three-peakers' and other dedicated fell-walkers.

It will have been repainted several times since then, but the
winds that sweep unceasingly across these lofty moors carry grit
in their teeth abrasive enough to undo the painters' work in a season
or two at most. When I arrived on this most recent occasion the

inn was looking even more desolate than usual, and the reason was a sad one indeed. The current landlord had installed gas-cylinder heating and cooking; only a fortnight before my arrival, two of the cylinders had exploded in the middle of the night and practically gutted the building; the wreckage had been extracted from within the enclosing walls, which were unaffected save by smears of smoke at the windows, but the whole of the interior had yet to be restored. With memories of that first visit, I had not the heart to go in, preferring to remember it as it had been on that first occasion, so long ago now, it seemed.

I was, as I have mentioned in connection with the inn at Edale, 'walking the Way', solo, pack on back. I had arrived at the end of a very strenuous day's walking, and went into the oil-lamp-lit kitchen-cum-bar-cum-living-room to ask for a bed for the night. A thin snow was being carried on the wind outside and in spite of the hard climb up West Stonesdale I was chilled to the marrow. The landlord, Peacock by name, shook his head. Their one room was in use by a shepherd lad. Fortunately for me Mrs Peacock spoke up : it was Saturday; the lad had gone home for the week-end. If it was for only one night, I could have his bed, if I liked.

'If I liked!' It was to a low-ceilinged room that I was shown, and a feather-bed. I will swear that the kidney-shaped curve in that mattress, which the shepherd lad had left behind him when he crawled out of it that morning was still warm from his sleeping there! I adapted myself to the shape, curled up and passed out for ten hours. I have never slept better in my life; I can *feel* that experience still!

Today there is a small signpost immediately opposite the inn, marked PENNINE WAY. It points north, over Sleightholme and Bowes Moor, and the route climbs almost unceasingly northwards until at long last you drop down into the Tyne Valley. There were no such signposts indicating the 'Way' when I did my journey, or for many years thereafter; there might not be any even today, had it not been for that champion of walkers' rights, Tom Stephenson, a name revered by everyone who has essayed this magnificent long-distance walk since it finally became established as a right-of-way. I thought back to the two students I had talked with at Edale, and wondered whether they had called in for a glass of beer (Oh, you and your *beer*! as their girl companion had said). They would have been disappointed. Luckily for them, they were equipped for sleeping rough, and would not have required a bed; in any case, the weather was better than it had been on that first memorable visit of mine.

Whether or no, they would not have been unduly disconcerted by the scene of desolation that now met my eye as they trod The Way northwards over Sleightholme, with so many miles ahead of them as well as behind them. I hoped that they had been, and were still, infused with the sense of splendid isolation, indeed of exaltation, that I recalled so well from that walk, the first of so many walks of several hundred miles each time, both in England and abroad, that I have been privileged to enjoy over the years. Indeed, it was almost with a feeling of shame that I stepped into my car and drove away from *Tan Hill*, the highest (by twenty-seven feet) inn in England and one of the high-spots (in more senses than one) of that first major solo walk that I had tackled when I was a much younger man. It would have served me right if my car had suffered four simultaneous punctures on the steep road that runs twisting down over the moor, past the little one-man coal-mine that old man Peacock had worked single-handed during all the spare hours of a long and strenuous life. He is remembered still by the oldest members of the little community at the foot of the dale with whom I lingered to talk of those far-off days.

The Lake District

Because of the immense and understandable popularity of this region as a resort for holiday-makers, whether just sightseers or climbers, a great many of its inns have been progressively enlarged to accommodate the many for whom climbers' huts are not their choice. But there do remain—and long may they so remain!—a few inns that have hardly changed in the many years that have elapsed since the period when they served chiefly as halting-places for the pack-horse trains that were really the sole means of transporting goods through such mountainous terrain. Because there are really only two main roads that run through the region, apart from the dull coastal road from Millom to Maryport, we may take these few inns more or less at random—as I myself did when I wandered about there on the lookout for anything that particularly caught my eye other than the superb peaks and glacier-carved valleys.

On the eastern fringe, for example, the *King's Arms* on the outskirts of Temple Sowerby. Standing as it does on one of the old main roads, one that has long been a link between Penrith and the Great North Road at Scotch Corner, it is obviously a former posting-house. It is built of the warm red sandstone that is so distinctive a feature of the Eden Valley, reminiscent of that of which so much of Chester was built, notably the wall that practically surrounds that city. Incidentally, it offers a satisfying contrast to the hard grey Cumberland stone of which almost all Lakeland dwellings large and small have been built ever since man first settled there.

It is an L-shaped building that stands at an angle to the main road, as does the *King's Head* at Thornham, Norfolk, where the small boy informed me that I had a broken windscreen. It encloses a courtyard entered through a roomy archway at the back, a courtyard surrounded by old stabling, some of it now converted into sleeping quarters. Here the stage-coaches halted for their horses to be watered or changed while the passengers snatched something to eat and drink and, in cold weather, thawed out in front of the open fires. Just inside the door there hangs a besom. I asked why such an object should be so prominently displayed, hanging there from a nail in the wall. An old woman who was sitting in a corner looked up at me. 'There's *always* a besom there,' she said, reproachfully, as though I should have known better than to put such a question. 'One goes, and another takes its place.'

She was sufficiently crone-like to have been a witch; had we been nearer to Pendle Hill in Lancashire she could well have been one of its denizens. She had remarked that the besoms come and go; had she personal knowledge of this? It was traditional that witches rode the air on just such broomsticks. But I hardly liked to remark upon this, in the circumstances. Probably the besoms that had gone had simply been taken by souvenir-hunters, but the landlord confirmed that they were always replaced. Indeed, the present one looked quite new. I asked as casually as I could why a besom was always kept hanging from that nail. Her reply, and his, were in identical, emphatic, terms: 'It sweeps away ill luck'.

On the west side of the Eden Valley runs the motorway, the M6; it is a relief to escape from the din of the traffic that roars ceaselessly along it north-bound and south and enter the first slopes of true Lakeland. Why, I asked myself, had the simple refrain from Tennyson's *The Lady of Shalott*—a poem I had not re-read for goodness knows how many years—crept into my mind? Why was I quietly humming 'Tirra, lirra, by the river, Sang Sir Lancelot?' And almost instantly I knew: I was headed for the minute hamlet of Tirril, between Penrith and Ullswater. A charming name, which a lark might well sing in full-throated joy.

I pulled up outside the *Queen's Head*. It was obvious at a glance that it had originally been a pair of cottages, like so many others throughout the country. The landlord was polishing glasses in readiness for the evening's trade. He was an unexpected type to find in so lowly an inn as this, and it did not surprise me to learn that he has ambitions. Astonishingly, he had already installed, of all things, a sauna bath, quite possibly the first to be installed anywhere in the Lake District. 'It'll increase the value of the place,' he said. Doubtless he knows what he is about, though I did wonder just what proportion of the clientele one would expect to find in his bar would be likely to avail themselves of the facility. Perhaps in addition to the locals there are Wordsworth devotees who come to Tirril to bow their heads beneath the low-beamed ceiling, and not only because it is so low; it happens that the Lakeland Bard actually lived here for a short while, indeed owned it, and in 1828 leased it to a friend for a quarterly rent of two peppercorns.

Three or four miles to the south, on the Earl of Lonsdale's Lowther estate, is another *Queen's Head*, at the entrance to the charming 'private village' of Askham. A long, low, white-painted inn with bright yellow woodwork as opposed to the more customary glossy black. It carries on its main wall a pair of wagon wheels which were salvaged by the present landlord when he heard that the nineteenth-century Bampton hearse was being broken up. Over the neat gabled porch hangs the portrait of the First Elizabeth, and a plinth of local stonework running the whole length of the façade is filled with shrubs and flowers, carefully tended and maintained.

Beneath the angle of this building a curious discovery was made some years ago when drains were being installed. Deeply embedded in the ground was a collection of bones. Excitement reigned in the small community: obviously, the villagers told one another, their cottages were built on some old battlefield! If so, then the battle must have been fought between giants, for the few bones that have been retained are more than man-size. And the skulls that were dug up among them were not those of men—even of Neanderthal Man—but quite manifestly of cattle. The simple, and disappointing, truth was, as research duly revealed, that there had once been a slaughter-house at this spot.

No long-distance coaches called at Askham en route between base and terminus; but pack-horse trains did, and what is now the dining-room was once the stabling where the animals were stalled while the men dossed down for the night. There are, inside this inn, fewer of the brass and copper pieces than might be expected; but the landlord is an original and has looked elsewhere for articles to catch the eye and stimulate the imagination. Certainly he has succeeded: he has arranged on his inner walls no fewer than forty calico-printing blocks, all of them dated around the year 1800, such fine specimens of the wood blocks from which the Lancashire textile designers printed their fabrics that many a museum curator has coveted them. They are not only ornamental in themselves but are notable examples of rugged strength combined with real artistry. Apart from this inn I have never found anything to compare with them, save in certain museums in Lancashire cotton towns.

I would gladly have eaten and slept at the *Queen's Head*, Askham, as I had done more than once in the past; but it was still only late afternoon and, even though the evening was at hand, I wanted to cover a little more ground before the end of the day. So, skirting the north end of Ullswater, I got on to the B5288 and followed the course of the River Glenderamockin by way of Troutbeck as far as Scales, just short of Threlkeld.

There stands the *White Horse*, as unassuming a little Lakeland inn as you could hope to find anywhere in its seven hundred square miles of mountains, valleys and fells. It looks out on to the old road that linked Keswick with Penrith, but in the interests of modern traffic this short stretch has now been bypassed. So, this very modest stone building, with its small, black-framed windows, possesses its own diminutive 'service road' that virtually crosses its threshold, while the replacement road runs past many feet below it, the cliff-like wall rejecting the sound of the traffic.

The front windows look out over the river and to Matterdale beyond; behind the inn, which gives the impression of having been carved out of the solid stone—almost like Nottingham's *Trip to Jerusalem* crouching beneath Castle Rock—the steep slope of Saddleback climbs to the skies, or at least to a summit at 2,847 feet, which is near enough. The steep slated roof seems almost to be a continuation of Saddleback's lowest slope. Inside, all is as cosy as you could wish. A fireplace at each end of the long, low-ceilinged room, again giving the impression that at some time two cottages were thrown into one; the beams, many of them unusually shaped, could well have originally been ships' timbers. The long cracks in these, the result of seasoning and drying-out in the heat of the open fires, are now filled with coins stuck into them in the cause of charity by customers filled with goodwill as well as the local brew. 'Last time I picked 'em out,' the cheerful North Country landlord told me, 'there was just thirty quids' worth. I sent the lot to the Spastics.' The beams are so low overhead that a drinker hardly has to lift his elbow higher than he would when drinking to push a coin into any one of them. I took the hint myself.

The relics here are more interesting than the customary brass and copperware, though there is plenty of this as well. Here the emphasis is on corn-dollies and also on stage-coachmen's long-handled whips and other whips; on hunting horns and stage-coach horns, on bridles and bits and harness buckles all scrupulously burnished; and behind the corner bar an unusual collection of old glass and stone bottles with their 'marbles' still in their bulging necks. Among the many specimens of work done in wheatstraw other than the corn-dollies, all of them the work of a craftsman who had spent all his working life in the East Riding of Yorkshire and then crossed over to the English Lakes for the last years of his life, the most impressive is a large plaque on the wall facing the door in which the words WHITE HORSE INN are set out in woven and plaited straw, the whole surrounded by a rope, from the ends of which straw dollies and tassels hang.

After the bar closed for the night the landlord took me to a cupboard set in the thickness of the wall against one of the fireplaces and removed from it an ancient Bible. Laying it on an oak table, he turned its gilt-edged pages slowly, and with reverent care. There were innumerable illustrations, in the fashion of the large family Bibles of the day. Its actual date was indecipherable and he could not enlighten me; but he did tell me that there was a clause in the Deeds of the inn stating that the Bible must never be taken from beneath its roof. Who laid down the edict, and when and why? Alas, he could not answer the questions. There was snow on the fell sides when I went to bed that night, glistening from afar under a brilliant cold full moon. There was more snow on the upper slopes of Saddleback above the inn as I departed next morning; and, from the feel of the air, more to come.

No one was able to tell me why the old *Hare & Hounds*, at the head of Elterwater, one of the Lake District's less-well-known lakes and for that reason less spoiled than the others are becoming, was changed to *Britannia*, the name it has borne since just after the Second World War. Anyhow, the large sign over the porch depicts a full-rigged man-o'-war somewhat reminiscent of the 90-gun frigate at the *Old Albion*, Crantock, in far-away Cornwall. It is the only ornamentation on the brilliant white-painted façade of the inn, a seventeenth-century structure scheduled, I learned, as Class II of the Historical Buildings Survey: 'Local stone walls, rough-cast, white, of simple proportions, with eighteenth- and nineteenth-century windows inset'.

It was in fact originally a cluster of small cottages occupied by quarrymen, on a site potentially very dangerous because it was one of five Lakeland gunpowder manufactories, though this was closed shortly after the First World War. It has been most skilfully re-organised, and unobtrusively so; if I had not been told, I doubt if I should have known. To stand beneath the tree in front of it, on a gentle downward slope and with one's back to the lake, is to be enchanted by its trimness and air of integrated self-sufficiency. There are many erstwhile-inns-become-hotels along the shores of Derwentwater, Bassenthwaite, Ullswater, Windermere, Rydal Water and Grasmere, but I can think of none more charming than the *Britannia*.

The view from its windows, too, is as satisfying as those from the other and better known, more pretentious places; not least because no main or even secondary road passes between it and the water. 'The name Elterwater,' the owner told me, 'comes from the Norse word *Hjoldr*, meaning a swan. Each year, to this very year, and for as long as I can remember, a score or so of whooper swans arrive, usually about the time of the full moon and when the first snows appear on the hill tops. They have probably come from Spitzbergen, and they remain here on Elterwater—the Lake-of-the-Swans—until about Eastertide. I await their arrival every year, as you may imagine, with the utmost eagerness, and am always unhappy when the time comes for them to leave. Yes, as you may guess, *Swan Lake* is my favourite ballet!' He reflected for a moment or two, and then added: 'But there is a wealth of wild-life hereabouts, too. Foxes, badgers, roe-deer, red squirrels, pine-martens; occasionally ravens, buzzards and herons. And of course we have mute swans on the lake all the year round.'

From the *Britannia* and its well-informed, enthusiastic owner I made my way leisurely back on to the A593 and came to the end of Coniston Water and Hawkshead, where Wordsworth went to school. Just beyond is Coniston, with a characteristic Lakeland inn, *The Ship*, its glossy-black window-frames staring eagle-eyed out of its dazzlingly white-painted walls. A few miles on, and I came as far south as I intended to come, for I had now crossed into that part of the Lake District which is also Lancashire. I vaguely remembered having passed a Church House inn somewhere near there and, being now so very far from South Devon, wanted to see whether my memory had betrayed me.

At Torver, sure enough, I did find the *Church House Inn*, standing hard up against St Luke's Church—separated from the church, in fact, only by a splendid specimen of a yew tree, as at the *Old Albion*, in Crantock, the small granite church built on the site of St Carantocus's fifth-century oratory is separated by the great cedar. Torver's *Church House Inn* does not, admittedly, begin to compare with those of Harberton and adjoining parishes. Nor was I able to elicit any information about this one from the landlord; for once— and how strong the contrast!—he simply did not want to know. Disappointed, I looked about me for a source of information.

Torver is a very small place indeed. There was a small railway there once, that ran from the industrial area of Millon northwards by way of Broughton to the slate and limestone quarries and the copper mines on the slopes of Coniston Old Man. It has long since been closed, but I called at one of a little group of cottages near where the railway halt had been, and struck lucky. An old age pensioner—in so remote a spot the alternative 'senior citizen' would really have seemed anomalous!—was working in his pocket-hand-kerchief-sized garden. He straightened his back as far as was possible for a man who, it turned out, had spent his whole long working life on the quarry face, and proved to be a fund of information. Yes, the inn was as old as the church, though much restored: both dated from the fourteenth century. When pressed, he admitted that what he really meant was that their foundations and part of the fabric of the church were of fourteenth-century origin. He knew nothing about the inn's having been used by the men who built the church, but mentioned 'the long room', over the bar and lounge. 'I read about it in a book I got from the library in Ulverston,' he explained. 'It was once the Court House and Hanging Room. That's where the sheep-stealers and the like were sentenced, you see.' His wife tapped at the window and signed to him that he was to 'bring the gentleman inside for a cup of tea.' It was cold in that garden in March, and I accepted gratefully.

It was even colder on the summit of Kirkstone Pass. I would not have lingered in anybody's garden, however avid for information, in such near-Arctic conditions as obtained later on that March day when I came to a halt outside the *Kirkstone Pass Inn*. It stands beside the A592 that links Windermere with Penrith, at the point where a steep minor road climbs from Ambleside to join it. It is another of that rare category that has its name printed on the motorist's map. A bleaker, more windswept spot it would be hard to find; even on a warm day the wind blows strongly here, and apparently from all directions at once. On the wide, uneven threshold you are 1,468 feet above sea level.

There has been a building here certainly for three hundred years and more; a rugged, stone-built, low-roofed, almost fortress-like place, with a massive porch into which you dart headlong, ducking beneath the curved lintel, in search of warmth. Look upwards, and you will see that the low-pitched roof is fastened down to the walls at the eaves as though there is a constant threat that the everlasting wind will lift it off and carry it across the fells until it disintegrates. It could of course simply be that those brackets are designed to buttress the guttering so that it can withstand the weight of accumulated snow that must press down upon it for months on end at such a height, though I prefer the first explanation. The chimneys are the characteristic squat Lakeland type: paired slates set deep in cement, edge to edge, to assist the smoke to escape and at the same time prevent the rain from flooding down the chimney to dowse the fire in the hearth. The slate roof of the porch is weighted down with rough stones cemented on to it; everything about the *Kirkstone Pass Inn* suggests preparations for a siege! Oddly enough, the place did not hold a licence until as recently as the middle of the last century. One wonders what the pack-horse train men drank. Were they really content with water, or with milk? Not —— likely! In all probability the owner of the place had his own resources—and the fewer the questions asked the better for all concerned. When it did obtain a licence, it was known as the *Travellers' Rest*. It is a pity that so evocative and appropriate a name as that was discarded for what is now really nothing more than an address.

Northumberland

Deduct the half-million or so inhabitants of Newcastle upon Tyne and the few other towns and it is hardly surprising that the remainder of its population is spread pretty thinly over the million acres of this, our fifth largest county. One might say as the old shepherd did when asked how many sheep he reckoned to graze to the acre: 'We don't reckon sheep to the acre, but *acres* to the *sheep*.' Where population is scanty and individual communities largely self-contained, inns tend to be scattered. Nevertheless they certainly are to be found here, and often in the unlikeliest places; they are almost invariably well worth seeking out. In their way they epitomise, or at least emphasise, what may be called the ethos of Northumberland.

On the border of this county with County Durham immediately to the south is the *Lord Crewe Arms*. The River Derwent, without question the most charming of the right-bank tributaries of the Tyne, forms the boundary between the two counties for some miles of its serpentining length. It flows practically through the hamlet of Blanchland, considered, and rightly I would say, to be the most beautiful in all Northumbria; indeed, some connoisseurs will declare that it is the most beautiful in the whole of the North Country, though I would dispute this.

Eight centuries ago there was a Premonstratensian monastery here—the abbey of the Order of White Canons, hence the name of the place, Blanch Land. It was largely destroyed by the Scottish raiders, but devotedly rebuilt, though of course abandoned at the time of the Dissolution. But though most of the abbey has vanished, its stonework was salvaged and, in the eighteenth century, a village built on its foundations. You enter by what still remains of the original gatehouse, to find yourself in what was the abbey's Outer Precinct. Here, immediately on your left, is the Abbot's Lodging; adjoining it is what was the Guests' Lodging. This is now the *Lord Crewe Arms*, one of the noblest hostelries in the whole country.

Curiously, it succeeds in blending what could be called 'Romantic-Gothic' and the characteristics of a fortified ecclesiastical edifice. Its walls are a yard thick—a reminder of its origins. There is an immense fireplace that unquestionably dates from the twelfth century and is still in use today. Inset in one of the inner walls, as so often in these very old buildings, there is the entrance to a Priest's Hide, not unlike some of those to be found in certain of our Stately Homes which harboured ecclesiastics during periods of religious persecution. What was formerly known as the Abbot's Cellar—a reminder, if such is needed, that austerity did not necessarily prevail at these establishments when it came to a question of entertainment of honoured guests by abbots and priors—is today, appropriately enough, a bar; because of its outstanding stonework and its certain origin, it is called the Crypt Bar. No other inn anywhere in the country, I think, possesses quite the atmosphere of the *Lord Crewe Arms* in the twelfth-to-eighteenth-century hamlet of Blanchland.

The county has been the setting for battles during nearly twenty centuries. Flodden Field, some miles to the north of Wark, may be the best known of them; but the Lords of Northumberland, the Percies and others, were incessantly engaged in warfare on a greater or lesser scale with the Scots beyond the Cheviot frontier and with one another; internecine warfare was a way of life. And long, long before that, Emperor Hadrian had made this the northernmost frontier of the vast, sprawling Roman Empire, and had his own problems in this respect in the early years of the Christian era.

The *Battlesteads Inn*, Wark, has little apart from its name to suggest that it was ever involved in warfare on however minor a scale. It is small, unobtrusive, remarkably picturesque, incidentally, in a region in which heavy hewn stone tends to predominate, cold and grey and forbidding. Over its small porch the date 1747 is inscribed on the lintel: initials, possibly those of the builder, can be faintly discerned alongside. But the inn is certainly at least a century older than that, or at least contains stonework of a much earlier date. Its name derives from the fact that troops are known to have been quartered here during more than one of the campaigns against the Scots, when this was both an inn and a farmhouse. Their horses were stabled in outbuildings that extended from the east end of the present building.

Today, as I saw for myself, the interior is cosy, unpretentious, not unduly ornamented with objects designed to catch the eye and promote speculation; certainly nothing could be further than the notion that alarums had once been sounded here. Yet, look out through one of its small windows in the considerable thickness of the wall and you will see immediately in front of the inn an unmistakable *motte*, or earthwork, such as the Normans turned to such good use in their day when establishing strongpoints that were later developed into virtually impregnable castles.

Local tradition, as outlined for me first by the young and enthusiastic landlord and subsequently by a farmer's wife in her farm kitchen on top of the earthwork, holds that this *motte* was built by the womenfolk of the district who carried up stones from the bed of the North Tyne that flows past its foot. It is as hard to believe as it is that Silbury Hill, in Wiltshire, is man-made, though this has been authoritatively established. It is known today as Mote Hill, which suggests that it is a natural mound, with an even earlier date, since in Saxon times the Mote, or local Parliament, could have been held there. Small as it is, Wark was formerly the administrative centre of a region known as Tynedale, and there are authenticated records of justice being meted out here for sheep stealing and other crimes. The village was occupied for a time by David I of Scotland, and the Scottish Court Sessions were held here because this part of Northumbria belonged, for a time at any rate, to Scotland.

As for the inn itself, it is unlikely that the building, at least as it appears today, could have been the actual setting for this Court; some more substantial building, of which there are a number in the village, may well have been used. Or, even more probably, the rugged building, now a farmhouse, on the very summit of the *motte*, in the kitchen of which, having climbed the tortuous spiral track that leads to it from the doorstep of the *Battlesteads Inn*, I had a fund of information, not all of it verifiable, handed out to me by a woman as interested in the place as the landlord of the inn down below which her farmhouse windows overlooked. The earthwork, she told me, was built for a garrison whose duty was to watch over a vital crossing of the Tyne, a ford of some military consequence. The very name, Wark, she added, referred to the earth-'wark' beneath the foundations of her house. Maybe; but somehow it struck me as just a little too obvious; almost on the same level as the popular but wholly spurious origin of the word, ostler, being a corruption of 'oat-stealer'.

A few miles away is the village of Wall. In this case the origin of the name is not only self-evident but beyond dispute. It stands almost on the line of Hadrian's Wall itself, a furlong or so to the south of the Tyne crossing at Chollerford. The builders of the village cannibalised the remains of this spectacular relic of the Roman occupation of this country, as builders have done wherever the Roman stonemasons' abandoned products lay readily to hand, whether in Italy, France, England, or elsewhere. You can see stones in almost any of the cottages, the walls and outbuildings, that were quite obviously hewn from the quarries near by on the orders of Emperor Hadrian early in the second century A.D.

Inevitably, the inn commemorates the man. *The Hadrian*, a Virginia-clad L-shaped building, offers a wide view over the Tyne Valley, the famous Wall itself, and the lower slopes of the Cheviots beyond. Undoubtedly there are Roman stones in its fabric, though these are less obvious than they are in so many of the buildings in the village on the fringe of which it stands. It is older by a good deal than it looks: three hundred and fifty years old at least; but, as with the *Battlesteads Inn* some ten miles away on the other side of the valley, the fact is not emphasised, structurally at any rate, and the rampant creeper imparts a cottagey appearance to the whole.

Within, the place is more than ordinarily interesting. The emphasis here, notably in the bar, is on weaponry; the landlord has assembled a remarkable collection of duelling-pistols and other fire-arms, and some highly unusual specimens of the swordstick. Even more eye-catching is a glass-fronted cupboard set in an unusually thick party-wall. It contains, imaginatively and effectively illumin-ated, an impressive display of Chinese *objets d'art*. Among these, at any rate to someone like myself who cannot claim to be knowledge-able about such matters, the most remarkable object is an ornate hollow ivory ball containing no fewer than twelve concentric hollow balls, each carved in a different pattern. A museum piece, surely? It must have occupied the dedicated craftsmanship of a lifetime. Apart from the famous Crystal Skull in the King's Gallery of the British Museum (which was the inspiration of a book I wrote long years ago), I do not think I have ever seen a museum piece that I have more greatly coveted. A visit to this inn is worth it for this alone.

There is nothing here to link the inn specifically with the Roman Wall after whose originator it is named—save the odd little detail that the bedroom doors are individually numbered in Roman style. An indication of the comparative ignorance of chambermaids drawn from the immediate district lies in the fact that almost without exception over the years they seem to have been unable to relate the Roman figures to the familiar 1, 2, and 3 of the Arabic numerals. I twitted one of them about this, and she not unnaturally bridled; and she added, for good measure: 'What's more, I don't like them ugly faces on the doors, either!' 'Them ugly faces' are in fact a series of classic portraits of Roman emperors, including, of course, Hadrian.

Far to the north, midway between Alnwick and the Border at Berwick upon Tweed, is the *Blue Bell*, at Belford. It stands at an angle to the most famous highway in Britain, the Great North Road. Fifteen miles short of the Scottish Border, seventy-five miles from Edinburgh, it was a posting-house during the heyday of the stage-coaches that took this route. As a building, it is something of a hybrid: an eighteenth-century façade is united unobtrusively with a seventeenth-century structure built of the local soft, warmly-tinted sandstone. The façade itself, however, is composed of bricks from a local brickworks that are smaller in depth by nearly an inch, a fact which is not immediately apparent unless you are interested in such detail, but does explain the particularly pleasing texture, so to speak, of the exterior. Large, white-painted Georgian-style windows light the front of the inn, but at the rear no two of the much smaller windows are on the same level, and the uneven sills and lintels are indicative of much earlier work. The solid stone outbuildings, where once horses were baited and stabled, give an air of self-sufficiency to the place which is echoed in the interior.

In the thickness of the wall there is still the somewhat cramped entrance (now no longer used) to the Minstrels' Gallery that overlooks the Banqueting Hall, a fine, generously proportioned room still used for special occasions in Belford. You approach it up a creaking staircase and along a corridor where, it would seem, even in daytime ghostly steps can be heard. I slept well there, nevertheless, and did not hear a sound even during the darkest watches of the night. But I do not think that, in such an atmosphere, I should have been worried even if ghostly steps had disturbed my sleep, or even if a ghost had materialised in the spacious room I occupied; if haunted at all, then it is haunted by happy ghosts . . .

Not far from the stairway a plaque on the wall reads—in part, for the whole is too long to record verbatim: 'We, being His Majesty's Justices of the Peace . . . do hereby authorise and empower Elizabeth Macdonald at the Sign of the Blue Bell to keep a Common Inn, Ale House or Victualling House, and to utter and sell in the house in which she now dwelleth and in the premises thereunto belonging, and not elsewhere, Victuals and all such Excisable Liquors as she shall be licensed and empowered to sell . . . provided that the true Assize in Bread and Beer, Ale, Cyder and all other Liquors be duly kept and that no unlawful Game or Games or Drunkenness or other Disorder be suffered in her House, Yard, Garden or Premises but that Good Order and Rule be maintained and kept therein, according to the Laws of this Realm in that Behalf made.' It is dated 12 September, 1812.

In 1971 Belford was declared the 'Best Kept Northumbrian Village'. It was a Belford inhabitant, who combined, as so often in former times, the craft of cabinet-maker, coffin-maker and undertaker, who proved a mine of information about the village generally and the *Blue Bell*. I met him in the morning, quite by chance: an old man, collecting his pension in the little post-office where I was buying a postcard. He took me by the elbow and led me to a vantage-point from which, he said, the old smugglers' track from Kirk Yetholm, on the Scottish Border, ran down by way of the pele tower

at Doddington to its terminus in Budle Bay beneath the shadow of
Bamburgh Castle. It passed within yards of the *Blue Bell*, and he
showed me just where. He spoke with such conviction that I could
almost believe that he himself had seen the smugglers on their ardu-
ous moorland journey between the Border and the North Sea. As
a youngster, he told me, he had tended horses in the ample stabling
behind the inn.

A corner of this stabling is now the studio-workshop of a man
who is still indulging in his lifelong hobby of clock making. He buys
odd parts here and there, up and down the country and quite far
afield, hoards them until a use for them arises, and then incorporates
them in his latest project. Seated at his well-lit bench, he was surrounded by clocks—long-case, or 'Grandfather', 'wag-o'-the-wall',
bracket, and other types, every one of them assembled or rebuilt
with his own hands.

I found him at work on a clock every single part of which he had
himself fashioned out of—hardwoods. He was using long-seasoned
beech, closer-grained than oak but almost as hard; for bearings he
was using *lignum vitae*. The cogs that he had cut by hand for the
escapement mechanism were as beautifully precise as if they had
been cut in brass by Thomas Tompion or Joseph Knibb himself. He
hoped to have the clock in full working order within six months, but
this was not an occupation that could ever be carried out—he smiled
at the metaphor trembling on his lips—'against the clock'. He obviously had had, throughout the whole of his long life, an obsession
with time-pieces. Yes, he knew most of the collections of these, including the little-known one at Bury St Edmunds. There was a sense of
timelessness in that homely workshop, a part of the *Blue Bell*, which
I found most rewarding; I could have stayed there all day, watching
him at work, his touch at once so firm and so delicate, his tools so
varied, so much an extension of his fingers. Having realised that I
myself was interested in craftsmanship, he opened out and confided
some of his ambitions. It did not surprise me to learn that his
crony in the village was the cabinet-maker from whom I had elicited
so much information about the *Blue Bell* and indeed the whole region
from Belford northwards to the vast emptiness of the high Cheviots.

The smugglers' track which he had described to me so graphically must have passed a little to the south of the site of the Battle of Flodden Field, on the eastern slopes of the Cheviots where they level out into the shallow valleys of the River Tweed and the smaller River Till, which join at Twizel Bridge. Nearby is Cornhill-on-Tweed, a small, straggling village dominated by the *Collingwood Arms*. The inn stands four-square, uncompromising, overlooking the main road that used to carry the Newcastle-Wooler-Edinburgh coach traffic. The hardness of its outline is mitigated by a creeper that covers much of the long, high façade; but this is always kept cut back sufficiently for the name of the inn to appear in its bold lettering, together with, as a reminder of the prime function of the inn in its heyday, the gold-blocked words: P O S T H O R S E S. By tradition, the front of the inn always carries a larger-than-life portrait of the current representative of the Collingwood family, from which of course the name of the inn derives. Over the bar there is to be seen a complete set of the Regimental Crests and the actual caps of the five Guards regiments: the Irish, the Welsh, the Grenadier, the Scots and, because of the locality, the most important of all—the Coldstreams.

Here, then, my zigzag journey through England came to an end. I had started in Cornwall; if I had moved even a few yards farther, I should have crossed the border into Scotland. Pure chance, of course, that there should be, here at the *Collingwood Arms*, in the most northerly part of our most northerly county, so positive a link with that tiny *Treguth Inn* in Holywell Bay on the Cornish Atlantic coast: in the one, an array of soldiers' cap badges; in the other, caps and crests complete of the five Guards Regiments. But then, had not my whole safari, spread over the months of two successive years, been marked by links and memories resulting from half a lifetime of exploring the country I have come to know, and love, so well?

Index

(References in bold type are to illustrations.)

243

Index

Index

Index